T0327083

Hellenic Studies 69

THE THEBAN EPICS

Recent Titles in the Hellenic Studies Series

THE THEBAN EPICS

by
Malcolm Davies

CENTER FOR HELLENIC STUDIES
Trustees for Harvard University
Washington, DC
Distributed by Harvard University Press
Cambridge, Massachusetts, and London, England
2014

The Theban Epics
By Malcolm Davies
Copyright © 2014 Center for Hellenic Studies, Trustees for Harvard University
All Rights Reserved.
Published by Center for Hellenic Studies, Trustees for Harvard University,
    Washington, D.C.
Distributed by Harvard University Press, Cambridge, Massachusetts and
    London, England

ISBN 9780674417243
Library of Congress Control Number: 2014953140

Contents

Preface

THIS BOOK IS THE FIRST IN A PLANNED SERIES of volumes consisting of commentaries on the surviving fragments of early Greek epic. The text and fragment numeration follow my *Epicorum Graecorum Fragmenta* (Göttingen 1988), and the project will end with a revised and improved edition of that work. The present volume deals with the three Theban epics which were included in the Epic Cycle, and also that enigmatic composition the *Alcmaeonis*, which, though probably not part of the Cycle, apparently shared some of its subject matter with the three poems that were. This seemed to justify treatment of it and its intriguing fragments here (the fragments are particularly interesting for the history of Greek religion).

The volume derives from a draft which seemed ready for publication at the end of the 1980s. Why the appearance of it and the other planned constituent parts was so long delayed would be tedious to explain; but the delay has brought various benefits, especially by allowing me to refer to secondary literature that has accrued in the interval. The present seems a particularly auspicious moment for publication since interest in early epic appears to be growing apace: the year 2013 saw the publication by the Oxford University Press of Martin West's *The Epic Cycle*, and 2015 will welcome the *Cambridge Companion to the Epic Cycle*, from both of which I have sought to profit. I was also fortunate enough to be able to consult Robert Fowler's commentary on the early Greek mythographers (Oxford 2013).

The present volume surveys the various traditions about the war of the Seven against Thebes, together with the story of Oedipus that led up to it and the sequel involving the Epigoni, from the perspective of the four early epics that treated them. A survey of these traditions from a different perspective, that of the treatment of them by Stesichorus, will be found in the forthcoming commentary on that poet by myself and Patrick Finglass, in the introductory sections on his compositions *Eriphyle* and *Thebaid*. In view of the recent publications on the Epic Cycle, I shall postpone my general introduction to the numerous issues arising from the Cycle, saving it for my later volume containing the *Titanomachia*, the first poem in the Cycle with extant fragments and thus a more logical location than one prefatory to the Theban epics.

The earlier draft referred to above was, at the relevant time, read and improved by Hugh Lloyd-Jones and Rudolf Kassel, while Anna Morpurgo and Eva-Maria Voigt provided very helpful advice and information on specific linguistic and philological issues. More recently Martin West read and improved the latest draft and stressed the importance of the mythographer Apollodorus as an actual or potential source of information concerning the Theban epics. This author certainly names, on occasion, *Thebais* and *Alcmaeonis* as sources for details (fragments 8 and 4, respectively) and elsewhere provides a narrative which matches details in other fragments of the Theban epics (e.g., *Epigoni* F3 ~ Apollodorus III 7.4 or *Alcmaeonis* F1 ~ Apollodorus III 12.6). The possibility of his preserving, without specific confirmation, details from the lost epics must therefore be taken seriously. On the other hand I am sympathetic to the skepticism of Alan Cameron, *Greek Mythography in the Ancient World* (Oxford 2004) 93–104 ("we must beware of assuming that even ... plausible citations ... are based on direct consultation of the sources named ... It is another matter altogether to assume that [Apollodorus] directly constructed his narrative from a firsthand study of the texts he cites"). My *Index Locorum Apollodoreorum* will help the reader to consult and decide on the more important passages. The issue becomes more complex (and more interesting) with the Trojan epics, where we have the summaries of Proclus to compare and contrast, and I shall have more to say in the future volumes dealing with those epics.

A review published over fifty years ago—of a book on a classical but very different topic from my own—suggested that "a little honest plagiarism would have made some parts of the book easier reading" because its author "sometimes sacrifices clarity of expression to an overconscientious desire to attribute each specific view to its originator" in an explicit "attempt to rescue meritorious works of the past ... from 'undeserved oblivion'" (*Classical Review* 4 [1954]: 142–143). Some may think or say the same of the present work. The motive is certainly the same.

Abbreviations of
Most Frequently Cited Works

ARV²	J. Beazley, *Attic Red-Figure Vase-Painters*, 2nd ed. (Oxford 1963)
EM	*Enzyklopädie des Märchens* (Berlin and New York 1977–2014)
FGrHist	F. Jacoby, *Fragmente der griechischen Historiker* (1923–)
GGL	L. Schmid, *Geschichte der griechischen Literatur*, vol. 1.1 (Munich 1929)
GP²	J. D. Denniston, *Greek Particles*, 2nd ed. (Oxford 1954)
Heldensage	C. Robert, *Bild und Lied: Archäologische Beiträge zur Geschichte der griechischen Heldensage* (Berlin 1881)
LfgrE	*Lexikon der frühgriechische Epos* (Göttingen 1955–1979)
LIMC	*Lexicon Iconographicum Mythologiae Classicae* (Zurich and Munich 1981–1999)
LSJ	Liddell, Scott, and Jones, *Greek–English Lexicon*, 9th ed. (Oxford 1940)
MW	R. Merkelbach and M. L. West, *Hesiodi Fragmenta* (Oxford 1967)
RE	*Real-Enzyklopädie des Klassischen Altertumswissenschaft* (1893)
Rohde	E. Rohde, *Psyche*, 9–10 ed. (Tübingen 1925)
Roscher	W. H. Roscher, *Ausführliches Lexikon der griechischen und römischen Mythologie* (Leipzig 1884)
Schwyzer, *Gr. Gr.*	E. Schwyzer, *Griechische Grammatik* (Munich 1939, 1950)
Stith Thomson	S. Thomson, *Motif-Index of Folk Literature*, 6 vols. (Indiana 1955–1958)
TrGF	*Tragicorum Graecorum Fragmenta* (Göttingen 1971–2004)

1

Oedipodeia

Title

ἡ Οἰδιποδ(ε)ία (*Tabula Borgiana* [T: see page 133 for text] and Σ Euripides *Phoenician Women* [F1: see page 133 for text]), meaning "the poem about Oedipus" (for the variation in spelling and [perhaps] the principle see Stesichorus' Εὐρωπ(ε)ία fragment 96 with Davies and Finglass *ad loc.*); or τὰ Οἰδιπόδια (*scil.* ἔπη) by analogy with the *Cypria* and *Naupactica* as Pausanias (F2: see page 134 for text) cites the work? There is not really enough evidence to decide, although Pausanias is the likelier to be wrong because his context provides more opportunity for corruption through assimilation (τὰ ἔπη ... ἃ ὀνομάζουσι). On the "Iliac tablets" exemplified by T, see M. Squire, *The Iliad in a Nutshell: Visualizing Epic on the Tabulae Iliacae* (Oxford 2010).

Authorship

In F1 and F2 the work is cited anonymously with the formula οἱ τὴν Οἰδ. γράψαντες / ὁ τὰ ἔπη ποιήσας ἃ Οἰδ. ὀνομάζουσι. There is no substantial difference between these two expressions. The once-popular notion (so, for instance, Rzach 1922:2358.7–8, etc.) that the plurals in the former (and in such analogous phrases as *Epigoni* F3 (see page 144 for text) οἱ τὴν Θηβαΐδα γεγραφότες, *Cypria* F21 οἱ τῶν Κυπρίων ποιηταί) indicate uncertainty as to authorship is illogical and unparalleled, and quite out of the question in the present instance. The use of plural for singular is idiomatic in this type of anonymous citation: see K. Alpers, *Das attizistische Lexikon des Oros* (Berlin 1981) 82n14. The *Tabula Borgiana*'s unique attribution of the work to Cinaethon must be viewed very skeptically, not because of the doubts as to its reliability expressed by W. McLeod ("The

'Epic Canon' of the Borgia Table: Hellenistic Lore or Roman Fraud?," *Transactions and Proceedings of the American Philological Association* 115 [1985]: 153–165; for a defense, see Squire 2011:44–47), but because of the general tendency of later writers to attach authors' names to epics earlier writers had cited anonymously.[1] Wilamowitz suggested his supplement for the relevant passage in 1884:334 purely *exempli gratia*. For its problematic relation to the space required see McLeod 1985:159–160. West's supplement is proposed in West 2013:3.

> Jedes Urteil über die älteste form wird dadurch erschwert, dass wir die thebanische Epen nicht wiederherstellen können.
>
> F. Dirlmeier, *Der Mythos von König Oedipus*[2] (Mainz 1964) 14

We would learn a good deal about the handling of the Oedipus legend by the Attic tragedians and later writers, and other similarly inestimable advantages would accrue, if only we possessed some reliable information as to the general contents of this early epic. Unfortunately, the number of actual fragments that we have is tiny, and no one would call them particularly informative. At least, F1 on Haemon's death at the claws of the Sphinx tells us relatively little, and F2 on the mother of Oedipus' children has been dismissed as no more helpful by several scholars. Other critics, however, are more sanguine, and suppose that, if combined with later sources, this latter fragment can be used to open up surprisingly wide areas of the now-vanished poem. Here, then, we already meet the two incompatible attitudes that will clash again and again in these pages: the sanguine and the skeptical. Needless to say, even the more optimistic scholars disagree among themselves, and are divided, for instance, as to which of our later sources can legitimately be combined with F2 of the *Oedipodeia* to produce valid evidence.

Both types of dissension are fully represented even in the short list of treatments of our epic that follows: Bethe 1891:1–23, Robert 1915:*passim*, but esp. 1.149–168; Deubner 1942:2–27 = 1982:636–661. There is a critique of these three fundamental studies in Stephanopoulos 1980:103–110. Note also de Kock 1961 (with bibliography in 13n35 and 15n43) and 1962, and Wehrli 1957 = 1972. For a more general bibliography of treatments of Oedipus see G. Binder, *Die Aussetzung des Königskindes: Kyros und Romulus* (Beiträge zur Klassischen Philologie 10 [Meisenheim 1964]), 142–143; Lowell Edmunds 1981a (with bibliography on 30–39) and 1981b:221–238; and T. Petit, *Oedipe et le Chérubin: Les sphinx leventins, cypriotes et grecs comme gardiens d'immortalité* (Göttingen 2011).

---

[1]   See my "Prolegomena and Paralegomena to a New Edition (with Commentary) of the Fragments of Early Greek Epic," *Nachrichte der Akademie der Wissenschaften in Göttingen, 1 philosophische-historische Klasse* (1986): 99–100.

Bethe's first chapter gives a brief, exuberant, and colorful sketch of the *Oedipodeia*'s contents as he thought they could be recovered from later sources. Robert brought a massive weight of learning to crush this rash attempt at expanding the boundaries of knowledge. Deubner, while admitting the justice of much of Robert's negative criticism, believed that more could be salvaged from the wreckage of Bethe's theory and more inferred from a careful analysis of some later evidence than Robert allowed, though he himself often disagrees with Bethe over the details of reconstruction.

Under the influence of Robert's destructive onslaught upon his predecessors, Wilhelm Schmid tried to confine his remarks on the poem in *GGL* 1.1.202 to what we certainly know. This proves to be circumscribed enough: the epic was 6,600 lines long; it mentioned Haemon as one of the Sphinx's victims; it gave the name of Euryganeia to the mother of Oedipus' children. Schmid relaxed his scruples enough to permit two inferences: Oedipus' rescue of Thebes from the Sphinx and his marriage to his mother must also have fallen within the poem's scope.

Even this rigorous approach may have admitted too many uncertainties: thus the cautious and skeptical Robert allowed the hypothesis that the *Oedipodeia* mentioned the Sphinx's riddle, something which other scholars find quite inconceivable (see pages 9–13 below). Clearly we must carry out a careful and scientific examination of the credentials of this and all other similar suggestions before we can allow them anything approximating a serious hearing.

The best way of proceeding seems to be to fix in our minds the outlines of the Oedipus story as familiar to us from later writers and then isolate each individual detail and ask what grounds there are (if any) for supposing that detail to have featured in our epic. But before embarking on this painstaking examination, we must first inspect the notorious "Pisanderscholion" which will form a suitable prelude to our task. For, according to Bethe, it handily contains within itself a summary of the contents of the whole epic, a ὑπόθεσις, as it were, for the entire *Oedipodeia*. After the onslaught upon it by Robert and then Deubner, this position seemed, for nearly a century, to have been abandoned as unsustainable; but finally it found perhaps surprising adherence in one of the last of Lloyd-Jones' contributions to classical scholarship. On the identity of Pisander see in particular Deubner 1942:5–18 = 1982:639–652; Keydell's article in *RE s.v.* "Peisandros (13)" (19 [1938]: 146–147); Jacoby *ad loc.* (1^A.493–494) and in his Nachträge thereto (1^A2.544–547); de Kock 1962; Ed. Fraenkel, "Zu den *Phoenissen* des Euripides," *Sitzungsberichte der Philosophisch-philologischen und der Historischen Klasse des Königlich Bayerische Akademie der Wissenschaften* 1 (1963): 6–7; Mastronarde's commentary on Euripides *Phoenician Women* (Cambridge, 1994) 31–38; Lloyd-Jones 2002 = 2003; N. Sewell-Rutter, *Guilt by Descent* (Oxford

2008) 61–65. The text to be discussed occurs in Σ Euripides *Phoenician Women* 1760 (1.44 Schwartz = *argumentum* 11 of Mastronarde's Teubner text of this play) = Peisandros *FGrHist* 16 F10.

"Pisander"

The first item concerns the reason for the Sphinx's sudden appearance within Theban territory: she was sent by Hera (presumably in her role as γαμοστόλος: cf. Lloyd-Jones 2002:9 = 2003:28) to punish the Thebans for their toleration of Laius' indulgence in homosexuality and his consequent abduction of Chrysippus. Before considering this section in full we must note (with Robert [1915: 151–155]) the presence within it of a digression on the Sphinx and her victims which one would not readily attribute to the same source as the surrounding context:

ἦν δὲ ἡ Σφίγξ, ὥσπερ γράφεται, τὴν οὐρὰν ἔχουσα δρακαίνης. ἀναρπάζουσα δὲ μικροὺς καὶ μεγάλους κατήσθιεν, ἐν οἷς καὶ Αἵμονα. τὸν
Κρέοντος παῖδα καὶ Ἵππιον τὸν Εὐρυνόμου τοῦ τοῖς Κενταύροις μαχεσα-
μένου. ἦσαν δὲ Εὐρύνομος καὶ Ἡιονεὺς υἱοὶ Μάγνητος τοῦ Αἰολίδου καὶ
Φυλοδίκης. ὃ μὲν οὖν Ἵππιος καὶ ξένος ὢν ὑπὸ τῆς Σφιγγὸς ἀνῃρέθη, ὁ
δὲ Ἡιονεὺς ὑπὸ τοῦ Οἰνομάου, ὃν τρόπον καὶ οἱ ἄλλοι μνηστῆρες.

At first sight, the agreement with F1 of the *Oedipodeia* over Haemon as one of the Sphinx's victims might seem to support Bethe's case. But in fact, it is the remainder of the account of the victims which undermines it. The strangely disproportionate attention (not taken into account by Lloyd-Jones [2002:4 = 2002:23] when he disputes Robert's claim) here paid to the strictly irrelevant Eurynomus and Eioneus indicates, as Robert (1915:154) saw, a source in the form of a "mythologische Traktat" which summarized the legend of the Lapiths' battle along much the same lines as Diodorus Siculus IV 99. This part of the scholion, then, can safely be segregated from any reconstruction of the *Oedipodeia*.

In much of the rest of his argumentation, Robert places an excessive reliance upon logic, which he applies keenly and unsympathetically in all sorts of inappropriate places in an attempt to expose the scholion as a mishmash riddled with internal inconsistencies. Thus his labors (1915:1.156–157) to reconstitute from the text at our disposal a narrative in which Hera's anger can most logically be justified seem to me quite misplaced: where in Greek literature is the anger of gods or goddesses grounded in reason and sense? Likewise his calculation that if Oedipus were aged around seventeen years at the time of Laius' death, the Sphinx must have been active for some eighteen years–during which she would have devoured (at the rate of one per day) 6,280 μικροὺς καὶ μεγάλους while Laius stood mysteriously inactive! Against this sort of misplaced realism[2] see the shrewd comments of Lesky (*RE* 3A *s.v.* "Sphinx" 3 [1928]: 1712–1713).

Nevertheless, even Bethe himself (1891:10–15) was obliged to argue that the pristine outline of the epic story had been blurred to obscurity by the interpolation of material from tragedies by Euripides and Sophocles. The razor-sharp intellect of Robert (1915:1.163–167) objected that, even if allowances were made for these alleged intrusions, the scholion remains as incoherent as before. We shall consider in a moment whether this is really so. Let us first register approval of Robert's point (1915:1.152; misunderstood by Lloyd-Jones [2002:9 = 2003:29] when he writes "even Robert allows that the marriage with Euryganeia comes from the *Oedipodeia*") that the mere mention of the name is no guarantee of epic origin (see page 22 below for other apparently independent testimonies which give this name to Oedipus' wife). From the assumption that epic origin was so guaranteed sprang Bethe's initial interpretation of the "Pisanderscholion" as a handy resumé of the *Oedipodeia*. The inadequacy of this approach must by now be plain.

But, of course, to exclude a given scholar's theory about epic sources is not definitively to rule out any hypothesis concerning an epic source. This could be done if there were grounds for confidence in a totally incompatible hypothesis, such as Deubner's notion that two tragedies by Euripides underlie Pisander's narrative. A brief examination of this influential idea will not, therefore, be totally irrelevant to a study of the epic *Oedipodeia*. Deubner argued (1942:6 = 1982:640) that in order to reject the picture of an epic source for this and most portions of the scholion, one need not resort to Robert's extreme interpretation of the whole as a confused *mélange* (attacked also by Lesky [1712.39–40], Jacoby [495], etc.). Robert was right to point to the inconcinnity involved in the clumsy change of subject at the climax of the narrative's first half:

ἀπελθὼν τοίνυν ἐφονεύθη ἐν τῆι σχιστῆι ὁδῶι αὐτὸς (*scil.* Λαῖος) καὶ ὁ ἡνίοχος αὐτοῦ, ἐπειδὴ ἔτυψε τῆι μάστιγι τὸν Οἰδίποδα. κτείνας δὲ αὐτοὺς [*scil.* Οἰδίπους] ἔθαψε παραυτίκα σὺν τοῖς ἱματίοις ἀποσπάσας τὸν ζωστῆρα καὶ τὸ ξίφος τοῦ Λαίου καὶ φορῶν κτλ.

But Deubner's economic hypothesis (1942:7–9 = 1982:641–643) was that between the two sentences Pisander has changed his source, and that the two different sources are to be equated with Euripides' *Chrysippus* and *Oedipus*. The former will have supplied all the information about Laius as πρῶτος εὑρετής

---

[2] "So kann kein halbwegs verständiger Dichter erzählt haben" is Robert's triumphant conclusion (1915:1.156) to this part of his argument. "So darf man aber in epischer Dichtung und in Dichtung überhaupt nicht rechnen," Lesky (1712.47–48) reasonably retorts.

of homosexuality and Hera's punishment, indeed everything down to ἔτυψε τῆι μάστιγι τὸν Οἰδίποδα, with the obvious exception of the digression on the Sphinx considered on page 4 above.

Must the passage's sources be dramatic? Must they be the two particular dramas envisaged by Deubner? Is there no other explanation of the grammatical inconcinnity? Deubner's treatment of these complex problems is not altogether satisfactory.[3] Thus the reconstruction of events which he finds so redolent of Greek tragedy is flawed by several misapprehensions, including his belief (1942:8 = 1982:642) that Chrysippus committed suicide because he was pilloried (perhaps by Tiresias) as "Ursache des Unheils." It is surely more reasonable to suppose (what our scholion implies) that Chrysippus killed himself out of shame over Laius' treatment of him (Kassel [*ap.* Lloyd-Jones 2002:6 = 2003:24n39] cites Aristotle *Rhetoric* I 14.1374^{B}34, where a similarly placed individual ἀπέσφαξεν ἑαυτὸν ὑβρισθείς). The Sphinx would then appear at once (because the Thebans οὐκ ἐτιμωρήσαντο Laius) and not at the later stage postulated by Deubner.[4] And on a more general level, the very important role assigned to Teiresias by our scholion is not necessarily and exclusively indicative of drama (compare his significance, for instance, in Stesichorus' poem on Theban matters [fr. 97 in Davies and Finglass]).

The second question posed above is rendered all the more difficult by the near impossibility of deciding on reliable sources for the reconstruction of these works. On Euripides' *Chrysippus* see the bibliography offered by de Kock (1962:31n97), and now Kannicht (*TrGF* 5.2.877–879). De Kock himself (1962:31–36) has no great difficulty in arriving at a reconstruction of the plot which is remarkable for its almost total lack of any common ground with the "Pisanderscholion." See further Mastronarde 33–34.

As for the *Oedipus*, here too scholars have disagreed over the details it will have contained. For a bibliography of recent attempts to reconstruct the play see D. Bain, "A Misunderstood Scene in Sophokles," *Greece and Rome* 26 (1979): 145 = *Greek Tragedy* (Greece and Rome Studies 11 [1993]), 93n17; and now Kannicht, *TrGF* 5.1.569–570. The play's most famous fragment (F 541 Kannicht), spoken by a θεράπων of Laius (ἡμεῖς δὲ Πολύβου παῖδ' ἐρείσαντες πέδωι | ἐξομματοῦμεν καὶ διόλλυμεν κόρας), has no counterpart in anything Pisander tells us of Oedipus' varied career, and Deubner does his case no good at all by seeking (1942:19 =

---

3   But perhaps de Kock's citation (1962:20n31) of Aristotle's characterization of the *Odyssey* as ἀναγνώρισις ... διόλου (*Poetics* 1459^{B}15) does not really meet Deubner's stress on the essentially dramatic nature of ἀναγνωρίσματα. One should not confuse the concrete objects that are the latter with the abstract process that constitutes the former.

4   For Deubner's "basic misreading of the chronological sequence implied by the Greek" here see Mastronarde 32–33.

1982:653) to declare this precious piece of evidence spurious. We must therefore ask ourselves whether Delcourt (*Oedipe et la légende du conquérant*[2] [Paris 1981], xviii) and de Kock (1962:22–23; cf. Lloyd-Jones 2002:8 = 2003:27) are not right to posit a deliberate anacoluthon or a minor lacuna as a simple, unmomentous solution for that awkward change of subject.

If we reject Bethe's picture of the source as epic, and Deubner's picture of the source as dramatic, and if we believe that Robert's contemptuous dismissal of the scholion as a hopelessly confused *mélange* goes too far, then we have precious little room for maneuver. Perhaps de Kock's hypothesis (1962:23–24) of a learned Hellenistic mythographer ingeniously and idiosyncratically combining older and newer motifs, some of them from drama, is not so far from the truth. We may, at any rate, heartily agree with his final conclusion on the passage of Pisander (1962:37): "the important deduction ... is that, because we cannot determine all its sources with absolute certainty, we have no right to rely on it alone in our reconstruction of the *Oedipodeia*."

Let us now turn to the main features of the Oedipus story as familiar to us from later authors and see whether there is any chance of gauging the likelihood that they featured in our epic.

Components of the Story

The Rape of Chrysippus

Lloyd-Jones states the facts with memorable precision: "Robert showed that Bethe had not proved that the *Oedipodeia* used the Chrysippus story, but he did not show that it cannot have used it" (*Justice of Zeus,* 120; cf. his later, fuller, but less cautious treatment 2002:5–6 = 2003:24–25). Given our present state of knowledge, we have no hope of deciding either way. It is, however, striking that so many scholars (especially Robert 1915:1.157) should have so vehemently denied the very possibility of the motif's occurrence in epic, and one cannot help concluding that prejudice rather than probabilities swayed their minds. The lack of any specific testimony concerning the legend before the time of Euripides' *Chrysippus* is no very impressive argument. And the tendency of some myths to gain a homosexual coloring in later authors (especially the Alexandrian poets: cf. Kroll, *RE s.v.* "Knabenliebe," 11 [1922]: 903; Dover, *Greek Homosexuality,* 199) does not entail that every legend containing such features must be late. Homosexuality is certainly absent from the world of the Homeric epics (cf. Dover 194 and 196–197; Griffin 1977:45 = 2001:378 and *Homer on Life and Death* [Oxford 1980] 104n4), and the absence is most easily recognized by the manner in which Hebe usually ousts Ganymedes as cupbearer to the gods (on *Iliad* XX 231–235 cf. Dover 196). But the likeliest explanation of this state of affairs lies in the sphere of deliberate omission on aesthetic grounds rather than mere ignorance, and we are by now perfectly familiar with the process whereby features specifically excluded from Homer's works reappear in later epics. It is therefore no surprise to find that the *Homeric Hymn to Aphrodite* 202–206 makes reference to Zeus' passion for Ganymedes (see Faulkner *ad loc.* and cf. J. Th. Kakridis, "Die Pelopssage bei Pindar," *Philologus* 85 [1930]: 463–474 = Μελέτες καὶ Ἄρθρα 55–63 = *Pindaros und Bakchylides* [*Wege der Forschung* 134 (1970): 175–190]), as does Ibycus fr. 289 PMGF; cf. Richardson's commentary on the *Homeric Hymn to Demeter* (Oxford 1974) 279–280, and Wilkinson's on the Ibycus fr. (pp. 253–258). The same lyric poet represents Rhadamanthus and Talos (Daedalus' nephew) as homosexual lovers (fr. 309 *PMGF*). The adjectives applied to Haemon in F1 of the *Oedipodeia* are very suggestive in this context (Thebes punished for the abduction and death of one handsome youth by the abductions and deaths of countless handsome youths?). Given the likely motive (see page 6 above) for Chrysippus' suicide, Lloyd-Jones (2002:5–6 = 2003:24) was probably right to argue that it is not unthinkable in early epic.

But if we have no evidence that the rape of Chrysippus was missing from the *Oedipodeia*, we have no evidence either of its presence. Wilamowitz (*Hermes* 59 [1924]: 270 = *Kleine Schriften* 4.363–364) thought he could produce the latter. In one of the letters of Julian the Apostate (80 [p. 97.19 Bidez-Cumont]) the paradosis runs ὥσπερ ἐξ ἁμάξης εἰπεῖν οἷα ψευδῶς ἐπὶ τοῦτ Λαυδακίδου Ἀρχίλοχος. For the corruption in the penultimate word Weil conjectured Λυκάμβου and this correction has been widely accepted (e.g., by M. L. West, who prints it in his edition of Archilochus [p. 64] among the *testimonia* for the epode dealing with the eagle and the fox with no indication that it is a conjecture). Wilamowitz, however, suggested a different remedy: Λαβδακίδου (i.e., Laius), with an insinuation of pederasty against Julian's acquaintance Lauricius. If Archilochus did indeed bring such a charge against his victim, he must have derived it from an earlier "Theban epic" (unknown to Julian, who therefore calls Archilochus' charge "false"). This conjecture hardly involves an alteration (for the interchangability of β and υ in manuscripts see Aristotle *Rhetoric* 3.14.1415^{B}38 [αὐτοκάβδαλα Α, -καυδαλα β]; Theocritus *Idyll* 5.109 and Gow *ad loc.*), but the hypothesis of derivation from an earlier Theban epic does not necessarily follow, and the question of an epic origin for the rape of Chrysippus must remain open.[5]

---

[5] For a list of scholars who supposed the *Chrysippus* to have introduced the story into Greek literature see de Kock 1962:27nn61 and 62. An origin in early epic (not necessarily the *Oedipodeia*) is preferred by e.g. Lamer (*RE* 12.1 [1925]: 477.32–35), Daly (*RE* 17.2 [1937]: 2110–2111), and K. Schefold (in *Classica et Provincalia* [Erna Diez Festschrift (1978)] 178–179), who deems the story "eine grossartige Konzeption, das Unheil des thebanischen und des mykenischen Königshauses auf einen gemeinsamen Ursprung, die Frevel an Chrysippos zurückzuführen," a characterization

The Oracle to Laius on the Consequences of Begetting a Son

On the sources and likeliest origin of this see Fontenrose, *The Delphic Oracle* (Berkeley 1978) 96–98 and 362–363. It might at first be thought that our views as to its presence or absence in the epic must depend on what we think of Chrysippus' presence or absence. Wehrli (1957:110 = 1972:63), however, though refusing that figure to our epic, is prepared to countenance an oracle which warned a *guiltless* Laius of the consequences of begetting a child. He compares the utterance to the blameless Croesus concerning his projected war on Persia (see Fontenrose 302) and the famous "son of Thetis" prophecy.

The Exposure of Oedipus

As Rzach stresses (1922:2360.50–62), our ignorance of the epic's contents is so comprehensive that we cannot tell whether the version familiar from tragedy was used (exposure on Mount Cithaeron) or the variant preserved in Σ Euripides *Phoenician Women* 28 (1.252 Schwartz): τινὲς δὲ ἐν λάρνακι βληθέντα καὶ εἰς θάλασσαν ῥιφέντα τὸν παῖδα προσπελασθῆναι τῆι Κορίνθωι φασίν. Both motifs are primitive and popular: on the former see Stith Thomson, *Motif-Index* R 131, S 301, on the latter S 141, S 331; Bethe 1892:72–73; A. B. Cook, *Zeus* (Cambridge 1925) 2.671–673; N. M. Holley, "The Floating Chest," *Journal of Hellenic Studies* 69 (1949): 39–47; G. Binder, *EM s.v.* "Danae" (3.264), and more fully in *Die Aussetzung des Königskindes*, 142–144 and index *s.v.* "Ödipusmythos."

The Parricide

On the general question of this episode's connection with the Oedipus legend see Edmunds 1981a:47–48. Mastronarde (34–35 and n2) observes that one feature of the Pisander scholion which looks relatively early is its location of Oedipus' killing of Laius on Mount Cithaeron, in contrast to the later almost-universal placing of it at the crossroads in Phocis. Lloyd-Jones (2002:7 = 2003:26) thinks Oedipus' exposure on Cithaeron may be from the *Oedipodeia*, and notes (9 = 28) the existence of a cult of Hera (see page 4 above) on the self-same mountain. See further Fowler 2013:403.

The Sphinx's Riddle

On the connection with the Oedipus legend see Edmunds 1981a, esp. 18–21; on the possibility of its appearance in epic, Lesky, *RE* 3A (1928), *s.v.* "Sphinx,"

---

he takes to favor a late archaic source. For a bibliography of scholars who suppose it to have featured in Aeschylus' Theban trilogy see Mastronarde 35n1 (adding now, e.g., Lloyd-Jones 2002:11 = 2003:31–32). Mastronarde himself (35–36) is skeptical.

1711–1712, *Mitteilungen des Vereines Klassischer Philologen im Wien* 5 (1928): 3–12 = *Gesammelte Schriften* 318–326; Lloyd-Jones, *Dionysiaca* (Page Festschrift [Cambridge 1978]) 60–61 = *Academic Papers* [I] 332–334; Petit, *Oedipe et le Chérubin, passim*). On the scene in art see Simon 1981:12–70; K. Schauenberg in *Praestant Interna* (Hausmann Festschrift [Tübingen 1982]) 230–235 (bibliography in 230 nn1–2); *LIMC* VII.1 V 3–9.

The riddle is reported in differing forms by different authors. I record here the text printed by Lloyd-Jones, to whom the reader is referred for details as to its sources and the significant verses (see too Edmunds 1981a:32n16):

ἔστι δίπουν ἐπὶ γῆς καὶ τετράπον, οὗ μία μορφή,
καὶ τρίπον, ἀλλάσσει δὲ φυὴν μόνον ὅσσ' ἐπὶ γαῖαν
ἑρπετὰ κινεῖται καὶ ἀν' αἰθέρα καὶ κατὰ πόντον.
ἀλλ' ὁπόταν τρισσοῖσιν ἐπειγόμενον ποσὶ βαίνηι,
ἔνθα τάχος γυίοισιν ἀφαυρότατον πέλει αὐτοῦ.

The particular question that concerns us is whether Robert was right to suggest (1915:1.56–57 and 168) that the lines (or something like them) emanate from an early epic such as the *Oedipodeia* or the *Thebais*. The original publication of a papyrus fragment belonging to Euripides' *Oedipus* (*TrGF* 5.1.573; cf. Edmunds 1981a:33n22) led Lloyd-Jones (*Gnomon* 35 [1963]: 447) to suppose that Robert's thesis had been strengthened: the fragment showed that Euripides used a different version of the riddle from that cited above: this latter must then have possessed considerably more authority than the tragedian's for it to survive so long and to be quoted by so many later authors. In the later treatment (from 1978), just cited, Lloyd-Jones displayed considerably more skepticism, largely due to his acquaintance with the second of Lesky's articles.

In his second article, after decisively establishing that the *Oedipodeia* is the only early epic in which the riddle could possibly claim to be both totally relevant and appropriate, Lesky turned to the disproving of Robert's thesis as applied to this poem. His counterarguments fall under the headings of the general and the specific, and within the former category belong his attempts to demonstrate that in the *Oedipodeia* the Sphinx does not yet seem to have featured as a poser of riddles: rather she was a mere brutal murderer. Intrinsic to this whole argument, of course, are the assumptions that this is exactly how the Sphinx operated in the earliest form of the legend of Oedipus' encounter with her, and that the familiar riddle version is a later intellectualizing refinement. Such a reconstruction has found favor with several scholars (especially Edmunds [1981a:18]), although few have expressed the view with the force and clarity that Lesky devoted to it in his *RE* article (1716–1717). His argumentation there rests on two types of reasoning.

First is the *a priori* intuition that in legends involving heroes, brute force must logically precede the more sophisticated employment of cunning and guile, so that a more straightforward version in which a normal unintellectual monster is crushed by strength of arm must be presupposed by the extant story of the riddle and a battle of wits to solve it. Second is the evidence of an often-cited lekythos now in Boston (97.374: *LIMC* VII.1 B2.78, *s.v.* "Oidipous"), which shows a naked man labeled as Oedipus wielding a club against the Sphinx, for all the world as if he were Heracles. The image on this vase can now be supplemented by several other artifacts (useful list and bibliography: Edmunds 1981a:35n37)[6] similarly suggestive of a tradition wherein Oedipus killed the Sphinx in straightforward manner, with sword or spear.[7]

The *a priori* arguments seem to me altogether too crude and simplistic. It would be one thing to insist that stories where heroes win through by strength and might are earlier in kind than stories where the hero relies on his wits; it is a quite different proposition to claim that all examples of the latter originally ran along the lines of the former, as if Odysseus' cunning escape from the Cyclops' den was originally effected by sheer brute strength! And indeed tales of cunning and stratagem seem basic to mankind in general (note in particular M. Detienne and J.-P. Vernant, *Les ruses de l'intelligence: La metis des grecs* [Paris 1974] = *Cunning Intelligence in Greek Culture and Society* [Sussex 1978] *passim*). The riddle in particular as a motif in folk-literature is both primitive and widespread: see Stith Thompson, *Motif-Index* 6 *s.v.* "Riddles: Guessing with life as wager," and especially the entries *s.v.* H 512, 541.1, and 541.1.1; H. Fischer's article *s.v.* "Rätsel" in *EM* 11.267–275; Edmunds 1981a:5–12; and M. L. West, *Indo-European Poetry and Myth* (Oxford 2007) 281.

As for the vase paintings and other artifacts which show Oedipus destroying the Sphinx by force, their artists may have thought the mere intellectual confrontation of the two protagonists excessively static and unexciting for visual representation.[8] The element of personal innovation and idiosyncrasy in the depictions under consideration should not be underestimated. See in particular the remarks of H. Walter ("Sphingen," *Archäologische Anzeiger* 9 [1960]:

---

[6] See too Krauskopf, *Der thebanische Sagenkreis und andere griechische Sagen in der etruskischen Kunst* (Mainz 1974) 89n334 and n8 below.

[7] Brief literary resumés which tell us Oedipus "killed" the Sphinx (cf. e.g. Wolff in Roscher 3.716.3–12) are, of course, nothing to the point. This is a perfectly natural condensation of "caused her to commit suicide."

[8] This seems especially probable in the case of Etruscan gems that show Oedipus stabbing with sword a sometimes unresisting Sphinx (instances discussed and illustrated by Krauskopf [as cited in n6 above] 52 and plates 19.8 and 9). Etruscan art often depicts Theban legends in a lurid and bloodthirsty manner: see pages 40n11 and 83 below on depictions of Tydeus' cannibalism.

69–70) and his verdict on the Boston lekythos: "Die Szene ... kann kaum mehr als ein Missverständnis dieses unbedeutenden Malers sein," and on other possibly relevant vases: "Diese mehr als provinziellen Bilder ... haben kein Gewicht gegenüber den klaren Aussagen bedeutender Darstelles des Themas mit Ödipus und der Sphinx."

There is more than a little to be said in favor of the hypothesis that the riddle was *ab initio* and always thereafter connected with the Sphinx (so, for instance, O. Crusius, *Literarische Zeitungsblätte* (1892) 1699; Walter 69–70). That does not entail, of course, that the version of the riddle now under discussion appeared in the *Oedipodeia*. Lesky's specific arguments against this possibility are more convincing than the general ones just examined. At least his linguistic observations seem irrefutable: verse 2's ἀλλάσσει is alien to epic (the word first occurs in Theognis 21; on ἐπαλλάξαντες in *Iliad* XIII 359 see *LfgrE* 1 col. 535), and τάχος ... ἀφαυρότατον in verse 5 presupposes for the adjective a sense unexampled in Homer (whence, presumably, the variant μένος ... ἀφ. offered by some authors). The use of hexameters is no necessary index of epic origin: see the fragment of Euripides' *Oedipus* mentioned on page 10 above and Radt, *TrGF* 4.237 (on F190). If Lesky is right, we need not seek (with Rzach [1922:2358–2358] and several other scholars: cf. U. Hausmann, *Jahrbuch der Staatliche Kunstsammlungen in Baden-Würtemberg* 9 [1972]: 20) to establish a connection between the *Oedipodeia* and the famous Vatican cup (Vatican H 569: *ARV*² 451 = *LIMC* VII.1 Vb.19, *s.v.* "Oidipous"; cf. Simon 1981:28–31 and plate 15) redated ca. 470 by Beazley *ap.* Fraenkel on Aeschylus *Agamemnon* 1258 (and in *ARV*² as cited), which shows the Sphinx addressing Oedipus from her column and beside her the words (κ)αὶ τρί(πουν) which begin verse 2 of the riddle. Simon (1981:30–31) revives the old idea that the vases may reflect Aeschylus' *Sphinx*. Other attempts to decide the issue either way are unsatisfactory. West's observation (on Hesiod *Works and Days* 533) that if the riddle "had come in the epic *Oedipodeia*, Athenaeus might have been expected to quote it from there instead of from Asclepiades *FGrHist* 12 F7" is not particularly convincing. Scholars have shown some skepticism about accepting the one fragment Athenaeus cites from the *Thebais* as evidence of direct knowledge of the original poem. In the case of the *Oedipodeia* there are no grounds whatsoever for thinking that Athenaeus had read the epic. (West has since changed his mind and prints the riddle as a fragment of our poem as preserved by Asclepiades on p. 40 of the Loeb *FGE* [2003].) Although the vase Rzach cited is no evidence for the supposition, he may still have been right (1922:2358.52–53) to suppose that our epic mentioned the Sphinx's riddle.

In spite of the above uncertainties as to the Sphinx's role, it seems safe enough to follow the vast majority of scholars in deducing from F1 (see page 18 below) that the hand of the queen (Oedipus' own mother) was the reward for the Sphinx's conqueror in our epic, together with royal rule. For this popular folk-tale motif see in particular Stith Thompson, *Motif-Index* 6 T 68, Wehrli 1957:113 = 1972:66n28.

The Dénouement and Its Consequences

> μητέρα τ' Οἰδιπόδαο ἴδον, καλὴν Ἐπικάστην,
> ἣ μέγα ἔργον ἔρεξεν ἀϊδρείηισι νόοιο,
> γημαμένη ὧι υἱῖ, ὁ δ' ὃν πατέρ' ἐξεναρίξας
> γῆμεν· ἄφαρ δ' ἀνάπυστα θεοὶ θέσαν ἀνθρώποισιν.
> ἀλλ' ὁ μὲν ἐν Θήβηι πολυηράτωι ἄλγεα πάσχων
> Καδμείων ἤνασσε θεῶν ὀλοὰς διὰ βουλάς.
> ἡ δ' ἔβη εἰς Ἀΐδαο πυλάρταο κρατεροῖο,
> ἁψαμένη βρόχον αἰπὺν ἀφ' ὑψηλοῖο μελάθρου,
> ὧι ἄχεϊ σχομένη. τῶι δ' ἄλγεα κάλλιπ' ὀπίσσω
> πολλὰ μάλ', ὅσσα τε μητρὸς Ἐρινύες ἐκτελέουσι.

Odyssey xi 271–280

Ever since Welcker (1865:2.313–314), many scholars have believed that the above lines provide, in effect, a handy summary of the latter part of the *Oedipodeia*. For a bibliography see Deubner (1942:34 = 1982:668n2), who himself advances further arguments in favor of the hypothesis. He has convinced many sober scholars even in recent times. Thus we find Griffin writing (1977:44n32 = 2001:375n38): "It was pointed out in antiquity (Pausanias IX 5.10) that the word ἄφαρ seems to rule out the production of children. This is the more striking as it has been shown by Deubner ... that this passage of the *Odyssey* is based on the version of the cyclic *Oedipodeia*, in which Oedipus had by her [*scil.* his mother] two sons, Phrastor and Laonytus." But it is my contention that Deubner has shown nothing of the sort, and that much of Griffin's article merely underlines the implausibility of the hypothesis he here accepts. Griffin himself (1977:44 = 2002:375) has established that the Odyssean episode takes its place within a series of passages where Homer has sought to eliminate grisly details of family murder and strife. He instances as analogous the omission of the tale of Iphigenia's sacrifice by her father and "the silence in the *Odyssey* about the way in which Clytemnestra died."[9]

In the present case the parricide and union with the mother are so basic to the story that they must be accorded a mention. But this mention is of the briefest, and nothing is said of Oedipus' self-blinding or of the unhappy children

---

[9] Just as failure to understand Homer's elimination of the gruesome led Bethe (*Homer* 2.2.268) to suppose that Homer's Clytemnestra committed suicide (refuted by Griffin [1977:44n32 = 2001:375n38]), so Wecklein (1901:683 and 688) inferred from *Odyssey* xi that Homer was unacquainted with the tradition of Polyneices and Eteocles as sons of Oedipus.

born of the incestuous relationship. With the latter omission we might compare Homer's refusal to bless the guilty liaison of Paris and Helen with children (see Griffin 1977:43 = 2002:373). Scholars are becoming gradually more willing to accept that idiosyncratic mythological details in Homer are much likelier to be the product of the poet's innovation in or reworking of myth than to represent an accurate and painstaking summary of some now lost epic for which they are a valuable source of information. This is true of the story of Meleager as it appears in *Iliad* 9 (see Davies and Finglass on Stesichorus fr. 183). I believe it is also true of the story of Oedipus in *Odyssey* xi.

No unbiased reader of *Odyssey* xi 275–280 would for one moment conclude that they were in any way compatible with (let alone suggestive of) a version in which, after all the dreadful revelations, Oedipus calmly proceeded to take a second wife and father four children upon her. But Deubner has not yet finished with the Odyssean passage: far from being content with reading into these lines the birth of four infants after the great dénouement, he goes on to extrapolate the birth of two infants before it!

Deubner, in common with many scholars, assumes that Pausanias can be trusted in his remarks upon the *Oedipodeia*'s presentation of the facts pertaining to its hero's married life. I myself prefer to follow Robert and others (see page 21n17 below) in supposing Pausanias to be guilty of a fairly elementary blunder in the matter of Euryganeia's identity (see page 21 below). That there is considerable danger in attributing to Pausanias an error of this kind in connection with a poem that has now vanished almost without trace I do not deny. But those who accept Deubner's views here are in no position to throw stones. Or are they unable to detect the inconsistency inherent in trusting Pausanias without demur when he is talking of a lost epic, while faulting him twice over in connection with an extant one? For if Deubner is right to suppose that Jocasta/Epicaste bore Phrastor and Laonytus to her son in the *Oedipodeia*, and if he is further right in conjecturing that the Odyssean lines are based on the *Oedipodeia*, then Pausanias must be doubly wrong, both in his particular interpretation of the word ἄφαρ, and in his general deduction that the *Odyssey* knew of no children begotten by Oedipus upon his mother.

Deubner (1942:36 = 1982:670) pleads for an "elastic" interpretation of ἄφαρ here and in the allegedly analogous instances at *Odyssey* ii 95 and 169 and in *Homeric Hymn to Demeter* 454. His claim will not survive a reading of the excellent article on this word that Führer has contributed to *LfrE*. ἄφαρ can indeed have a nontemporal signification and it is under this heading ("2 modal: in der Tat, wirklich, schon") that *Odyssey* ii 169 appears (1697.70–72). The other Odyssean passage is ranked under subsection Id ("sogleich") at 1697.35–37 and *Homeric Hymn to Demeter* 454 under Ia 1696.15–16 ("erstaunlich, schnell"). These are all accepted meanings for the word and so is that assigned to the passage under discussion (Ib: "schnell, gar bald" [1696.53–57]), with a reference to the implied absence of incestuous offspring in the version here followed. Deubner's claim—that the word need not exclude an interval of a year between marriage and the emergence of the truth—is most decidedly to be rejected. See further Fowler 2013:404n25 against other ancient and modern misreadings of the relevant Greek word.

And who, after all, are the two sons Phrastor and Laonytus whom Deubner wishes to have brought into the world during this year's interval? Why, they figure in Pherecydes *FGrHist* 3 F95:

Οἰδίποδι (φησί) Κρέων δίδωσι τὴν βασιλείαν καὶ τὴν γυναῖκα Λαΐου, μητέρα δ' αὐτοῦ Ἰοκάστην, ἐξ ἧς γίνονται αὐτῶι Φράστωρ καὶ Λαόνυτος, οἳ θνῆισκουσιν ὑπὸ Μινυῶν καὶ Ἐργίνου< *lac. stat.* Jacoby>. ἐπεὶ δὲ ἐνιαυτὸς παρῆλθε, γαμεῖ ὁ Οἰδίπους Εὐρυγάνειαν τὴν Περίφαντος, ἐξ ἧς γίνονται αὐτῶι Ἀντιγόνη καὶ Ἰσμήνη, ἣν ἀναιρεῖ Τυδεὺς ἐπὶ κρήνης, καὶ ἀπ' αὐτῆς ἡ κρήνη Ἰσμήνη καλεῖται. υἱοὶ δὲ αὐτῶι ἐξ αὐτῆς Ἐτεοκλῆς καὶ Πολυνείκης. ἐπεὶ δὲ Εὐρυγάνεια ἐτελεύτησε, γαμεῖ ὁ Οἰδίπους Ἀστυμέδουσαν τὴν Σθενέλου.

Even Bethe, who is as eager as Deubner to posit the *Oedipodeia* as source for both Pherecydes[10] and the Odyssean lines, supposes that Phrastor and Laonytus have been foisted upon the former by an interpolator (compare Fowler *ad loc.* [2013:407]: "Pherecydes has taken the first part of this fragment from one source, and the second and third marriages from another"). And, since Pausanias fails to tell us that the *Oedipodeia*'s wife was succeeded by Astymedusa, the case for this tradition's appearance in our epic is reduced to a position of extreme implausibility.

Both Bethe (followed in the main by Jacoby on Pherecydes F95 [1^A 416]) and Deubner (1942:29–33 = 1982:663–667) place much stress upon the information provided by Σ A *Iliad* IV 376:

Οἰδίπους ἀποβαλὼν Ἰοκάστην ἐπέγημεν Ἀστυμέδουσαν, ἥτις διέβαλε τοὺς προγόνους ὡς πειράσαντας αὐτήν.[11] ἀγανακτήσας δὲ ἐκεῖνος ἐπηράσατο αὐτοῖς δι' αἵματος παραλαβεῖν τὴν χώραν.

---

[10] His narrative is also derived from the *Oedipodeia* by C. Kirchoff, *Der Kampf der Sieben vor Theben und König Oidipus* (Berlin 1917) 65; Wecklein 1901:676 and 681.

[11] On the general "Potiphar's wife" motif see the article *s.v.* "Joseph, der keutsche" by Reents and Köhler-Zülch in *EM* 7.640–648 and W. Hansen, *Ariadne's Thread: A Guide to International Tales Found in Classical Literature* (Ithaca 2002) 332–352. Cf. Davies, "'The Man Who Surpassed All Men in Virtue': Euripides' *Hippolytus*," *Wiener Studien* 113 (2000): 55n8.

Both attribute these contents to the *Oedipodeia*, though they disagree as to the exact implications of ἀποβαλών, with Bethe picturing Oedipus as expelling his wife from the city (cf. LSJ *s.v.* ἀποβ. 2a) and Deubner envisaging the king as losing his wife by death (cf. LSJ *ibid.* 3). It is hardly worth expending energy on a choice between the two interpretations, since both fall foul of the objections lethally leveled by Robert (1915:1.109–110) against the earlier. Either approach inevitably presupposes that the name which follows the disputed verb is an error for Euryganeia. And yet why not accept Robert's infinitely simpler explanation: that the Iliadic scholion's source has merely eliminated Euryganeia from Pherecydes' account and represents (*Heldensage* 133n2) "Mythenklitterung übelster Art"? In other words, both Σ *Iliad* IV 376 and Pherecydes[12] represent the same story, and there is not the slightest reason to suppose that story featured in the *Oedipodeia*. It is hard to disagree with the overall verdict delivered by Jacoby (416 as cited): "kontaminiert hat Ph. sehr naiv, indem er aus den verschiedenen namen für die muttergattin eine reihe von ehen machte" (cf. Schmid, *GGL* 1.1.202n6 for whom Pherecydes' version is "ein Logographenkompromiss, der zugleich pragmatisch und moralisch ist"; *contra* Fowler on the fragment of Pherecydes: 2013:405).

These issues are vitally important, for several scholars have drawn conclusions crucial for the character of our epic (and for the "evolution" of the Oedipus legend) from the identification of the traditions supposedly represented by *Odyssey* xi, Pherecydes, and Σ A *Iliad* IV 376 with what once stood in the *Oedipodeia*. Thus Deubner (1942:38 = 1982:672) infers an "epic" tradition in which Oedipus figured as a much more robust character than his counterpart in Attic tragedy: he does not blind himself, he can bring himself to marry again, he continues to rule over the Thebans, and he finally dies in battle. This is an archaic, and therefore the oldest and original, presentation of the hero. Likewise de Kock, who on other topics arrives at conclusions that drastically disagree with Deubner's, claims (1961:16–17) that in the *Oedipodeia* "we find ourselves in a world completely different from that of the tragedy," and that this epic presents us with "a hero who is clearly not deeply affected by the effects of patricide and mother marriage." If this last remark were true it would be a remarkable epic indeed, and a remarkable mental attitude to incest and murder within the family, very important for studies of the development of Greek morality. Similarly now Fowler 2013:404–405: "the incestuous offspring [were] germane in tragedy, but absent from epic ... the tragedians ... raised the level of horror."

---

[12] I do not intend to delve into the textual problems raised by the phrase ἐπεὶ δὲ ἐνιαυτὸς παρῆλθε in Pherecydes' fragment. Jacoby *ad loc.* posits a lacuna before the phrase, since he takes it that the year elapsed after the death of Jocasta. Deubner (1942:29 = 1982:663) prefers to suppose that the year in question is to be dated after the death of the two sons.

And so it is worth stressing that this picture is largely based upon the very economic summary in the *Nekyia* from which it would be unreasonable to expect a detailed account. In such a context, "Homeric decorum" (Mastronarde p. 21) will have found it easy (and congenial) to skirt the awkward and fearful questions of incestuous children and Oedipus' guilt. It is hard to see how an epic whose very title implies a detailed account of the career and suffering of the hero could ever have similarly avoided these basic issues.

Nor is this what our general experience of comparing Homer's treatment of myth with the Epic Cycle's had led us to expect. What Homer sedulously avoided in the field of the fantastic or the bloodcurdling they happily reinstated (see Griffin's article *passim*). The *Thebais*'s presentation of Oedipus, as revealed in F2 and F3, is already remarkably similar to the rash and choleric hero of tragedy, as de Kock (1961:18) accepts. We should not be in a hurry to assume that the *Oedipodeia*'s treatment of this figure was so remarkably different, especially when we discover that the alleged difference is built upon details extracted from the *Odyssey*'s passing summary.[13]

Fragments

F1 (*see page 133 for text*)

On the relationship between the textual tradition of the Euripidean scholion and the *Hypothesis* he numbers 11, see Mastronarde's Teubner edition of the *Phoenician Women*, p. 10, speculating that the latter derives from a fuller version of the former than now survives. It is obvious that the quotation itself is incomplete. In the words of Valckenaer (*Euripidis Tragoedia* Phoenissae [1802] *Scholia* p. 165) "qui haec pauca de multis excerpsit literator ... vetusti carminis versus describere neglexit, praeter hos duo suavissimos, quorum sensus ab illis pendet qui perierunt, aliunde tamen non difficulter eruendus." One may disagree with the literary criticism here (perhaps excessively influenced by ancient critics' views of the effects of epithets)[14] but no one will seriously try to deny that in the

---

[13] J. Bremmer in *Interpretations in Greek Mythology* (London 1987) 52 has tried to accept and make sense of the idea of an early Oedipus who remarries, but I find his arguments ("the wedding may well have been a poet's solution to the question 'what happened next?' In a way, the myth was finished ... but an audience always wants more ... to be a widower was not a permanent male status") singularly unconvincing. J. March, *The Creative Poet: Studies on the Treatment of Myth in Greek Poetry* (*BICS* Suppl. 49 [London 1987]), 122, is another relatively recent adherent of the notion of an early epic tradition featuring a non-incestuous family, with the incest motif an Aeschylean invention.

[14] E.g. Hermogenes on Stesichorus (Tb 28 Ercoles): σφόδρα ἡδὺς εἶναι δοκεῖ διὰ τὸ πολλοῖς χρῆσθαι τοῖς ἐπιθέτοις.

original epic the two verses must have been followed by others mentioning the Sphinx and containing a verb of which the Sphinx was subject and Haemon, as he features in the couplet preserved, the object.

On the plurals in οἱ ... γράφοντες see page 1 above. The phrase which in our MSS immediately precedes the quotation (οὐδεὶς οὕτω φησὶ περὶ τῆς Σφιγγός) has been variously emended or deleted. Vian's suggestion οἱ τὴν Οἰδιποδείαν γράφοντες, οἵτινές εἰσιν, made in 1963:207n5, takes its inspiration from the idioms used in quoting such epics of uncertain authorship as the *Titanomachy* (T2) and the *Cypria* (F7). If the epic's allusion to the Sphinx has dropped out, then the disputed phrase requires no remedy, since for all we know the sequel to the two extant lines presented the Sphinx in a unique way. The unparalleled nature of this epic's treatment of Haemon as victim of the Sphinx is stressed by Vian (1963:207–208), and this may be what our scholion originally intended to convey.

That "the Sphinx is a secondary element in the Oedipus legend, added at some point ... in order to motivate the hero's marriage to his mother," has been powerfully argued by Edmunds (1981a:12–16) on the ground of "the awkwardness of the Sphinx's position in the plot of the legend," and because comparison with analogous folk-tales reminds us that "the Sphinx is not integral to the plot ... which easily finds other ways to motivate the marriage of son and mother." But "the modification of the legend which brought the parricide closer to Delphi also drew it too far from Thebes and thus it was necessary to add the Sphinx in order to motivate the hero's marriage to the widowed queen of Thebes."[15] On the nature of the Sphinx as a monster and its particular predilection for young men like Haemon as its victims see Vian 1963:206–207.

It would perhaps be misleading to suggest that there is anything strictly and literally unique about the epic's presentation of Haemon as a victim of the Sphinx. This is a tradition which recurs in at least three other authors. We have already encountered it in "Pisander" (see page 4 above), where it is said of the Sphinx that she ἀναρπάζουσα μικροὺς καὶ μεγάλους κατήσθιεν ἐν οἷς καὶ Αἵμονα τὸν Κρέοντος παῖδα. A more detailed description of the exact circumstances of Haemon's destruction is to be found in Apollodorus III 5.8:

χρησμοῦ δὲ Θηβαίοις ὑπάρχοντος τηνικαῦτα ἀπαλλαγήσεσθαι τῆς Σφιγγὸς ἡνίκα ἂν τὸ αἴνιγμα λύσωσι, συνιόντες εἰς ταὐτὸ πολλάκις ἐζήτουν τί τὸ λεγόμενόν ἐστιν, ἐπεὶ δὲ μὴ εὕρισκον, ἁρπάσασα ἕνα

---

[15] Edmunds' position here is assailed by Bremmer (as cited page 17n13 above) 46, who to my mind merely succeeds in showing (what we all knew) that the Sphinx had been integrated into the story by the time of the earliest evidence of literature and art.

κατεβίβρωσκε. πολλῶν δὲ ἀπολομένων, καὶ τὸ τελευταῖον Αἵμονος τοῦ Κρέοντος, κηρύσσει Κρέων τῶι τὸ αἴνιγμα λύσοντι καὶ τὴν βασιλείαν καὶ τὴν Λαΐου δώσειν γυναῖκα.

A similar picture of Theban deliberations, but without the detail of Haemon's death in Σ Euripides *Phoenician Women* 45 (1.255 Schwartz) = Asclepiades *FGrHist* 12 F7[B]. These passages may all, as Vian (1963:207–208) suggests, derive from the *Oedipodeia*.

Vases often depict the Sphinx carrying off a youthful male victim which clings beneath her belly (see *LIMC* VIII.1 IVB, *s.v.* "Sphinx," esp. 3–4 [p. 1161], Simon 1981:16, K. Schauenberg, in *Praestant Interna* [U. Hausmann Festschrift (1982)] 232, and Petit, *Oedipe et le Chérubin*, 123–124 on "le sphinx ravisseur"). The late black-figure lekythos painter who repeats this subject four times was therefore awarded the title of the "Haemon Painter" by E. Haspels, *Attic Black-Figured Lekythoi* (Paris 1936) 130–141. The name is convenient and probably harmless, so long as we remember the warning delivered by its inventor (130n3): "I do not wish to imply ... that the victim of the Sphinx on our vases is necessarily" Haemon or, indeed, any other definite and specific person. Most scholars have assumed that in the *Oedipodeia*, as in Apollodorus, Haemon was the last of the Sphinx's victims. The ἔτι and the superlatives in the first line of our fragment are consistent with, though not in themselves indicative of, such a hypothesis. However, as Lesky stresses (see page 10 above), the very logic of the story also points in this direction: the death of the Theban regent's son and heir finally creates an overwhelming crisis concerning the city's future and Creon is forced to adopt the expedient (so familiar in folk tale: see page 13 above) of offering the kingdom to whatever stranger shall rescue the city. Haemon's death, Creon's proclamation, and Oedipus' success must follow closely on each other's heels for the story to work. So too concludes Vian (1963:206).

Whether the *Oedipodeia* placed the death of Haemon in the same circumstances as those reported by Apollodorus we have no means of knowing. I do not accept, however, that Lesky has decisively excluded any link between the riddle and this epic in general or our fragment in particular. As part of his attempt to establish that the riddle cannot have featured in the *Oedipodeia* (see page 11 above), this scholar argued that Asclepiades' version of events can have nothing to do with the epic and must be a relatively late attempt to reconcile the familiar picture of the riddling Sphinx with the alleged earlier picture of the Sphinx as a normal ravening monster. Inevitably the same objections must apply to Apollodorus' version, which inserts Haemon's death into the background of events established by Asclepiades.

I have already explained my reluctance to accept the popular reconstruction of the "original" form of Oedipus' encounter with the Sphinx (page 12 above). In the present case, one must add that Lesky's approach leaves no room for *any* early version linking the riddle with the death of Haemon (or, indeed, any other Theban). Why such a version should be excluded on principle I cannot see: granted the possibility of the coexistence of a riddling Sphinx and Haemon's death at her hands, Apollodorus' is the only conceivable way of combining the two motifs, and there seems to me to be nothing obviously absurd or redolent of a late compromise in his version of events. The famous Hermonax pelike (Vienna 3728: *ARV²* 1.485.24 = *LIMC* VII.1 VA2.490, *s.v.* "Oidipous"), which shows eleven Theban elders deliberating over the riddle while the Sphinx looks on ominously, perched upon a pillar, has therefore been taken to derive from our epic (Robert 1915:1.168, Rzach 1922:2358.22–28, etc.; cf. Petit, *Oedipe et le Chérubin*, 127 on "le sphinx à la colonne"). Although unconfirmable, the possibility should not be excluded as categorically as it is by Lesky.

   1. κάλλιστόν τε καὶ ἱμεροέστατον ἄλλων: the language seems surprisingly erotic for epic: cf. Theogn. 1117 = 1365: (Πλοῦτε, θεῶν | ὦ παίδων) κάλλιστε καὶ ἱμεροέστατε πάντων (cf. Ibyc. S 173.7 *PMGF*]ιστε παιδῶν [(where Page suggested κάλλ]ιστε). This may be connected with the original conception behind the Sphinx's addiction to the snatching up of young men: see Vian 1963:206–207. There is no call to suppose (with e.g. Küllenberg, *de imitatione Theognidea* (1877) 23, van Groningen on Theogn. 1117) that our epic is the inspiration for the verses of Theognis cited above. As Wilamowitz observed (*Sappho und Simonides* 120n1, followed by J. Kroll, *Theognisinterpretationen* (1936) 7n18 and Vetta on Theogn. 1365) the *Oedipodeia's* use of accusatives "ist ganz schlecht aus dem Vocativ ... gemacht: hier ist das Epos jünger, nicht notwendig als diese Verse, aber wohl als diese Wendung in einem erotischen Trinkverse." **ἱμεροέστατον**: the LSJ entry *s.v.* ἱμερόεις is deficient and erroneous: the word is only used of things by Homer (ἀοιδή, ἔπεα, ἔργα, etc.). Hesiod applies it to females: *Th.* 359 (of Calypso as in *HHDem* 422) and fr. 291.3 MW. LSJ should not have cited Pind. fr. 33ᶜ (= 87) 2 Sn. as an instance of its application to persons (thereby misleading e.g. Page, *Sappho & Alcaeus* 59 and Gow, *Theocr.* 2. *Addenda* [p. 592]): the reference there is to the island of Delos. The only other early example besides the present where it is attached to a young man has a decidedly homoerotic tinge: Theogn. 1365 (cited above). Note, however, Wilamowitz's popular supplement at Sappho fr. 17.10: Θυώνας ἱμε[ρόεντα παῖδα: see Page as cited. For its use (often homosexual) of persons in Alexandrian authors see Theocr. *Id.* VII 118 and Gow *ad loc.*, Kost on Musaeus *Hero and Leander* 20.[16] On vase-paintings which depict the Sphinx snatching up desirable young men see page 19 above. The superlative plus genitive construction is guaranteed by the two Theognidean verses cited above. It is fairly common in Homer: see *Iliad* I 505–506 ὠκυμορώτατος ἄλλων | ἔπλετ'. For further examples and discussion see Schwyzer, *Gr. Gr.* 2.116n1 and Chantraine, *Gramm. hom.* 2.60.

   2. Κρείοντος ἀμύμονος: on the meaning of the epithet here see A. A. Parry,

---

[16]   Kost omits our passage and says "von einer Person zuerst" (*Homeric Hymn to Demeter* 422).

Blameless Aegisthus (*Mnemos.* Suppl. 26 [1973] 78) who argues that "in view of the emphasis on [Creon's] son's beauty, the reference is surely to Creon's looks." *Non sequitur.*

On Creon's role in Theban myth see Vian 1963:183–193; on his son's, 206–208.

F2 (*see page 134 for text*)

On ancient traditions regarding Oedipus' wife/wives see in general Fowler 2013:403–408. On attempts to amplify our fragment by reference to Pherecydes *FGrHist* 3 F95 and Σ A *Iliad* IV 376 see pages 15–16 above. It is important to reconstruct the stages in Pausanias' argument here, leading up to the mention of the *Oedipodeia*'s version: (1) Pausanias takes *Odyssey* xi 271–280 to entail that Epicaste/Jocasta bore Oedipus no children. (2) Pausanias' reason for this inference is that in these lines Oedipus' murder of his father and marriage to his mother are followed shortly (ἄφαρ) by the gods' disclosure of those deeds. (3) *Therefore* Epicaste/Jocasta can have had no time before the disclosure to bear to Oedipus as many as four children. (4) Rather, the four children were begotten by Oedipus upon an entirely different woman, to wit Euryganeia. (5) And this latter personage is alluded to in the *Oedipodeia*. (For the use of δέ here to answer a question [πῶς οὖν ... τῶι Οἰδίποδι; ἐξ Εὐρυγανείας δὲ τῆς Ὑπέρφαντος ἐγεγόνεσαν] see Denniston, *GP*² 171 [ii b].)

Those scholars are right then (e.g. Deubner 1942:34–37 = 1982:668–671; Jacoby on Pherecydes *FGrHist* 3 F95 [1.417]; Stephanopoulos 1980:105) who stress that Pausanias' argument only works if Epicaste and Euryganeia are two different women. But unfortunately such a conclusion does not exclude the possibility that Pausanias has made a crass error. And it is precisely such a possibility that is urged by Robert (1915:1.110–111),[17] to the dismay of many of the scholars named above.[18] According to Robert, the truth distorted by Pausanias' error is that Oedipus' mother and wife was called Euryganeia in the relevant epic, just as she was called Epicaste in the *Odyssey*, Jocasta in the Greek tragedians and Pherecydes as cited, Eurycleia in Epimenides 3 B15 DK (Ἐπιμενίδης Εὐρύκλειαν τὴν Ἔκφαντος φησὶν αὐτὸν [*scil.* Λάϊον] γεγαμηκέναι, ἐξ ἧς εἶναι τὸν Οἰδίποδα), and Astymedusa in Σ A *Iliad* IV as cited. The *Oedipodeia*'s version of events will then have corresponded with what we find in Apollodorus III 5.8: εἰσὶ δὲ οἳ γεννηθῆναι τὰ τέκνα (i.e. Polyneices and Eteocles, Antigone and Ismene) φασίν ἐξ Εὐρυγανείας αὐτῶι τῆς Ὑπέρφαντος (Aegius: Τεύθραντος).

---

[17] Followed by several scholars (bibliography in de Kock 1961:15n45: add J. T. Sheppard, *The Oedipus Tyrannus of Sophocles* [Cambridge 1920] xviin3).

[18] For a list of opponents of Robert's approach see de Kock 1961:16n46. Add de Kock himself, Stephanopoulos 1980:105, Simon 1981:9n10, Mastronarde 21n3, etc.

Now clearly, if this were the case, step (5) in Pausanias' argument would simply not apply and the presumption that Euryganeia is a separate personality would have no basis in epic. Pausanias must be credited with a crude blunder, a hypothesis that is in no way inconsistent with the poor view taken of him as a writer by the late nineteenth and early twentieth century in general and by Robert in particular. Robert's conviction[19] that Pausanias cannot have known the original epic directly but must have gathered his knowledge from late prose intermediaries fits in with this picture as a whole and makes the assumption of a blunder all the more likely. However, it should be said that his interpretation of the present fragment is based on more than an instinctive tendency to disparage Pausanias which many scholars would now regard as outdated.

This is just as well, for if the idea of Euryganeia as the sole mother and wife of Oedipus has the support of those ancient authors quoted above, the alternative interpretation of her as a second spouse whose union with Oedipus is quite free from incest was obviously widespread in antiquity. We have already seen the testimony offered at the end of 'Pisander''s narrative:

> φασὶ δὲ ὅτι μετὰ τὸν θάνατον τῆς Ἰοκάστης καὶ τὴν αὐτοῦ τύφλωσιν
> ἔγημεν Εὐρυγάνην παρθένον, ἐξ ἧς αὐτῶι γεγόνασιν οἱ τέσσαρες παῖδες.

Pherecydes too (*FGrHist* 3 F95) has a similar tale:

> Οἰδίποδι (φησί) Κρέων δίδωσι τὴν βασιλείαν καὶ τὴν γυναῖκα Λαΐου,
> μητέρα δ' αὐτοῦ Ἰοκάστην, ἐξ ἧς γίνονται αὐτῶι Φράστωρ καὶ Λαόνυτος,
> οἱ θνήισκουσιν ὑπὸ Μινυῶν καὶ Ἐργίνου <lac. stat. Jacoby>. ἐπεὶ δὲ
> ἐνιαυτὸς παρῆλθε, γαμεῖ ὁ Οἰδίπους Εὐρυγάνειαν τὴν Περίφαντος, ἐξ
> ἧς γίνονται αὐτῶι Ἀντιγόνη καὶ Ἰσμήνη, ἣν ἀναιρεῖ Τυδεὺς ἐπὶ κρήνης
> ... υἱοὶ δὲ αὐτῶι ἐξ αὐτῆς Ἐτεοκλῆς καὶ Πολυνείκης. ἐπεὶ δὲ Εὐρυγάνεια
> ἐτελεύτησε, γαμεῖ ὁ Οἰδίπους Ἀστυμέδουσαν τὴν Σθενέλου.

However, the value of the former is highly dubious (see pages 4–7 above). As for the latter, even Jacoby (*ad loc.*, p. 416), who refuses to accept Robert's approach to the present epic fragment, is obliged to admit of the Pherecydean version "kontaminiert hat Ph. sehr naiv, indem er aus den verschiedenen namen für die muttergattin eine reihe von ehen machte." (Fowler *ad loc.* [2013:406] is a little more reluctant to accuse Pherecydes of "such an elementary lack of understanding.") Stephanopoulos (1980:105–106) has tried to use Pherecydes' fragment as a means to refute Robert's interpretation of Pausanias' words. But his first argument merely terminates in the conclusion that *Oedipodeia* and *Thebais*

---

[19] Accepted by most scholars, even those (e.g. Stephanopoulos who wish to accept Pausanias' testimony.

are unlikely both to have called Oedipus' wife and mother Euryganeia. Since this is no essential part of Robert's reading of the present fragment, little is achieved by the denial. The second argument asks why, on Robert's reckoning, Pherecydes should make Euryganeia, rather than Jocasta, bear Oedipus the four famous children. But nothing is achieved either by wondering why Pherecydes chose this rather than that form of contamination. The proliferation of extra children and wives for Oedipus is reminiscent of the way in which late authors devise increasingly numerous husbands for Helen, and increasingly numerous offspring for her and for Menelaus (cf. Griffin 1977:43 = 2001:373). Robert's argument is at its strongest when it concerns itself with the basic significance of the Oedipus story as a whole. It is instructive to pose the question "Can we imagine the Sophoclean Oedipus marrying again?," even though whether the epic hero begot children on his mother like his counterpart in tragedy is precisely what we are disputing, and it is equally unproven, in fact, that epic's Oedipus blinded himself. Nevertheless, the dread and terror of the original myth surely derive from the fact that the hero marries his own mother and has children by her. The grimness of his and his offspring's dilemma is absurdly diluted if their mother is not his too, and if Oedipus proceeds to behave like a Tacitean Claudius *caelibis vitae intolerans*. The introduction of additional and normal wives, for Oedipus to have normal children by, looks very like a later attempt to purge the story of some of its horror.[20]

An analogous effect is aimed at in the brief narrative of *Odyssey* xi 275–280, where Oedipus is implicitly denied any offspring by Epicaste. But there the legend is only referred to elliptically and in passing and the elimination of children is quite in the manner of the Homeric epics, with their notorious aversion for grim tales of strife within the family. On the whole, the other early epics seem to have differed from Homer's in this respect (see Griffin's article *passim*). They showed little inclination to omit such horrors and had little opportunity to do so since these horrors were often basic to the plot. As soon as we have any specific information about epic's presentation of Oedipus (witness the two curses he delivers in the *Thebais*) we are able to recognize a figure not so very different from the character familiar to us from Attic tragedy (see page 60 below).

As Dirlmeier (*Der Mythos von Konig Oedipus*[2] [Mainz 1964] 21 [cf. 14]) remarks: "der Name Oedipus von allem Anfang an in sich schliesst, dass der Träger eine Unglücksgestalt war und dass also die Ehe mit der Mutter von allem Anfang an eine schauerliche Tat gegen die Natur gewesen ist." I too detect an indissolubly

---

[20] Compare, perhaps, the tradition of Meleager's heroic death in battle in Hesiod fr. 25.9–13 MW, which seems to follow the *Iliad*'s playing-down of the horrific elements in the legend. On Bremmer's attempt to interpret the remarrying Oedipus as an early and explicable feature see page 17n13 above.

close link between Oedipus' incestuous union with his mother, the birth of ill-starred sons, their father's cursing of them, and their death in the Theban War. Some scholars,[21] who reject any such close connection between the first of these elements and the rest, nevertheless admit that Oedipus' curse presupposes the incestuous origin of Polyneices and Eteocles and their death at Thebes. Unconvinced by Robert's interpretation of Pausanias IX 5.10–11, they are obliged to infer for the *Oedipodeia* a rather novel version of the legend: the two brothers are free from the slightest taint of incest, they do not suffer their father's curse (in strongest possible contrast to events in the *Thebais*, where they are cursed twice), and they do not perish in battle before Thebes.

One must not dogmatize as to the contents of epics which have vanished with such approximation to totality as the *Oedipodeia*. Nevertheless, I find it next to impossible to believe that an epic ever existed in which Polyneices and Eteocles lived quietly unexceptionable lives and the Theban War did not take place. One would require more direct and convincing testimony for so remarkable a scheme of events than is afforded by Pausanias. It may be objected that the fortunes of Polyneices and Eteocles lay outside the scope of the *Oedipodeia*. The objection is inept: we do not know at what point in the saga the epic closed, and even if it did exclude this particular area, its composer must have drawn upon *some* tradition which will have supplied him with ideas about the fate of Oedipus' sons.

Suppose, however, that the *Oedipodeia* did lack the motif of incestuous offspring, but still envisaged the father's curse upon his sons and their death at Thebes. Difficulties still arise. As we shall see, the vast majority of scholars suppose that the brothers featured as incestuously begotten in the *Thebais*. Is it really plausible that so infinitely more compact and logical a schema should have occurred to one epic poet but not the other?

Onasias' Painting: *LIMC* VII.1 *s.v.* "Septem" I.3 (p. 710)

I have so far postponed consideration of this important (but no longer extant) artifact which Pausanias mentions immediately after his reference to F2 of the *Oedipodeia*. "A grief-stricken Euryganeia at the battle of her sons" is compatible with either interpretation of the afore-mentioned fragment. It fits perfectly, of course, with the idea that Euryganeia was Oedipus' second wife, not his mother, and bore him four children. But it is equally consistent with the notion that Euryganeia is merely another name for the mother of Oedipus upon whom he begets incestuous offspring. In this latter case we must suppose that Onasias was following a tradition whereby this woman survives the catastrophic

---

[21] In particular Wehrli (1957:112 = 1972:65) followed by de Kock (1961:16).

revelations like Stesichorus' queen (see Davies and Finglass on fr. 97 of that poet) or Euripides' Jocasta (in the *Phoenician Women*); unlike Homer's Epicaste (*Odyssey* xi 271–280) or Sophocles' Jocasta (in the *Oedipus Rex*). How a painter could have signified which of the two (second wife or surviving first wife) he was actually depicting is not very clear.

Difficulties do push themselves forward, however, when we try to delve further into the exact relationship between Onasias' vanished painting and our literary sources.[22] Our particular concern here is whether this artifact reflects in some way the version used in the *Oedipodeia*. A negative answer is entailed by Deubner's thesis (see page 16 above) that this epic included the death of Euryganeia, Oedipus' marriage to a third wife (Astymedusa), and that hero's curse upon his sons as engineered by her cruel machinations. However, we have already seen good reason to reject this hypothesis (page 17 above).

Should we therefore agree with, for example, Bethe and Stephanopoulos (see the latter 1980:107 and n12) that Onasias' painting reflected a scene described in the *Oedipodeia*? P. Corssen (*Die Antigone des Sophokles* [Berlin 1898] 22 [followed by Rzach (1922:2359.30–53)]) had already argued that, if the *Oedipodeia* did indeed contain such a scene, Pausanias (or his source) would have continued to cite it, rather than turning to Onasias as if he supplied a detail missing from the epic. Besides, we should not be in too much of a hurry to assume that the *Oedipodeia* closed at so relatively late a stage in the story and included so much of matter that must also have occurred in the *Thebais*.

Εὐρυ-γάνεια as daughter of Ὑπέρ-φας is discussed by M. Sulzberger in "ONOMA et ΠΡΑΓΜΑ: Les noms propres chez Homère et dans la mythologie grecque," *Révue des Études Grecques* 39 (1926): 395, as an example of the widespread tendency, in early myth and epic in particular, for minor characters to have parents with similar names. He compares Καλητώρ son of Κλυτίος in *Iliad* XV 419. In fact, it is the variation in the form of both daughter's and father's name that provides most of the problems from this stage onwards. Let us put behind us the controversy over the number of Oedipus' wives and concentrate on nomenclature. Apollodorus III 5.8 clearly entails precisely the same tradition as our fragment: εἰσι δὲ οἳ γεννηθῆναι τὰ τέκνα φασὶν ἐξ Εὐρυγανείας αὐτῶι τῆς Ὑπέρφαντος (Aegius: Τεύθραντος). Cf. Σ Euripides *Phoenician Women* 13 (1.249 Schwartz): καὶ τὸν Οἰδίποδα δέ φασιν Ἐπικάστην τε τὴν μητέρα γεγαμηκέναι καὶ Εὐρυγάνην. This version of the name recurs in "Pisander": ἔγημεν Εὐρυγάνην παρθένον. For the alternative forms compare Εὐρώπεια / Εὐρώπη and see page 1 above.

---

[22] For a survey of attempts to identify extant artifacts as dependent upon Onasias' painting, see J. P. Small, *Studies Related to the Theban Cycle on Late Etruscan Urns* (Rome 1981) 142–145.

Hyperphas' name too seems capable of metamorphosis. At least, Ὑπέρφας is presumably to be equated with the Περίφας whom Pherecydes *FGrHist* 3 F95 makes father of Εὐρυγάνεια. (For the phenomenon of "minor variation of the same name" see Henrichs in *Interpretations in Greek Mythology*, ed. J. Bremmer [London 1987] 251). And Epimenides fr. 15 DK is represented by Σ Euripides *Phoenician Women* 13 (1.249 Schwartz) as stating that *Laius* married Εὐρύκλειαν τὴν Ἔκφαντος ... ἐξ ἧς εἶναι τὸν Οἰδίποδα (rightly denounced by Fowler [2013:408] as "a mishmash ... from which it is difficult to extract a coherent account").

Pausanias' argument clearly implies that in our epic Oedipus begot upon Euryganeia not only Eteocles and Polyneices but also Antigone and Ismene. (Robert [1915:1.181] goes so far as to state that the pair of sisters are explicitly ["ausdrücklich"] attested for the *Oedipodeia*.) This is rather more remarkable than scholars have generally recognized, since Antigone and Ismene are conspicuous by their absence from Homer, Hesiod, Bacchylides, Pindar, and almost all of the remains of early Greek lyric and elegiac poetry. The earliest secure reference to both is Pherecydes *FGrHist* 3 F95. One wonders how much area the plot of the *Oedipodeia* would have had to cover before either sister could have had any significant part to play. Still, although we should not forget that, in the words of Wilamowitz (1914:93), "eine Person, die nichts zu tun bekommt, kann die Sage nicht brauchen," we should also not forget post-Homeric epic's fondness for minor characters and superfluous children (see Griffin 1977:43 = 2001:373), or Attic tragedy's tendency to bring into sudden prominence such previously subordinate figures (Chrysothemis is a case in point).

2
Thebais

If it were possible to choose a lost work of Greek literature for recovery, the epic *Thebais* would come high on a preference list. It would answer more questions about Homer than all the deciphering of Mycenaean tablets and excavating of tholos tombs.

Willcock 1964:144 = 440

Dass es der Dichter der *Thebais* war, d. h. der Epiker, welcher den Zug der Sieben für alle Zeiten in den Grundzügen feststellte, ist selbstverständlich.

Wilamowitz 1891:224–225 = 1971:59

Ein Epos hatte ... eine ganz bestimmte, künstliche, hochgezüchtete Heroenwelt als Objekt seiner Darstellung; in dieses epische Alterweltsmilieu wurden alle bestehenden Sagen umgeformt und erweitert; so auch der Zug der Sieben. Das bekam ihm nicht gut; seine Herkunft stand einem freien Wachstum in Wege; zu viele störende Elemente trug er in sich. Trotzdem sich ihm bedeutende Talente widmeten, wiewohl er durch die Vereinigung mit der Ödipussage neuen Aufschwung bekam und dichterische Steigerungsmöglichkeiten von grösster Eindrücklichkeit in sich barg, so erwiesen sich doch manche andere Sagenkreise als zukunftsreicher und durchschlagender als der Zug der Sieben; vor allem die trojanischer Sagen. So trat das Epos, das ihn darstellte, in den Hintergrund.

Howald 1939:17–18

Testimonia

T1 *(see page 135 for text)*

These remarks of Pausanias constitute one of the most important documents for the history of early Greek literature. Their implications for the authorship and date of our epic are very considerable, and several other weighty inferences have been built upon them (see, for instance, Grote's *History of Greece* [twelve-volume edition (London 1884)] 2.129).[1] Of course one cannot divorce the problem entirely from the more general question of those passages which have seemed to many to imply that Ὅμηρος was often used as a "collective name" for early epic. However, I must discuss these elsewhere. In the present place I shall endeavor to analyze the passage on its own merits.

Since the original words to which Pausanias alludes here are no longer extant, we must obviously proceed with the greatest caution. Nevertheless, I think that the evidence at our disposal is enough to enable us to rule out the most extreme example to date of skepticism as to this testimonium's worth. I refer to J. A. Scott's unfortunate conglomeration ("Homer as the Poet of the *Thebais*," *Classical Philology* 16 [1921]: 20–26 = *The Unity of Homer* [California 1921] 15–22) of mistranslation and misinterpretation.[2] Mistranslation, for who will accept Scott's statement (p. 16) that Pausanias tells us how the man whose name begins with Καλ- "*regarded* the author as Homer" (my italics), or "*regarded* the author as *an* Homer" (my emphasis again)? Misinterpretation, for the purpose of the tendentious paraphrase just cited is to ease our transition to the following conclusion (p. 16): "all this passage is intended to show is the high estimate in which the *Thebais* was held and that even here the author of that poem is regarded as an equal with the great Homer." Our journey to this deduction is further facilitated by the doubt which Scott casts upon Sylburg's emendation of the manuscripts' Καλαιν- (an emendation accepted by practically every scholar who has considered the passage, even those most hostile to its worth) and by his stubborn refusal to equate the Καλλῖνος thus emended with the elegist of that name. The information that the emperor Hadrian preferred Antimachus' *Thebais* to Homer (Dio Cassius LXIX 4 = T32 Matthews) is next dragooned into service and we are presently being assured (p. 17) that "there is nothing in Pausanias to show that he is not referring to Antimachus." From Pausanias, then, we are to infer that the mysterious Calaenus, unlocatable in time or place, set Antimachus on a level equal with Homer.

---

[1] "For the title of the ... *Thebais* to be styled Homeric depends upon evidence more ancient than any which can be produced to authenticate the *Iliad* and the *Odyssey*."

[2] On the general nature of Scott's reasoning in these works see Dodds, *Fifty Years (and Twelve) of Classical Scholarship* (Oxford 1968) 9–10.

Scholars have rightly failed to take this assault very seriously. There is, however, scope for a more reasoned skepticism. E. Hiller ("Beiträge zur griechischen Litteraturgeschichte," *Rheinisches Museum* 42 [1887]: 324–326) and Ed. Schwartz ("Der Name Homeros," *Hermes* 75 [1940]: 3–4) reached (independently, it would seem) the same conclusion on many important issues. In an attempt to narrow down the range of possibilities concerning the nature of Callinus' reference to Homer, each saw that a specific and direct citation of the *Thebais* by title would be alien to the manner of early elegy. Both were also aware that the quite categorical statement "Homer composed the *Thebais*" is likely to be an inference drawn by a later and learned writer (Pausanias or his source)[3] from some less definite remark by Callinus himself.

But what is the most probable reconstruction of this remark? Hiller saw two possibilities:[4]

(i) Callinus mentioned a detail (which later writers recognized in the narrative of the *Thebais*) and attributed it to Homer. In this case one should presumably accept Schwartz's inference (p. 3) that Callinus himself had cause to mention the Theban expedition as context for this attribution.

(ii) Callinus directly quoted as "Homer's" some words or phrases which later writers recognized as occurring in the text of the *Thebais*. The obvious elegiac analogy to this is the famous "quotation" of *Iliad* VI 146 given by Semonides (= Simonides fr. 8.1–2 W):

ἓν δὲ τὸ κάλλιστον Χῖος ἔειπεν ἀνήρ

«οἵη περ φύλλων γενεή, τοίη δὲ καὶ ἀνδρῶν.»

Hiller seems to think that alternative (ii) offers less scope for confusion and error on the part of the later writer, though even here we must bear in mind the carefully formulated warning of J. A. Davison ("Quotations and Allusions in Early Greek Literature," *Eranos* 53 [1955]: 137 = *From Archilochus to Pindar* [London 1968] 81–82): "All that we can feel sure of is that Pausanias (or his authority) found in Callinus a phrase or phrases ascribed to Homer which resembled some words in the *Thebais* closely enough to lead him to infer that Callinus was actually quoting the *Thebais* and ascribing it to Homer." How much more uncertainty would be uncaged if (i) were the truth! Hiller does well to stress (p. 326) the large number of admittedly brief and passing references to the Theban saga in the *Iliad* and

---

[3] Schwartz (3n1) mentions Demetrius of Scepsis as a possibility, since this writer, as source in turn for Strabo, would seem to have often quoted Callinus (cf. Schwartz, *RE* 4 [1901]: 2811.41–42). On Demetrius see Pfeiffer, *History of Classical Scholarship*, 1: *From the Beginnings to the Hellenistic Age* (Oxford 1968) 249–251 and 259.

[4] O. Crusius ("Litterargeschichtliche Parerga," *Philologus* 54 [1895]: 723) appears to find Hiller's approach excessively skeptical. I cannot agree.

the *Odyssey*. If an allusion to one of these from Callinus was misinterpreted we should be in a sorry way. Enough said, then, to put us well on our guard against any smooth and unpremeditated deduction from this notorious passage. Wilamowitz's cautious summing up (1916:364n1) can hardly be bettered: "Ob die bis in das dritte Jahrhundert gelesene *Thebais* mit der, welche Kallinos vor sich gehabt hatte, ausser dem Stoffe noch irgend etwas gemein hatte, wusste niemand."

The famous tradition of Cleisthenes of Sicyon's hostility towards Adrastus and Argos (Herodotus V 67.1; see page 135 for text) has been seen by some scholars[5] as relevant to the present question: Κλεισθένης γὰρ Ἀργείοισι πολεμήσας τοῦτο μὲν ῥαψῳδοὺς ἔπαυσε ἐν Σικυῶνι ἀγωνίζεσθαι τῶν Ὁμηρείων ἐπέων εἵνεκα, ὅτι Ἀργεῖοί τε καὶ Ἄργος τὰ πολλὰ πάντα ὑμνέαται (details of his hostility to Adrastus follow). In spite of LSJ *s.v.* ὑμνέω (1.1), the final phrase does not have to mean "(the Argives) *are* everywhere *praised*." See Hiller (326–327) and Powell's *Lexicon to Herodotus s.v.* (p. 364), where the word's two occurrences are rendered "*celebrate* anyone *in song*."[6] τὰ πολλὰ πάντα may be deliberate exaggeration, intended as an index of Cleisthenes' unreasonableness.

We may therefore conclude that, though the Argives, Argos, and Adrastus would be mentioned far more often in the *Thebais* and the *Epigoni* than in the *Iliad* and the *Odyssey*, nevertheless they are mentioned enough in the latter pair of poems (evidence marshaled by Hiller [327–328] and Scott [22–24 = 18–20]) for the story to work perfectly well if τῶν Ὁμηρείων ἐπέων as a phrase bears the meaning that a present-day reader would naturally place upon it. And (*pace* e.g. How and Wells or Cingano) it would surely be a little odd if Herodotus, who at IV 32 = *Epigoni* T1/F2 expresses doubt concerning the Homeric authorship of the *Epigoni*, were here calmly to couple it with the *Thebais* and label the combination τὰ Ὁμήρεια ἔπεα.

Two other passages have wrongly been thought to contain traces of this tradition of Homer as the *Thebais*'s author: (i) Antigonus of Carystus 25 (*Rerum naturalium scriptores graeci minores* p. 9 Keller) attributes to ὁ ποιητής a line and a half of gnomic advice which some have assigned to the Ἀμφιάρεω Ἐξελασία,

---

[5]   One of the earliest is Grote (*History of Greece* 2.129n3). Perhaps it was expressed most extremely by Wilamowitz (1884:352: "es ist … nur sinn in dieser geschichte, wenn Homer als der dichter der *Thebais* verstanden wird"; cf. 1914:102). The same view is taken by for instance, Stein (2.68) and How and Wells (2.34) in their Herodotean commentaries *ad loc*. Further bibliography is in Rzach 1922:2363.22–24. See more recently E. Cingano, "Clistene di Sicione, Erodoto e i poemi del ciclo tebano," *Quaderni Urbinati di Cultura Classica* 20 (1985): 31–40. Opposition already came from Welcker (1865:2.474n27).

[6]   Admittedly, Powell's translation of the present passage (2.381) renders the verb "extolled." But as we shall see (page 70 below), the *Thebais* is unlikely to have depicted the Argives in any very favorable light, a point not taken by, e.g., Cingano, as cited in the previous note.

a work most plausibly interpreted as part of the *Thebais* (as we shall see pages 99–102 below). But though we may accept that ὁ ποιητής is here equivalent to Homer, the rest of the hypothesis does not follow at all (see pages 101–102 below). Nor should (ii) Horace's *Ars Poetica* 146 (*nec reditum Diomedis ab interitu Meleagri* [*orditur*]) be taken even as necessarily referring to the *Thebais*, and still less as implying the Roman poet's attribution of that epic to Homer: see Brink, *Horace on Poetry: The Ars Poetica* (Cambridge 1963–1982) 442.

By contrast, the fragment of Dionysius of Samos (ὁ κυκλογράφος) cited as T4 (see page 136), which claims Homer as a contemporary of the Theban as well as the Trojan War, does seem to reflect the tradition. So, for instance, among earlier scholars, Grote (*History of Greece* 2.129n2), and Felix Jacoby, among the more recent (in his commentary *ad loc.* [1ᴬ.492]), have inferred.

We must now face another, scarcely less important, issue. When Pausanias introduces his remarks on the *Thebais* and its authorship with the statement ἐποιήθη δὲ ἐς τὸν πόλεμον τοῦτον καὶ ἔπη Θηβαΐς, he has just been describing the siege of Thebes as the climax of the Epigoni's campaign against that city. One might, then, expect "this war" to refer most immediately to this second, successful enterprise as well as the earlier failure. The fact has not escaped the attention of those scholars who believe the epic known as the *Epigoni* was part of a larger *Thebais* (so especially Bethe [1891:36–37 and 122]) and they triumphantly cite our passage as an evidence of this theory (see page 107 below). Even the cautious Rzach, who rejects the more extreme forms of this dogma, deduces from Pausanias' words (1922:2374.42): "er wählt also eine Gesamtbezeichnung." One can see why they came to this conclusion. But a closer examination of the structure of Pausanias' whole argument here will also show the needlessness of such an inference.

Pausanias' summary of the wars successively waged by the Seven and then the Epigoni against Thebes is very effectively framed within an introductory and a concluding passage. In the first, imitating the grand historical manner,[7] he tells us that he regards this war as the most noteworthy fought in the heroic age by Greek against Greek. The "this" is given reference by the previous sentence's mention of Capaneus' death (IX 8.7) in the midst of his attempt to scale the Theban battlements. In the second, concluding, passage, the initial emphasis is recapitulated in the statement that the *Thebais* was about this war and that Pausanias agrees with those who rank that epic third only to the *Iliad* and the *Odyssey*. Suppose the latter mention of "this war" is to be limited to that waged by the Seven: how could Pausanias have made this clearer? τὸν δὲ

---

[7] Compare esp. Thucydides I 1 (Θουκυδίδης ... ξυνέγραψε τὸν πόλεμον τῶν Πελοποννησίων καὶ Ἀθηναίων ... ἐλπίσας μέγαν τε ἔσεσθαι καὶ ἀξιολογώτατον τῶν προγεγενημένων). See further Nisbet and Hubbard, *Horace Odes* 2 p. 9.

πόλεμον τοῦτον (IX 9.1) in the introductory paragraph and τὸν πόλεμον τοῦτον (IX 9.5) at the conclusion will both refer to the same event, the war of the Seven against Thebes. If Pausanias had endeavored to make clarity doubly clear by placing the allusion to the *Thebais* immediately after the initial statement of the war's importance, he would have incurred several disadvantages: the present smooth continuity between this initial statement about the war and the narrative concerning that self-same war would have been disrupted, and Pausanias would have deprived himself of the impressive *coda* which IX 9.5 supplies in the text as it actually stands. This latter disadvantage would have arisen if Pausanias had placed the mention of the *Thebais* in the only other available position, at the start of IX 9.4, in between the narratives of the Seven and the Epigoni. And such a placement would again have ruptured a desirable continuity with the interposition of a piece of literary criticism that functions far better in its present place.

The relevance of Thucydides' proem was grasped by, for instance, Robert (*Heldensage* 3.1.932n3). With the notable exception of Wilamowitz[8] (1891:228n2 = 1971:63n1; cf. 1884:364n1), scholars have perhaps taken Pausanias' high valuation of the now-lost epic a little too seriously. They certainly seem to have adopted too automatically the terms of literary criticism he employs. Thus George Grote (*History of Greece* 1.261) concluded that the *Thebais* possessed "distinguished poetical merit." "Zweifellos enthielt das berühmte Gedicht gar manche dichterische Schönheit," Rzach (1922:2372.48–49) assures us. And Severyns (1928:211) talks of "*La Thébaide*, le plus ancien et le plus beau poème du Cycle après l'*Iliade* et l'*Odyssée*." It is hard to see how the few extant fragments could possibly justify such extravagant praise, and, consciously or not, these scholars must have been guided by Pausanias' verdict. But Rzach himself admits (1922:2361.37) that this very verdict was "offenbar überkommenen."

Homer and the *Thebais*

The relationship between the *Iliad* and the *Thebais* has long been a matter of debate and dispute. Four older treatments of the topic still repay attention: Welcker 1865: 2.320–332, Bethe 1891:174–147, Robert 1915:1.185–199, and Friedländer 1914: 317–329 = 1969:34–42. Of these, the last two, which originally appeared at about the same time and do not, therefore, show awareness of each other's conclusions, are the most rewarding. Robert's analysis is the fuller and more detailed, but labors under the disadvantage of approaching the topic via the not particularly fruitful conviction (needlessly stressed at every turn of the argument) that the author of the relevant Iliadic passages cannot be the author of the *Thebais*.

---

[8] In both passages he shows himself characteristically eager to stress that Pausanias can have had no direct knowledge of the *Thebais*'s text.

Friedländer's more concise study shows a greater awareness of the principles that underlie the whole issue. A Spanish monograph by José B. Torres-Guerra, *La* Tebaida *Homérica como fuente de* Iliade *y* Odisea (Madrid 1995), with English summary pp. 78–82, fails to take into account the monograph of Ø. Andersen (1978), the best treatment of the issue to date.

> Von einer sorgsamen Prüfung der Homerstellen auszugehen ist allerdings die eine Pflicht der Untersuchung. Man darf sich wohl auch gestatten, diese fragmentarischen Bilder mit aller Vorsicht aus der Gemeinsage zu ergänzen, wo sich solche Ergänzung aufdrängt. Aber man wird nicht glauben, damit den besonderen Stoff der *Thebais* wiedergefunden zu haben. Es könnte sehr wohl sein, dass dieses Epos jünger oder überhaupt anders ist als die Form der Sage vom Thebanischen Krieg, die sich aus der *Ilias* als "vorhomerisch" ergibt. Selbst diese Sagenform wird man nicht mit Gewissheit als einheitlich in Anspruch nehmen dürfen, da die verschiedenen "*Ilias*dichter" verschiedene Fassungen oder Entwicklungsstadien der thebanischen Sage voraussetzen können.
>
> Friedländer 1914:318 = 1969:34

TYDEUS

Perhaps the most interesting and important region of the present investigation concerns this hero, whose exploits in connection with the campaign against Thebes are described with particular detail in two passages:[9]

(i) *Iliad* IV 365–400

Here Tydeus' activities are described by Agamemnon in order to supply an exhortatory paradigm for Tydeus' son Diomedes, whom the leader of the Greeks mistakenly supposes to be skulking away from the battle, quite unlike his father. Diomedes' alleged cowardice is in especially striking contrast to Tydeus' behavior about the time he accompanied Polyneices on a peaceful embassy to Mycenae in the hope of gathering forces for the expedition against Troy. Mycenae would willingly have supplied such troops but παραίσια σήματα from Zeus deterred her (line 381). At a somewhat later stage, when the expedition was already under way, Tydeus was sent on another mission, this time to the enemy capital. At Thebes he went to the palace of Eteocles (line 386), challenged the

---

[9]   On these and the following passages see the work of Andersen (1978: *passim*, esp. 33–94), who gives the best exposition to date of the paradigmatic effect of the four passages (the first in particular) and shows that the poet's invention is often a more plausible hypothesis than his use of some such source as the *Thebais*.

Thebans to an athletic contest, and beat them all easily, with Athena's help. The angry Thebans set an ambush for him as he returned to the expedition, but here too Tydeus emerged victorious and killed all his assailants except for Maeon, whom he spared and sent back to Thebes, θεῶν τεράεσσι πιθήσας (line398).

(ii) *Iliad* V 793–813

Here again Diomedes is the recipient of a paradigmatic exhortation whose main theme is his inferiority to his father. This time the speaker is Athena, who recalls with authoritative knowledge an occasion when Tydeus went alone as a messenger to Thebes (lines 803–804) and was invited by its inhabitants to a feast. Instead, he challenged them to a contest and vanquished them all easily, thanks to Athena's help.

Less detailed but still important are the two following passages:

(iii) *Iliad* X 284–289

This time Diomedes himself reminds Athena (in a prayer designed to win her support by appeal to the principle "help now, as in the past"):

σπεῖό μοι ὡς ὅτε πατρὶ ἅμ' ἕσπεο Τυδέϊ δίωι
ἐς Θήβας, ὅτε τε πρὸ Ἀχαιῶν ἄγγελος ἤιει.
τοὺς δ' ἄρ' ἐπ' Ἀσωπῶι λίπε χαλκοχίτωνας Ἀχαιούς,
αὐτὰρ ὁ μειλίχιον μῦθον φέρε Καδμείοισι
κεῖσ'. ἀτὰρ ἂψ' ἀπιὼν μάλα μέρμερα μήσατο ἔργα
σὺν σοί κτλ.

(iv) *Iliad* V 115–120

In a very similar context (a prayer introduced by exactly the same formula of address to Athena) Diomedes requests aid εἴ ποτέ μοι καὶ πατρὶ φίλα φρονέουσα παρέστης | δηΐωι ἐν πολέμωι. Diomedes also makes general reference to his father's career in the Theban War at *Iliad* VI 222–223 and XIV 110–132.

Welcker (1865:2.328–329) *suo modo* took (i) to be derived from the *Thebais*; B. Niese (*Die Entwicklung der Homerischen Poesie* [Berlin 1882] 129) thought it free invention. Bethe was unimpressed by the first two passages, dismissing them as "Prahlereien" (1891:175). More reasonably, Friedländer (1914:320–321 = 1969:36) notes how consistent are the premises of their story of Tydeus with the more general context of the Theban War both as revealed in the other Iliadic references and as more explicitly set out by later sources: Athena's support is common to both accounts, for instance, and to the third version recounted in *Iliad* X (cf. *Iliad* V 115–116). Tydeus' transference from Aetolia to Argos (*Iliad* XIV 119) explains his presence on the Argive side in the war against Thebes (see further page 121 below) and *Iliad* IV's παραίσια σήματα recur in Pindar

Nemean IX 19–20 and Euripides *Suppliant Women* 155–160, for example. Andersen (1976:36) also observes that the very phrase παραίσια σήματα is a ἅπαξ in Homer, which may perhaps imply an epic source. Friedländer concludes that "ein altes Epos genau so erzählt hat," without, of course, necessarily equating that epic with the *Thebais* (see page 33 above). An epic source is also presupposed by, for instance, Aly (*RE* 7ᴬ [1948]: 1706.2–3) and Leaf (on *Iliad* IV 384).

Robert's attitude is more complex and skeptical, but in fact the difficulties he raises need not be fatal to the cautious findings of Friedländer and others. So, for example, he rightly draws attention to the awkwardness that arises when we ask ourselves how Agamemnon came to possess his knowledge of Tydeus' prowess (1915:1.190). If Tydeus' mission to Thebes involved (as we are explicitly told) no companion, and if all his comrades perished with him finally before the walls of that city, what can possibly be the identity of those informants of Agamemnon οἵ μιν ἴδοντο πονεύμενον (*Iliad* IV 374)? But the oddities that are revealed when we pose such exceedingly realistic and overlogical questions relate only to the frame that encloses the story of Tydeus' mission. They are oddities caused by the transformation of a straightforward narrative into a paradigmatic exhortation placed in the mouth of Agamemnon.[10] That transformation, with all its attendant problems, we can attribute to the poet of the *Iliad*, while leaving the core of the narrative intact. The self-same consideration will amply meet Bethe's objection (1891:175) that one would not expect the *Thebais* to have elevated the role of Argive heroes such as Tydeus: see in particular Andersen 1978:36–37.

Such a conclusion still allows considerable scope and freedom for Homer's own innovating hand. Take, for instance, the names of the two leaders of the Theban ambush: Μαίων Αἱμονίδης ... | υἱός τ' Αὐτοφόνοιο, μενεπτόλεμος Πολυφόντης (*Iliad* IV 394–395). Robert (1915:1.192) and Willcock (145 = "Mythological Paradigms in the *Iliad*," in *Oxford Readings in Homer's* Iliad [Oxford 2002] 441) think (to quote the latter) that "Maeon son of Haemon has a Theban-sounding father" (Haemon is the son of Creon in F1 of the *Oedipodeia*: see page 18 above) "and may be authentic; noticeably he is the only survivor." The suspiciously murderous-sounding Polyphontes and his father Autophonus have, on the contrary, often passed as Homeric inventions (for invented names in Homer cf. Willcock 144–145 = "Mythological Paradigms," 440; L. P. Rank, *Etymologiseering en verwante verschijnselen bij Homerus* [Assen 1951] 130–135; cf. E. Risch, *Eumusia* [Howald Festschrift (Zurich 1947)] 72–91 = *Kleine Schriften* 294–313; H. von Kamptz, *Homerische Personennamen* [Göttingen 1982] 25–28, on "redende Namen" in early epic). But if Homer

---

[10] τὰ Ὁμηρικὰ ἐγκώμια is how this and the other Iliadic allusions to Tydeus are summed up by Σ Aeschylus *Seven Against Thebes* 377 (2.2.180 O. L. Smith) and the accuracy of such a description is proved by Andersen's work.

could invent appropriate names in this manner, so perhaps could other, earlier, epic poets. They could conceivably be the source for the present passage. Tydeus' sparing of Maeon is explained by the bafflingly elliptical phrase θεῶν τερά-εσσι πιθήσας (line 398), the type of abbreviated reference which is often taken to represent compression of a preexisting narrative (cf. *Iliad* VI 183 for precisely the same phrase, and G. S. Kirk, *The Songs of Homer* [Cambridge 1962] 165). Andersen, too, is prepared to take seriously the idea that Maeon's sparing represents an earlier tradition (1978:44n11). Here also, of course, there is room for dispute, since Niese (*Die Entwicklung der Homerischen Poesie* [Berlin 1882] 128), who believes the whole scene to be based on Bellerophon's adventures in *Iliad* VI 187–211, takes the phrase in *Iliad* IV to be derived from that in *Iliad* VI. And the later details as to Maeon which we find in other authors may be spun out of Homer rather than stretching back to the *Thebais* (Andersen 1978:38).

The striking detail of a Mycenae ready to act as ally in the war against Thebes but deterred by signs from Zeus (see pages 33–35 above) is often interpreted as having been introduced to explain why that great city and its Pelopid rulers were conspicuous by their absence from the roll call of cities participating in the Theban War. If this is so, who first perceived the need of such an explanation? The composer of the *Iliad*, or the author of the epic which some suppose to underlie this and similar passages? Robert (1915:1.191: cf. *Heldensage* 3.1.932) followed by Andersen (1978:35) says the Pelopids can have played no part in the *Thebais*. We know too little of the poem to make such a generalization with utter confidence. But the surviving traces of the tradition, as Andersen stresses, do bequeath a picture of Adrastus and Amphiaraus as the leaders of all Argos and Achaea: the Pelopids need not have featured at all. Andersen again backs up Robert, who noted (1915:1.35) how the very fruitlessness of the visit to Mycenae (together with the superfluity of Polyneices in the Homeric context) might be thought to create a "Präjudiz für Erfindung." The motive for such an invention is well conveyed by Andersen: it is once more paradigmatic. As Agamemnon's forebears were willing to help Tydeus, so that hero's son should now help Agamemnon.

Like Andersen (1978:44n9; cf. 45n20), I cannot accept Robert's view of *Iliad* IV 365–400 as a "stümperhaftes Autoschediasma" (1915:1.191) deriving from *Iliad* V 793–813. For instance, modifying his earlier remarks in *Studien zur Ilias* (Berlin 1901) 185, he rather perversely tries to discover minor inconsistencies between the two sections that will confirm such a relationship (1915:1.188–189). But set these two passages side by side:

πολέας δὲ κιχήσατο Καδμεΐωνας
δαινυμένους κατὰ δῶμα βίης Ἐτεοκληείης ...

... ὅ γ' ἀεθλεύειν προκαλίζετο, πάντα δ' ἐνίκα
ῥηϊδίως ...

Iliad IV 385–390

and

δαίνυσθαί μιν ἄνωγον [*scil*. Καδμείωνες] ἐνὶ μεγάροισιν ἔκηλον
αὐτὰρ ὁ ...
κούρους Καδμείων προκαλίζετο, πάντα δ' ἐνίκα
ῥηϊδίως ...

Iliad V 805–808

Is it really natural to take the former as a misunderstanding of the latter, the second passage picturing a Tydeus invited to a feast and proudly challenging his hosts to a contest, and the first transforming this into a chance stumbling upon the feasting Thebans and a blatant provocation? Against Robert's view see further Andersen 1978:44n9 (who rightly concludes that Robert "hier ... legt viel zu viel in den Text hinein") and 79–82.

The *Doloneia*, of course, occupies a special position, though even if it did not I doubt whether I should be impressed by Robert's claims (1915:1.194) that X 289's μάλα μέρμερα μήσατο ἔργα rings odd of Tydeus' self-defense against an ambush, or that we must be disturbed by the specifying of Tydeus' ἀγγελία as a μειλίχιος μῦθος (implying a special negotiation?) and the absence of any reference to Tydeus' challenge. Andersen (1978:130) very sensitively explains the reason for these and other apparent divergences. We here find a concentration upon the μέρμερα ἔργα perpetrated by Tydeus on his way back from the embassy to Thebes because these and these alone are relevant to the situation in the *Doloneia* (where Diomedes is hardly likely to penetrate the capital of the enemy forces!). The same explanation applies to the new detail of Athena as helper to Tydeus in this encounter too (an *ad hoc* invention, thinks Andersen, designed to bring the situations of father and son into the closest possible similarity).

Other discrepancies between what the *Thebais* and what the *Iliad* have to say about the career of Tydeus allow of an easy explanation along lines that are by now very familiar (see page 14 above): the wish to avoid grim and grisly stories and (a point particularly stressed by Andersen [1978:17 and 141]), the need to preserve Tydeus as a suitable paradigm for his son. Both considerations will make clear at once why the cannibalistic propensities revealed in *Thebais* F5 (see page 140 for text) get no mention in the *Iliad*. Likewise this poem says nothing of the tradition that Tydeus killed one of his uncles or the son of one of his uncles (on which see page 121 below), a tale we know to have appeared in the *Alcmaeonis* and may guess to have featured in the *Thebais*. The *Iliad* does indeed name the uncles (XIV 115–118) and Σ AB *Iliad* XIV 120 notes that the verb πλαγχθείς may be a covert allusion to the exile that resulted from this killing. Again, the *Iliad* has nothing to say of the role of the Delphic oracle and its prophecy about the boar and the lion (see page 63 below). But even if we were not aware that Homer generally shies away from excessive dependence on the oracular and the prophetic (see Griffin 1977:48 = 2001:383) we might observe (with Robert himself 1915:1.196) that Tydeus' story is after all told allusively, and that the Delphic origin of this oracle is by no means guaranteed (see page 64 below).

The basic presuppositions of the *Iliad* and the *Thebais*, then, are similar. As to their relationship, our initial antithesis between Welcker's derivation of Iliadic details from *Thebais* and Niese's free invention may not, after all, be so absolute. As Andersen puts it (1978:36–37), the picture of Tydeus' single-handed expedition, if not a total invention, has at least been reshaped to give that hero the prominence required by the paradigmatic context.

MECISTEUS

Εὐρύαλος δὲ οἱ οἶος ἀνίστατο, ἰσόθεος φώς,
Μηκιστῆος υἱὸς Ταλαϊονίδαο ἄνακτος,
ὅς ποτε Θήβασδ' ἦλθε δεδουπότος Οἰδιπόδαο
ἐς τάφον. ἔνθα δὲ πάντας ἐνίκα Καδμείωνας.

Iliad XXIII 677–680

Friedländer rightly observes (1914:318–320 = 1969:34–37) that here, as with the Iliadic references to Tydeus, a few lines imply and conjure up a rich hinterland of mythical presuppositions which are fully consistent with the traditions of the Theban War as we recover them from later writers. As one of the seven Argive chieftains and a hero who fell before Thebes (see page 70 below), Mecisteus can only have participated in the funeral games of Oedipus if they were celebrated prior to the outbreak of hostilities. In other words, Oedipus' death is here conceived as occurring in Thebes and before the expedition of the Seven against that city, precisely the same conception that is entertained in Sophocles' *Antigone* and several other later works of literature. And there seems to be at least one further parallel for the friendly relations envisaged as existing between Thebans and Argives at this stage: Σ *Iliad* XXIII 679 (5.472 Erbse) saw the relevance of the version whereby Ἡσίοδός (fr. 192 MW) φησιν ἐν Θήβαις αὐτοῦ [scil. Οἰδίποδος] ἀποθανόντος Ἀργείαν τὴν Ἀδράστου σὺν ἄλλοις ἐλθεῖν ἐπὶ τὴν κηδείαν τοῦ Οἰδίποδος. One would naturally suppose that the marriage between Argeia and Polyneices (on which see page 63 below) is to be connected in some way with this visit, though precisely how one need not venture to speculate. Mimnermus fr. 21 W may also belong here: M. δέ φησι τὴν μὲν Ἰσμήνην προσομιλοῦσαν Περικλυμένωι (see page 96 below) ὑπὸ Τυδέως κατὰ Ἀθηνᾶς ἐγκέλευσιν τελευτῆσαι. As Friedländer observes (1914:319 = 1969:35n48), these events seem unlikely in wartime, and if the exiled Tydeus had proceeded first to Thebes and only afterwards to Argos, he could have participated in Oedipus' funeral games, and killed Ismene before encountering Polyneices at the gates of Adrastus' palace.

CONCLUSION

Die *Ilias* kennt offenbar wenn nicht eine *Thebais*, so doch Gedichte, aus denen eine *Thebais* auf demselben Wege entstehen konnte wie die *Ilias* enstanden ist.

Wilamowitz 1914:104

Homer's numerous references to the Theban War do indeed presuppose a tradition very similar to what we would independently guess to have stood in the *Thebais*. The Theban and Trojan wars "dominated epic tradition" (West on Hesiod *Works and Days* 162), and it is almost unthinkable that the composer of the Iliadic passages considered above was ignorant of some poetic work on the earlier war. The relationship of this work to the cyclic *Thebais* must remain obscure, but it cannot have been very different in content. On the other hand, Homer's tendency to invent mythical details for his own purposes must not be underestimated, and several features which earlier scholars derived from the *Thebais* may rather be explained, with Andersen, as *ad hoc* creations, or at the very least careful adaptations to fit the new context.

The relationship between the *Iliad* and the *Thebais* is very much a special one. Other works, of course, have been thought to reflect the now-lost epic. It will be convenient to examine below under the relevant headings such writers as mention the Seven against Thebes, the striking of Capaneus by Zeus' thunderbolt, and so on. In what follows I merely list, with a few appropriate comments, some studies not covered on pages 2–3 above in connection with the *Oedipodeia*, involving those authors that are most frequently supposed to have drawn upon the *Thebais*. On the origins of the story as a whole see Ernst Howald 1939—hard to get hold of, but stimulating. Also Dirlmeier 1954:151–158 = 1970:48–54, which, by accumulating potentially relevant material from the ancient Near East, interestingly anticipates the thesis of Burkert (1981:29–48 = 2001:150–165) on the eastern origins of the story. On Pindar's indebtedness to the *Thebais* there is a useful article by Stoneman (1981:44–63), whose main fault is an occasional

uncritical acceptance of some of the reconstructions produced by Bethe, Friedländer, and the rest. For further bibliography see Kühr 2006. Finally, we should
bear in mind that Statius, the one poet to have composed an epic *Thebaid* that is
still extant, "die *Thebais* notorisch nicht gelesen hat" (Robert 1915:1.228–229; cf.
1.172, 202, etc.). See also R. Helm, *RE* 18.3 (1949): 996.49–55; D. Vessey, *Statius and
the* Thebaid (Cambridge 1973) 60, etc.

The Evidence of Art

Robert (1915:1.181–182) claimed that the artistic evidence afforded little help in
reconstructing our lost epic, and that continues to be true, by and large, in spite
of the accretions to our knowledge since he wrote. Artifacts will be mentioned
as and when they seem likely to be relevant.

Here we may note a few general studies. For whatever reason,[11] Etruscan
artists and their clients seem to have found this circle of stories particularly
interesting, and the most useful resumés of this area of our topic occur in books
that start from studies of Etruscan artifacts. See especially R. Hampe and E.
Simon, *Griechische Sagen in der frühen etruskischen Kunst* (Mainz 1964), "Sieben
gegen Theben" (Hampe) 18–28 (with the critique by T. Dohrn in *Mitteilungen des
Deutschen Archäologischen Instituts, Römische Abteilung* 73 [1966]: 15–28 [for a bibliography of other reviews of the book see 15n2]; there is a reply by Hampe and
Simon in *Jahrbuch des Römisch-Germanischen Zentralmuseums Mainz* 14 [1967]: 79–
98). The main contention of Hampe and Simon—that the Etruscans had a direct
knowledge of the *text* of Greek epics—has found little support; see Krauskopf,
Der Thebanische Sagenkreis und andere griechische Sagen in der etruskischen Kunst
(Mainz 1974); J. P. Small, *Studies Related to the Theban Cycle on Late Etruscan Urns*
(Rome 1981). A general survey, with further bibliography, can be found in M. J.
Heurgon, "L'adoption et l'interprétation de l'Epopée grecque par les Etrusques"
(*Actes du Xe Congrès G. Budé* [Toulouse 1978] 1980) 37–44.

---

[11] Cf. Beazley, "The World of the Etruscan Mirror," *Journal of Hellenic Studies* 69 (1949): 1: "Nearly
always the subject chosen testifies only to the boundless love of the Etruscans for Greek heroic
legend and Greek heroic characters. ... Some legends are represented with more circumstance
on Etruscan mirrors than in any extant Greek monument"; and *Etruscan Vase Paintings* (Oxford
1947) 8: "Against certain crude or brutal traits in the Etruscan there is something to set. I cannot
believe that the intense interest in the great heroic and tragic figures of Greece ... was due to
no more than the love of exciting tales of adventure and violence; but must suppose that there
was a heroic strain in the Etruscan character to which these figures made a natural appeal." For
a more negative and reductive approach see Dohrn, 26: "Die Etrusker haben offenkundig nicht
genug Phantasie gehabt, um sich selbst einen Mythos zu schaffen." For another less idealized
view see the study entitled "Banalizzazioni etrusche di miti greci" by G. Camporeale in *Studi in
onore di Luisa Banti* (Rome 1965) 111–120. There is a balanced summary of the issue in Boardman's
review of Hampe and Simon, *Journal of Hellenic Studies* 85 (1965): 241 (stressing the possibility that
Greek artists were involved). Cf. Heurgon (1980) as cited above; and for "Etruria Hellenised" see
now e.g. N. Spivey, *Etruscan Art* (London 1996) 53–80.

Title

On the correct quantity of the middle vowel (Θηβᾰις) see Housman, "Notes on the *Thebais* of Statius (Continued)," *Classical Quarterly* 27 (1933): 72–73 = *Classical Papers* 3.1221–1222. The adjective κυκλικός is appended to the title, presumably to distinguish it from Antimachus' epic, by the quoters of F2, F3, and F7 (see *ad locc.* for the ultimate sources of these passages).

T3 (*see page 136 for text*)

The *Thebais*, like the *Epigoni*, is said to have contained seven thousand lines, a fact which excited Roscher (*Die Sieben- und Neunzahl im Kultus und Mythos der Griechen* [Leipzig 1904] 47–48) to the conclusion that each epic was divided into seven books of a thousand lines each, "ein deutlicher Beweis, wie weit in diesem Falle die Zahlensymbolik gegangen ist." The allusion is to the seven gates of Thebes, but even if we are as impressed by the coincidence as Roscher himself was, we will only have obtained a small insight into the perverse mentality of some anonymous scholar. On book-division in general see S. West, *The Ptolemaic Papyri of Homer* (Cologne 1967) 18–24; S. West and M. L. West, "Comment," *Symbolae Osloenses* 74 (1999): 68–73 = M. L. West, *Hellenica* 1.182–187.

In fact we have no evidence at all as to the number of books into which the *Thebais* was divided.

Date

Scholars once assumed that the legend of the Seven against Thebes originated in the Mycenaean age of Greece (discussion and bibliography in Dirlmeier 1954:154 = 1970:53; cf. J. T. Hooker, *Studies in Honour of T. B. L. Webster* [Bristol 1988] 2.61 = *Scripta Minora* p. 279). More recently, Burkert has ingeniously and persuasively argued that "the tale of the 'Seven against Thebes' is the epic transposition of a purification ritual of ultimately Babylonian origin" (1981:42 = 2001:160). He notes several potential parallels between the Greek story and an Assyrian magical text involving "Seven Demons with formidable wings," or rather figurines thereof, which are opposed by figurines of seven protective deities, and also "twins fighting each other in the gate" (1981:41–42 = 2001:159). But examination of the question as to when such Oriental influence can have made its influence felt in Greece leads Burkert to a conclusion he himself finds disturbing: "If any connection between the Babylonian and the Theban 'Seven' is accepted, the tale cannot have been created in Greece before 750 B.C." (1981:44–45 = 2001:161).

Now the reason Burkert is disturbed by this date is that it supplies "a rather later *terminus post quem* for the evolution of an oral tradition in Greek epic art."

But perhaps it is the theory of the oral nature of the *Thebais* rather than the idea of Babylonian influence that needs to be jettisoned (though against the latter see H. W. Singor, "The Achaean Wall and the Seven Gates of Thebes," *Hermes* 120 (1992): 410–411). By an analysis of both F2 of our epic and fragments of comparable length from the *Cypria* and *Ilias Parva*, J. A. Notopoulos ("Studies in Early Greek Oral Poetry," *Harvard Studies in Classical Philology* 68 [1964]: 28–77) convinced himself that their "solidly formulaic texture, exhibited also in all the smaller fragments, constitutes the *sine qua non* test of the oral character of these early epics." A similar[12] investigation of F1, F2, and F3 of the *Thebais* likewise leads Burkert to talk of the *Thebais*'s "unreflected (*sic*) use of 'Homeric,' formulaic technique" (1981:37 = 2001:156) and to conclude that "the *Thebais* was composed on (*sic*) the same technique as *Iliad* and *Odyssey*, in an identical oral style" (1981:38 = 2001:157).

Both sets of findings are at odds with the stress on "late" linguistic features in those fragments initiated by Wilamowitz and Wackernagel, and taken over by scholars like Bethe and Rzach or (more recently) Kirk and Griffin ("Die erhaltenen Verse sehen nicht danach aus, als hätte sie Kallinos gelesen" [Wilamowitz 1914:104]). They also raise important questions of principle, especially regarding the relationship between formulaic style and oral composition. Notopoulos' simplistic assumption that the former is in itself sufficient guarantee of the latter receives specific refutation in Kirk's important study of "Formular Language and Oral Quality" (*Yale Classical Studies* 20 [1966]: 153–174, esp. 169–174 = *Homer and the Oral Tradition* [Cambridge 1976] 183–200, esp. 195–200). Several studies have called into doubt the once-popular assumption that formulaic composition automatically entails orality: for a useful summary of their conclusions see Lloyd-Jones, "Remarks on the Homeric Question" (in *History and Imagination* [Trevor-Roper Festschrift (1981)] 7–10 = *Academic Papers* [I] 18–21; to whose bibliography add M. L. West's "Is the 'Works and Days' an Oral Poem?" [in *I poemi epici rapsodici non omerici e la tradizione orale* (Padua 1981) 53–67 = *Hellenica* 1.146–158]), with its stress on the possibility that oral and literary modes of composition need not represent absolute alternatives. See also R. Janko, *Homer, Hesiod, and the Hymns* (Cambridge 1982) general index *s.v.* "formula, definition of" and "orality, criteria for"; West, in *Der Übergang von die Mündlichkeit zur Literatur* (Tübingen 1990) 33–50 = *Hellenica* 1.159–175.

---

12 And apparently independent, but considerably more cautious. Burkert's definition of "formulaic language" restricts itself (1981:47 = 2001:163) to "words with at least three syllables or groups of at least two words in the same metrical position." A much less well defined and more chaotic notion of "formula" underlies Notopoulos' statement (1964:28) that "almost one hundred per cent of the verses [from the three fragments analyzed] exhibit formulae, ready-made or created by analogy to pre-existing systems."

Doubtless Burkert is right to draw the distinction he does (37 = 156) between the formulaic character of the *Thebais*'s fragments and, on the one hand, the allusive and playful adaptations of Homeric phraseology practiced by Panyassis and, on the other hand, the *Meropis*'s totally un-Homeric style. But no one has ever suggested that the *Thebais* was as late a composition as Panyassis' *Heracleia*. It does not follow that it was contemporary with the *Iliad* or the *Odyssey*. On the question of the relationship between the *Iliad* and the *Thebais* (or an earlier form thereof) see pages 32–40 above. On the more general issue of relative dating of early Greek epic see *Relative Chronology in Early Greek Epic Poetry*, ed. Andersen and Haug (Cambridge 2012), esp. the final chapter by West (pp. 224–241).

Fragments

F1 *(see page 136 for text)*

Ἄργος: for "the very first word" of a poem as indicating "the singer's subject" see West on Hesiod *Theogony* 1. Within the sphere of epic as narrowly defined we think at once of μῆνιν ἄειδε θεά (*Iliad* I 1), ἄνδρα μοι ἔννεπε Μοῦσα (*Odyssey* i 1), Ἴλιον ἄειδω (*Ilias Parva* fr. 1.1). See further B. A. van Groningen, *The Proems of the* Iliad *and the* Odyssey (*Mededeelingen der Koninklijke Nederlandsche Akademie van Wettenschappen, afdeeling Letterkunde* 9 [1946]) 6–7, W. H. Race, "How Greek Poems Begin," *Yale Classical Studies* 29 (1992): 20. Willcock on *Iliad* I 1 observes "the first word ... shows that the plot of the *Iliad* is to be primarily psychological, and that at any rate we do not have here a simple chronicle of the fighting at Troy," and compares the first word of *Odyssey* i 1. By contrast, the cyclic epics, as Aristotle and Horace saw (cf. Brink on Horace *Ars Poetica* 143–144) give what Griffin (*Homer on Life and Death* [Oxford 1980] 1; cf. "Critical Appreciations VI: Homer, *Iliad* 1.1–52," *Greece and Rome* 29 [1982]: 129 = *Homer* [Oxford 1998] 69) calls the "straightforward narrative of an obviously significant event—the war of the gods and the Titans, the whole Theban War, the capture of Troy." But given this, it is odd that an epic called the *Thebais* should begin with a reference to Argos: see pages 45–46 below.
ἄειδε: in early epic the verb is equally applicable to the activity of the Muse and that of the poet inspired by the Muse: see W. Kranz, "Sphragis: Ichform und Namensiegel als Eingangs- und Schlussmotiv antiker Dichtung," *Rheinisches Museum* 104 (1961): 6 = *Studien zur antike Literatur und ihrem Fortwirken* (Heidelberg 1967) 29n5.

ἄειδε θεά: of course the same pair of words occurs in the same metrical *sedes* in the first line of the *Iliad*. L. E. Rossi ("Estensione e valori del colon nell'esametro omerico," *Studi urbinati di storia, filosofia e letteratura* 39 [1965]: 250n33 and "La fine alessandrina dell'*Odissea* e lo ζῆλος Ὁμηρικός di Apollonio Rodio," *Rivista di filologia e di istruzione classica* 96 [1968]: 160) has interpreted this as a direct allusion to that poem by the composer of the *Thebais*. Kranz (6–7 = 29–30) had already expressed a more cautious attitude, preferring to think in terms of a general stylistic feature of ancient epic as opposed to the obvious imitation of Homer with which we are presented by Orphic fr. 48 Kern: μῆνιν ἄειδε θεὰ Δημήτερος ἀγλαοκάρπου. See further J. Redfield, "The Proem of the *Iliad*: Homer's Art," *Classical Philology* 74 (1979): 98–99 = *Oxford Readings in Homer's* Iliad 460.

Θεά: for this way of referring to the Muse at the start of a poem see Davies and Finglass on Stesichorus fr. 90.9.

πολυδίψιον: the attachment of such an epithet to the indicated subject of the poem immediately before a relative clause is a further regular feature of early epic: *Iliad* I 1 μῆνιν … οὐλομένην, *Odyssey* i 1 ἄνδρα … πολύτροπον (taken by Rossi as the direct model for our present passage; but for the feature as a regular device cf. *Ilias Parva* fr. 1.1: Δαρδανίην εὔπωλον); van Groningen, however, observes a significant discrepancy between the Homeric and the "cyclic" poems: "neither εὔπωλον in the *Little Iliad* nor πολυδίψιον in the *Thebais* are [*sic*] in any way connected with the following idea. They are merely adorning epithets." Contrast the highly pertinent nature and effect of the Homeric instances.[13] πολυδίψιον is again applied to Argos in *Iliad* IV 171 and Quintus Smyrnaeus III 570. Compare (with Bethe 1891:38n15) εὔπωλον at the start of *Ilias Parva*. Since the Argive plain is notoriously well watered by the river Inachus (see e.g. Euripides *El*.1 with M. W. Haslam, "'O Ancient Argos of the Land': Euripides, *Electra* 1," *Classical Quarterly* 26 [1976]: 1), Welcker (1865:2.546), following the lead of several ancient commentators (see Erbse on Σ *Iliad* IV 171 [1.482]), rejected the epithet's obvious meaning ("very thirsty") in favor of a ludicrous equation with πολυίψιος ("much-destroyed": cf. Sophocles *TrGF* 4 F296 with Radt's note *ad loc.*). Others (like Aristarchus *ap.* Hesychius δ2032 [1.466 Latte] δίψιον Ἄργος) took it as equivalent to πολυπόθητος ("much thirsted after"): cf. Strabo VIII 6.7, Athenaeus X 433[E]. The simplest answer is to suppose that the word possesses the signification we should normally assign to it and refers to the tradition alluded to by Hesiod fr. 128 MW Ἄργος ἄνυδρον ἐὸν Δανααὶ θέσαν Ἄργος ἔνυδρον. See further Cook, *Zeus* (Cambridge 1925) 3.894; R. Drews, "Argos and Argives in the *Iliad*," *Classical Philology* 74 (1979): 134–135 = *Oxford Readings in Homer's* Iliad 441 (arguing that "Peloponnesian Argos [was], not always without difficulty, attached to many of the legends … in Pelasgic Argos," a large area in Greece which could be contrasted with the greener and lusher Ionia).

ἔνθεν: for "the expansion by means of a relative clause of the subject of song initially named" as "a regular feature of epic proems" see West on Hesiod *Theogony* 2. Compare in particular *Iliad* I 2 (μῆνιν) … | … ἣ μυρί᾽ Ἀχαιοῖς ἄλγε᾽ ἔθηκε; *Odyssey* i 1 (ἄνδρα) … ὃς μάλα πολλά κτλ.; *Ilias Parva* fr. 1.2 (Δαρδανίην) … | ἧς πέρι. For Latin examples see Coleman on Statius *Silvae* 4.22.

ἔνθεν ἄνακτες: the absense of initial ϝ at the start of ἄνακτες here was claimed by Wilamowitz (1884:366n45)[14] as a sign of "lateness," a claim implicitly rejected by Wackernagel (1916:181 and n2). The failure of ϝ here to "make position" is no particular evidence of a late date for the *Thebais*, as *LfrgE* s.v. ἄναξ (M4 [col. 782] with literature) confirms by listing seventeen other epic examples of a like failure. Slightly more reliable evidence for the dating of our poem may conceivably be afforded by the difficulty we encounter in attaching a satisfactory meaning to ἄνακτες here. The word obviously refers to the Seven against Thebes (a conclusion we may safely draw even when taking into account the lack of context), but precisely how is a mystery. *LfgrE*, C4 (col. 790) is divided between (i) a signification it recognizes as subcategory 1b,

---

[13] On the emotional force of the *Iliad*'s οὐλομένην, for instance, see J. Griffin, "Homeric Pathos and Objectivity," *Classical Quarterly* 26 (1976): 171 = *Homer on Life and Death* (Oxford 1980) 118.

[14] Followed by Blass, *Interpolationen in der Odyssee* (Halle 1904) 290.

where ἄναξ occurs with the name of the relevant hero—we must then assume that the names of the Seven were given in the following lines, though even so the plural ἄνακτες in this sense seems anomalous, with only *Odyssey* xii 290 (θεῶν ἀέκητι ἀνάκτων) providing anything like a parallel; (ii) the possibility of a development from the *Lexikon*'s category 3aδ, where ἄναξ is used of slaves speaking of masters. It compares Euripides *Suppliant Women* 636 (θανόντων ἑπτὰ δεσποτῶν), which is indeed to be explained by noting that the speaker is Καπανέως ... λάτρις (see Collard *ad loc.*).

1-2. ἄνακτες ‖: even in the absence of the next line we can see that there was enjambement between it and the first verse of the poem, and this feature is the third of Rossi's reasons (for the other two see above on ἄειδε θεά and πολυδίψιον) for supposing that the very opening of the *Thebais* specifically imitated the openings of the *Iliad* and the *Odyssey*. The latter's initial verse and its sequel are indeed enjambed in an equally striking fashion: ὃς μάλα πολλά ‖ πλάγχθη. But even here I prefer to talk in terms of a general stylistic feature common in early epic rather than specific copying. A line from a later poem such as Apollonius of Rhodes IV 2-3 ἦ γὰρ ἔμοι γε ‖ yields more readily to an interpretation as allusive imitation of the feature. Our instance and the *Odyssey*'s provide a case of "necessary enjambement": see Milman Parry, "The Distinctive Character of Enjambement in Homeric Verse," *Transactions of the American Philological Association* 60 (1929): 200-220 = *The Making of Homeric Verse* (Oxford 1971) 251-265; G. S. Kirk, "Have We Homer's *Iliad*?," *Yale Classical Studies* 20 (1966): 105-152 = *Homer and the Oral Tradition* (Cambridge 1976) 146-182; G. P. Edwards, *The Language of Hesiod in Its Traditional Context* (Cambridge 1971) 85-100; Richardson, *Homeric Hymn to Demeter* pp. 331-338; Janko, *Homer, Hesiod, and the Hymns* (Cambridge 1982) general index *s.v.*, etc. For Argos as the point of departure for another great expedition celebrated in epic cf. Euripides *Electra* 1-3 (ὦ γῆς παλαιὸν ἄρδμος [Herwerden, Haslam: ἄργος codd.] Ἰνάχου ῥοαί, | ὅθεν ποτ' ἄρας ναυσὶ χιλίαις Ἄρη | ἐς γῆν ἔπλευσε Τρωιάδ' Ἀγαμέμνων ἄναξ. There, of course, the situation is slightly different, since the farmer is apostrophizing the locale in which the play is set.

Some scholars have drawn perfectly unsupportable conclusions from this initial reference to Argos. So, for instance, Wehrli (1957:113n27 = 65-66n1)[15] infers that at the very start of the poem the Argives are already advancing on Thebes, which conclusion "schliesst also eine ausführliche Behandlung von Oidipus' Schicksalen als Vorgeschichte aus" and proves that F2 and F3 on Oedipus' cursing of his sons cannot derive from the same epic as F1 (an earlier work limited to the expedition of the Seven and to be distinguished from the later cyclic poem of wider scope). This is absurd: as de Kock (1961:16-17n50) rightly (if inelegantly) states: "in no epic known to us the opening of the poem is necessarily also the strict chronological beginning."

A more popular misapprehension (bibliography in Stephanopoulos 1980: 114-115n40)[16] is that the initial allusion to Argos entails a bias towards that city

---

[15] A not dissimilar inference is already in Wecklein 1901:676-677.

[16] One of the earliest offenders was the great Grote: see his history of Greece 1.262: "The *Thebais* was composed more in honour of Argos than of Thebes, as the first line of it ... betokens." Cf. 2.129n2. Add to Stephanopoulos' bibliography van Groningen (as cited on page 46 above) 4n9;

in the rest of the epic. Stephanopoulos rightly comments (p. 115) that one might with as much reason deduce a pro-Trojan stance from the opening words of the *Ilias Parva* (Ἴλιον ἀείδω καὶ Δαρδανίην ἐΰπωλον). In fact, with far greater plausibility, Reinhardt inferred that the *Thebais* manifested a bias in favor of the beleaguered city (see page 70 below). Nor, of course, does the initial apostrophe to Argos imply that the epic continued the thread of its narrative until the final victory of that city as won by the Epigoni. Rzach (1922:2374.45–46) rightly warns against this misreading.

F2–F3

Howald (1939:7) convincingly argues that the stories of Oedipus and of the Seven against Thebes were originally independent entities: each is too complex and elaborate to be prologue or sequel to the other, and each has a quite distinct character. The two have been artificially united by the device of Oedipus' curse on his sons, and this expedient may well have been the invention of the *Thebais*. On curses in early Greek literature see Watson 1991, esp. 12–18. On ancestral curses in particular see West in *Sophocles Revisited* (Lloyd-Jones Festschrift 1999) 31–45 = *Hellenica* 2.287–301; R. Gagné, "The Sins of the Fathers ...," *Kernos* 24 (2008): 109–124; and N. Sewell-Rutter, *Guilt by Descent* (Oxford 2008). On Oedipus' curses in general W. Bühler, *Zenobii Athoi Proverbia* 5 (Göttingen 1999) 452–458.

It will be worth our while to spend some considerable time on a general consideration of these two fragments, since the relationship between them is easily misunderstood. Indeed, before Welcker's lucid exposition (1865:2.333–340), scholars were prepared to entertain the possibility that the fragments emanated from different epics,[17] and this in spite of the fact that the respective citers of the two extracts categorically name the author of each as ὁ τὴν κυκλικὴν Θηβαίδα πεποιηκώς or ποιήσας. Even now, after most of the truth about these passages has emerged and won recognition, Fowler can still write (2013:408): "It is probably wasted ingenuity to explain how these two curses consorted within the same poem; much easier to suppose that one is actually from the *Oedipodeia* or some other poem," though admitting the curses "are effectively the same."

In some respects the two fragments are very similar: in both, Oedipus becomes angry; in both the result of that anger is that he curses his two sons. But whereas in F3 the action that angers him is perpetrated by both sons so that

---

Burkert, *Museum Helveticum* 29 (1972): 83 = *Kleine Schriften* 1.147; P. Vicaire (as cited below page 90), p. 6; E. Cingano, "Clistene di Sicione, Erodoto e i poemi del ciclo tebano" (as cited n5 above), 37, etc.

[17] See e.g. L. C. Valckenaer, *Euripidis Tragoedia* Phoenissae (Leiden 1802) 194; G. Hermann, *De Aeschyli Trilogiis Thebanis* (Leipzig 1835) 10–11 = *Opuscula* 7.199.

the joint curse is instantly explicable, in F2 only Polyneices seems responsible; nevertheless, Eteocles too falls under his father's curse. Furthermore, the action that evokes the curse in F2 is on the face of it designed to honor Oedipus, so that Oedipus' response seems at first paradoxical. And the contents of the curse are different, though closely connected: in F2, despite the abrupt termination of the extract, war between the two brothers is clearly prophesied; F3 more specifically mentions their deaths at each others' hands. This climax in clarity and grimness (cf. my note on Sophocles *Trachiniae* [Oxford 1991] lines 43–48) suggests that in the original epic the two episodes did indeed stand in this order (cf. Welcker 1865:2.334–335). For the principle that a similar event's happening twice constitutes decisive proof of an underlying tendency see C. W. Müller, "Der 'zweite Beweis' als Wahrheitskriterium," *Hermes* 127 (1999): 493–495 = *Kleine Schriften* 182–185, esp. Erbse's citation *ap.* n12 of the present two fragments. Both filial misdemeanors concern τροφή, which is the reason given for anger and curse at Aeschylus *Seven Against Thebes* 786 and Sophocles *Oedipus at Colonus* 1265–1266, 1362–1369.

Robert (1915:1.169) appropriately stresses the flexibility of the curse motif in Oedipus' saga[18] (see in general O. Wolff, Roscher 3.2664–2665; Watson 1991: general index *s.v.* "Oedipus"). For instance, Sophocles *Oedipus at Colonus* 1370–1396 takes it over but deliberately postpones it until shortly before its fulfilment so that its delivery may be depicted on stage (see further Robert 1915:1.179). According to Σ A *Iliad* IV 376 (see page 15 above), Oedipus cursed his sons for attempting the virtue of their stepmother Astymedusa. In Apollodorus III 5.9 and in Zenobius *Century* V 43 (1.139 Leutsch–Schneidewin) the curse is for failing to help their aged father when he was expelled from the city; in Euripides *Phoenician Women* 875, it is for not driving him out. In Sophocles *Oedipus Rex* 236–258 the hero unwittingly curses himself, and by implication his mother curses *him* at *Odyssey* xi 272. See further Edmunds 1981b:227–228.

F2 (*see page 137 for text*)

Let us now confine ourselves for the moment to F2. We shall try to obtain a clearer picture of events: first and foremost, why is Oedipus so angry? Polyneices sets before him a fine silver table that had belonged to Cadmus, and also (presumably on it) a fine golden goblet full of wine. The possessions are then described as the precious γέρα of Oedipus' own father, Laius, so one presumes that the goblet too once belonged to Cadmus and that it and the table were handed down within the family from father to son. Athenaeus adds to this picture by claiming that Oedipus had previously forbidden the goblet to be brought before him. Whether

---

[18] It seems not to have featured in the Stesichorean treatment: see Davies and Finglass on fr. 97.

he derives this information from elsewhere in the epic or is merely making an obvious inference, one would suppose the ban to apply to the table also. The only conceivable motive for Oedipus' extreme vexation at the presence before him of these family heirlooms and kingly symbols must be that devised by Welcker (1865:2.334) in the wake of Eustathius and accepted by Bethe (1914:102–103), Robert (1915:1.175), Rzach (1922:2364.21–22), and practically all scholars: Oedipus does not want to be reminded by these objects of the father he had unwittingly killed and supplanted. Perhaps, too, as Robert added, he does not wish to be reminded by these royal tokens of his former prosperity and happiness. Erika Simon objected (1981:10 and n13) that the tokens had earlier belonged to Labdacus and Cadmus, and advanced the novel hypothesis that Oedipus was vexed because in setting before him the utensils used in the hero-cult of Cadmus, his sons were treating him as if he were already dead. But our fragment says nothing of Cadmus' hero-cult or the practice of "Totenmahl" (on which see page 119 below). It does, however, stress (lines 5–6) that the objects belonged to *Laius*. Perhaps this is another un-Homeric feature: the dining table is not the symbol of social harmony (see my remarks in "Feasting and Food in Homer: Realism and Stylisation," *Prometheus* 23 [1997]: 97–107), but a source of discord.

Most scholars (especially Robert [1915:1.175]) have deduced from Polyneices' role here that the *Thebais* already represented him as the wicked and impious brother familiar from later literature. The sinister etymology of his name would seem to bear this out (cf. Aeschylus *Seven Against Thebes* 577, 658, 829; Sophocles *Antigone* 110–111, etc.). For a bibliography of modern explanations of the name see Wolff, Roscher *s.v.* (3.2661.48–49); cf. Fraenkel (1957:44 = 1964:1.312–313), who even excogitates from Euripides *Phoenician Women* 1494 an epic hexameter beginning ὦ Πολύνεικες, ἔφυς νεῖκος πολύ. It is hard to accept Friedländer's counterassertion (326n1 = 40n55) that such a view betokens lack of "Sprachgefühl" and that Πολυνείκης "ist kein Schimpfname." On significant names in epic see page 35 above. On their frequent appearance within the legend of Oedipus see Dirlmeier 1954:157 = 1970:53. According to Robert, Polyneices' present access to the inherited possessions of the Labdacids looks forward to his appropriation of a further item from the same treasure-store: the girdle of Harmonia. Bethe too (1891:99) thinks Polyneices bribed Eriphyle in our epic: most of our sources[19] give him this role. The prominence of Polyneices here and the apparent absence of Eteocles led Bethe (1891:107) further to suppose that the former was already considered the elder as in Sophocles *Oedipus at Colonus* 374–375, 1294–1295, 1422. For other views in antiquity and modern times as to which brother was elder see Wolff, Roscher 2662.41–60.

---

[19]   On the alternative tradition whereby *Adrastus* bribes Eriphyle see page 125 below.

Finally, here are a few minor comments on the context of the present quotation in Athenaeus. Kaibel wished to delete the words δι' ἐκπώματα. The plurality need not disturb us (cf. A. C. Moorhouse, *The Syntax of Sophocles* [*Mnemosyne* suppl. 75 (1982)] 4–5 on plurals for instruments and tools) but the phrase is unnecessary and, worse, inadequate as a motivation for the curse, since (as we have seen [page 47 above]), the silver table plays its part too in angering Oedipus. However, as Robert pointed out (1915:2.66n28), Athenaeus is citing the whole passage for this one detail of the cup, and the double mention is appropriately emphatic. Athenaeus also seems to err in stating that both sons placed the cup before Oedipus (παρέθηκαν) but the mistake is venial, especially when it occurs in a sentence that began with the perfectly accurate statement that the incident led to the cursing of both sons. Eustathius has taken over from Athenaeus both of these small errors, and also the failure to refer to the silver table (irrelevant, as we have just seen, to the context in which Athenaeus cites the epic lines).

1. αὐτὰρ ὁ διογενὴς ἥρως: cf. *Iliad* XXI 17 αὐτὰρ ὁ διογενὴς δόρυ μὲν λίπεν κτλ.; *Odyssey* xxiii 306 αὐτὰρ ὁ διογενὴς Ὀδυσσεύς κτλ.; *Iliad* V 308 αὐτὰρ ὅ γ' ἥρως |, IV 489 | Αἴας διογενής. In a list of adjectives ending in -ης which can also operate as proper names, Σ A *Iliad* XVI 57 (4.173 Erbse) happens to juxtapose αὐτὰρ ὁ διογενής from the above passages with Πολυνείκης, but (*pace* e.g. Welcker; Schneidewin, "Zu den bruchstücken der homerischen dichter," *Philologus* 4 [1849]: 747; Nauck, *Mélanges gréco-romains*, 374; Allen, Oxford Text of Homer vol. 5, p. 113) this is fortuitous and has nothing to do with our line. **ξανθὸς Πολυνείκης** | : cf. *Iliad* III 284 = XVII 18 ξανθὸς Μενέλαος |; Hesiod *Theogony* 947 ξανθὴν Ἀριάδνην |. For other instances of the epithet in this position within the hexameter see W. D. Meier, *Die epische Formel im pseudohesiodeischen Frauenkatalog* (diss. Zurich 1976) 157.

2. | πρῶτα μέν: cf. *Odyssey* xxii 448 | πρῶτα μὲν οὖν; xxiii 131 | πρῶτα μὲν ἄρ; *Iliad* VI 179 πρῶτον μὲν ῥα. **Οἰδιπόδηι**: for the various forms of this name in epic and tragedy see A. Sideras, *Aeschylus Homericus* (*Hypomnemata* 51 [1971]) 101. **καλὴν παρέθηκε τράπεζαν**: cf. *Odyssey* v 92 θεὰ παρέθηκε τράπεζαν |; i 138–139 ξεστὴν ἐτάνυσσε τράπεζαν | ... ταμίη παρέθηκε φέρουσα.

2–3. παρέθηκε τράπεζαν | ἀργυρέην: for the enjambement cf. *Odyssey* i 441–442 θύρην δ' ἐπέρυσσε κορώνηι | ἀργυρέηι; xv 103–104 υἱὸν δὲ κρητῆρα φέρειν Μεγαπένθε' ἄνωγεν | ἀργυρέον. It is of the type that Milman Parry (as page 45 above) termed "unperiodic enjambement ... the addition of an adjectival idea ... describing a noun found in the foregoing verse" ("The Distinctive Character of Enjambement in Homeric Verse," 206 = *The Making of Homeric Verse* 255), and Kirk ("Have We Homer's *Iliad*?" [as on page 45 above] 107 = *Homer and the Oral Tradition* 149) "progressive enjambement."

3. Κάδμοιο θεόφρονος: see Kirk, "Formular Language and Oral Quality" [as on page 42 above], 169 = *Homer and the Oral Tradition* 195 for the epithet ("a compound unique in the epic tradition") as "a clear departure from the thrift of the oral epic. The standard laudatory epithet for this position in the verse is δαΐφρονος (28 times in Homer)." θεόφρων again only in Pindar *Olympian* VI 41. **αὐτὰρ ἔπειτα** |: the notorious cyclic formula: cf. Pollianus *Palatine Anthology* XI 130.1–2 τοὺς κυκλί<κ>ους τούτους, τοὺς 'αὐτὰρ ἔπειτα' λεγόντας | μισῶ, λωποδύτας ἀλλοτρίων ἐπέων (on which see Cameron, *Callimachus and His Critics* [Princeton 1995] 396–398; Griffin 1977:49; Campbell on Quintus Smyrnaeus XII 139). The phrase at line-end is not unknown to Homer (see Campbell) but in the present case one is reminded of the naïve repetition of ἔπειτα in our earliest examples of Greek prose: cf. Ed. Fraenkel, "Additional Note on the Prose of Ennius," *Eranos* 49 (1951): 50–56 = *Kleine Beiträge zur klassischen Philologie* 2.53–58, Dover in *Classical Contributions* (McGregor Festschrift 1981) 24–25 and n47 = *Greek and the Greeks* 29 and n46.

4. δέπας ἡδέος οἴνου |: the same phrase ends a line at *Odyssey* iii 51. The double absence of digamma (ϝηδέος ϝοίνου) is striking in both passages and a probable index of "lateness" (Wilamowitz 1884:366n45; Bethe 1891:40n20). On the line-end phrase μελιηδέος οἴνου see Chantraine, *Gramm. hom.* 1.123; on other Homeric instances of ἡδύς and οἶνος sans ϝ see 151 and 145 respectively. Most are easily removed. For the adjective's application to wine see Arnott on Alexis fr. 46.9 KA.

5. αὐτὰρ ὅ γ' ὡς: the same collocation of words at the start of a line in *Iliad* XII 40, XXI 550; cf. *Iliad* V 308, cited on line 1. On the stylistic implications of this third instance see Griffin 1977:49. **φράσθη**: the meaning is that given by LSJ s.v. II 4 ("perceive, observe"). Compare ἐνόησε in fr. 3.1 (Oedipus is again the subject). In other words, φράσατο would supply the same sense. For the form cf. (ἐπ)ἐφράσθης in *Odyssey* v 183, xix 485, xxiii 260. On its relatively recent development see Chantraine (as cited on line 4), 1.405–406 **πατρὸς ἑοῖο**|: same phrase, same position in *Iliad* XIV 11, XXIII 360; Hesiod *Theogony* 472.

6. τιμήεντα γέρα: cf. *Odyssey* i 312 (|τιμῆεν), xiii 129 (| τιμήεις). **μέγα οἱ κακὸν ἔμπεσε θυμῶι**: for a full and excellent analysis of the oddity of this phrase see Kirk, "Formular Language and Oral Quality" (as cited on page 42 above) 169–171 = *Homer and the Oral Tradition* 195–197. The poet seems to have conflated "two distinct formular applications of ἔμπεσε: an emotion 'falls upon' the spirit, an evil 'falls upon' a house." But in the present case, muddle-headedly, "an evil" (κακόν rather than, e.g., ἄχος) falls upon Oedipus' spirit. Did the poet mean κακόν to be equivalent to ἄτη? For ἔμπεσε θυμῶι | of emotion see *Iliad* IX 436, XIV 207, 306 (ἐπεὶ χόλος ἑ. θ.), XVI 206 (κακὸς χόλος ἑ. θ.), XVII 625 (δέος ἑ. θ.). For ⌣–κακὸν ἔμπεσεν οἴκωι | cf. *Odyssey* ii 45, xv 375. **μέγα οἱ**: ϝ is hardly ever neglected before third-person sing. οἱ: see West, *Hesiod's Theogony* p. 100, his note on Hesiod *Works and Days* 526 (p. 291), Edwards, *Language of Hesiod*, 138n48.

7. |αἶψα δέ: these two words begin a line in *Iliad* II 664, *Odyssey* xvi 359. **μεταμφοτέροισιν**: It is difficult to know what to make of this. If we are supposed (i) to detect here an example of the verb μετ' ... ἧρᾶτο in tmesis, we will look in vain for an entry s.v. μεταράομαι in our lexica. And the search s.v. ἀράομαι for the construction ἀρὰς ἀ. μετά τινι in place of the normal ἀρὰς ἀ. τινι will be equally futile. But emendations do not convince: ἑοῖσιν ἐπ' ἀμφοτέροισιν *coni.* H. van Herwerden, "Notulae ad Athenaeum," *Mnemosyne* 4 (1876): 313, *prob.* Nauck, *Mélanges gréco-romains*, 374–375, and seriously considered by Wackernagel (1916:181n2); κατ' ἀμφοτέροισι *coni.* R. Peppmüller, "Zu den Fragmenten der griechischen Epiker," *Neue Jahrbücher für Philologie und Pädogogik* 133 (1886): 465, comparing κατηράτο in *Iliad* IX 454. The two likeliest solutions for the problems raised by the paradosis are (ii) to associate it with the Homeric construction (Schwyzer, *Gr. Gr.* 2.483) whereby we find a verb with μετά + dative plural as prepositional object rather than with the simple dative that later suffices. Especially enlightening are instances where tmesis would be ruled out by the resultant form (e.g. μεταπολεμίζω) or by other considerations (*Iliad* I 525–526 τοῦτο γὰρ ἐξ ἐμέθεν γε μετ' ἀθανάτοισι μέγιστον| τέκμωρ). Alternatively, if not repelled by its remarkable equation of σύν with μετά, one may suppose that we have here (iii) the form μεταμφοτέροισι as an alternative to συναμφοτέροισι, though it must be admitted that (iii) is no less a stranger to LSJ than (i) and (ii). This third interpretation is adopted by scholars of the calibre of Wilamowitz (1884:366n45) and Wackernagel (1916:181n2), who take it as a further index of the relative recentness of the poem, the latter observing that (a) the equivalence between μετά and σύν thus implied is unknown to early epic, where the former means "amid" (see further Schwyzer, *Gr. Gr.* 2.481–482); (b) the word to which our form is an alternative, συναμφοτέροι, is itself not found until the fifth century (though cf. Theognis 820 συναμφοτέρους, which there seems no reason to date so late). M. Leumann, *Homerischer Wörter* (Basel 1950) 94n56 takes this explanation a stage further: starting with the tmesis in Homeric phrases like μετὰ Τρωιῆισιν ἔειπεν (*Iliad* XXII 476), μετὰ δ' Ἀργείοισιν ἔειπεν (XXIII 781), Τρώεσσι μεθ' ἱπποδάμοις ἀγορεύσω (VIII 525), ταῦτα μετ' Ἀργείοις ἀγορεύεις (X 250), he suggests that, in a manner constantly presupposed by his book, such extensions of the tmesis as μετ' ἀμφοτέροισιν ἔειπεν (*Iliad* III 85 = VII 66; cf. too the similar examples ἄριστα / ἔρισμα μετ' ἀμφοτέροισι γένηται at *Iliad* III 110, IV 38, ἔργα μ. α. ἔθηκε at *Iliad* III 321, φιλότητα μ. α. βάλωμεν / τίθησι at *Iliad* IV 16/83, ἔριν Ἀτρεΐδηισι μ. α. ἔθηκε at *Odyssey* iii 136) have been misunderstood and μεταμφότεροι created by misinterpretation. **ἐπαράς**: *Iliad* IX 456.

7–8. ἐπαράς | ἀργαλέας ἤρατο: comparable enjambement in *Odyssey* xi 291 (289: βόας) ...|... ἀργαλέας (cf. Hesiod fr. 37.2 MW), *Iliad* XI 3–4 ἔριδα ... | ἀργαλέην. With ἐπαράς ... ἤρατο cf. *Iliad* II 788 ἀγορὰς ἀγόρευον and in general Fehling, *Die Wiederholungsfiguren und ihr Gebrauch bei den Griechen vor Gorgias* (Berlin 1969) 156–157. For the adjective ἐπάρατος in real-life curses see Watson 1991:37.

8. θεῶν δ' οὐ λάνθαν' ἐρινύν: for a useful survey of references to Erinys or Erinyes in early Greek epic see A. Heubeck, "Ἐρινύς in der archaischen Epik," *Glotta* 64 (1986): 143–165. He finds θεῶν here eccentric ("auffällend": 152–153), without noting that it is Meineke's conjecture for—or, rather, reinterpretation of—the manuscripts' ΘΕΟΝ (proposal made in *Analecta Critica ad Athenaei* Deipnosophistas [Leipzig 1867] 211). I accept it, and certainly find it preferable to Rohde's θοήν (*ap.* C. F. H. Bruchmann, *Epitheta Deorum Quae apud Poetas Graecos Leguntur* [Leipzig 1893] 100): cf. Quintus Smyrnaeus V 454 θοαὶ ... ἐριννύες; Sophocles *Electra* 486–491 πολύπους ... ἐρινύς (cf. Finglass *ad loc.*). The Erinyes are ὠκύδρομοι at *Orphic Hymns* 69.9, although they are tardy elsewhere (e.g. ὑστερόπους at *Orphic Argonautica* 1162–1163). For the genitive compare Sophocles *Antigone* 1075 Ἅιδου καὶ θεῶν ἐρινύες (against Dawe's tampering [*Studies on the Text of Sophocles* [Leiden 1978] 3.114–115] see Lloyd-Jones and Wilson *ad loc.* [*Sophoclea* 143]): cf. Sophocles *Electra* 112 σεμναὶ ... θεῶν παῖδες. As Robert observes (1915:2.67), this genitive is different in kind from those which occur in such familiar phrases as πατρός, μητρὸς ἐρινύες where they represent the directly injured party (see E. Rohde, "Paralipomena," *Rheinisches Museum* 50 [1895]: 10–11 = *Kleine Schriften* 2.233–234). The manuscripts' θεόν may not be impossible as an interpretation of the original ΘΕΟΝ: cf. *Odyssey* xv 234 = Hesiod fr. 280.9 MW (θεὰ δασπλῆτις Ἐρινύς) and for the general idiom thus exemplified (θ. preceding the deity's name) West on Hesiod *Works and Days* 73. For feminine θεός in epic see West on Hesiod *Theogony* 442–443,

Richardson on *Homeric Hymn to Demeter* 1. Compare in particular Aeschylus *Seven Against Thebes* 720–723 (in the context of Oedipus' curse) τὰν …| θεὸν, οὐ θεοῖς ὁμοίαν, | … | … Ἐρινύν.[20] Or, with Robert 1915:2.67n2, we may simply emend to θεάν. But I prefer θεῶν because, as Deubner (1942:35 = 1982:669) observes, the shared responsibility of gods and Erinyes seems more in the epic manner. He compares *Iliad* IX 454–457 στυγερὰς δ' ἐπεκέκλετ' Ἐρινῦς, |…|… θεοὶ δ' ἐτέλειον ἐπαράς,| Ζεύς τε καταχθόνιος καὶ ἐπαινὴ Περσεφόνεια. See too *ibid.* 569–572 Meleager's mother curses her son: τῆς δ' ἠεροφοῖτις Ἐρινὺς | ἔκλυεν ἐξ Ἐρέβεσφιν κτλ.) and *Odyssey* xi 274–280 (ἄφαρ δ' ἀνάπυστα θεοὶ θέσαν ἀνθρώποισιν | … (Epicaste dies and bequeaths to Oedipus) ἄλγεα… | πολλὰ μάλ', ὅσσα τε μητρὸς Ἐρινύες ἐκτελέουσι). On the interaction of gods and Erinyes in epic see further Dietrich, *Death, Fate, and the Gods* (London 1965) 233–234, Watson 1991: general index *s.v.* "Erinyes, execute curses," esp. 30n133, and index of curse themes *s.v.* "gods' anger in curses." On Oedipus' links with Erinyes see Edmunds 1981b:225–231. **ἐρινύς** or **ἐρινῦς** at line-end in *Iliad* IX 454, 571, and XIX 87.

9. οὗ οἵ†: μή is tentatively suggested by Hutchinson in his commentary on Aeschylus *Seven Against Thebes* (Oxford 1985) xxix, but for the digamma see above on line 6. For a list of early attempts to solve the crux see W. Ribbeck, "Zu den Fragmenten der griechischen Epiker," *Rheinisches Museum* 33 (1878): 457. Best, perhaps, was Hermann's πατρώϊ ἐνηείηι φιλότητος, which Ribbeck himself adapted to π. ἐνηέϊ <ἐν> φιλότητι (so too, independently, Peppmüller, "Zu den Fragmenten" [as in 7n above], 465, comparing for the hiatus in the bucolic caesura ἔγχεϊ ὀξυόεντι in *Iliad* V 50, etc.). Kaibel's edition of Athenaeus placed Ribbeck's conjecture in the actual text of the fragment. Robert, however (1915:2.67), argued that both lines of approach are vitiated by the fact that Homer only employs ἐνηής of an ἑταῖρος or person (contrast Hesiod *Theogony* 651 μνησάμενοι φιλότητος ἐνηέος, cited by Ribbeck). The same charge may be leveled against O. Rossbach's ἐνηῆι φιλότητι ("Epica," *Neue Jahrbücher für Philologie und Pädogogik* 143 [1891]: 82) and a similar one (as seen by Robert and Peppmüller) against Meineke's ἐν ἠθείηι φιλότητι (*Analecta Critica*, 212), since Homer never bestows this (or any other) adjective upon this noun when it bears the nonsexual signification required here. However, Robert's criteria so drastically exclude most corrections from consideration that a reminder is necessary of the numerous other un-Homeric features that this fragment and others of our epic contain. Perhaps Ribbeck's suggestion is the least unsatisfactory after all. **φιλότητι** | in *Odyssey* viii 313, x 43 (in the last passage meaning "friendship").

9–10. (πατρώϊα …) | δάσσοντ': apart from πατρώϊων χρημάτων δατῆροι at Aeschylus *Seven Against Thebes* 711 (two lines after a reference to Οἰδίπου κατεύγματα), compare the terms of Oedipus' curse at 788–789 of the same play: καί σφε σιδαρονόμωι | διὰ χερί ποτε λαχεῖν κτήματα (see too the references to κτέανα and κτήματα in 729 and 817 and cf. Lloyd-Jones, *Classical Review* 28 [1978]: 214), at Euripides *Phoenician Women* 67–68 (ἀράς) … | θηκτῶι σιδήρωι δῶμα διαλαχεῖν τόδε and at [Plato] *Alcibiades.* (2) 138ᶜ ὥσπερ τὸν Οἰδίπουν αὐτίκα φασὶν εὔξασθαι χαλκῶι διελέσθαι τὰ πατρῶια τοὺς υἱεῖς. Hermann's conjecture δάσσαιντ' (made in the note on *Oedipus at Colonus* 1377 in his 1827 revision of Erfurdt's commentary [2.435]) held the stage until Wackernagel

---

[20] On the Erinys in this play see e.g. F. Solmsen, "The Erinys in Aischylos' *Septem*," *Transactions of the American Philological Association* 68 (1937): 197–211 = *Kleine Schriften* 1.106–120; and N. Sewell-Rutter, *Guilt by Descent* (Oxford 2008) 83–109.

(1916:254–255) objected that Homer only uses ὡς plus optative in indirectly quoted prayers (*Odyssey* xvii 243, xxi 201), and proposed δάσσοντ' on the basis of *Odyssey* v 23–24 = xxiv 479–480 (ἐβουλεύσας| ... ὡς ... ἀποτείσεται). The comparison is apt; only (unlike Wackernagel) we must take ἀποτείσεται and δάσσοντ' plus ὡς as exemplifying "the transition from modal to final use" (Schwyzer, *Gr. Gr.* 2.665 on *Odyssey* v 23–24, with which he compares *Iliad* VIII 36–37 βουλὴν ... ὑποθησόμεθ' ... |ὡς μὴ πάντες ὄλωνται). W. Headlam ("Emendations and Explanations," *Journal of Philology* 30 [1907]: 307), citing Sophocles *Oedipus Rex* 1270–1274 (Oedipus' curse on his sons) αὐδῶν τοιαῦθ' ὁθοῦνεκ' οὐκ ὄψοιντό νιν, conjectured δάσσοιντ', approved by Pearson (*Euripides' Phoenissae*, p. xxn2), but for future indicative rather than imprecatory optative in curses see Watson 1991:23–24 (cf. 40) and on Horace *Epode* V 89.

10. ἀεί: cf. *Iliad* XII 211 Ἕκτορ, ἀεὶ μέν πώς μοι ἐπιπλήσσεις ἀγορῇσιν, XXIII 648 ὥς μευ ἀεὶ μέμνησαι ἐνηέος, οὐδέ σε λήθω, *Odyssey* xv 379 οἷά τε θυμὸν ἀεὶ δμώεσσιν ἰαίνει. The short α in these passages is regarded as an Atticism by Wackernagel (1916:146), who rejects the notion of an East Ionic origin. Chantraine demurs (*Gramm. hom.* 1.167). But as Shipp, restating Wackernagel's case, observes (*Studies in the Language of Homer*[2] [Cambridge 1972] 49), "if Ionic it is late, as αἰεί persists into the inscriptions ... and is usual in MSS of Herodotus." Hermann's ἔοι (suggested in the note on *Oedipus at Colonus* 1377 cited above on lines 9–10), resembles Schneidewin's αἰεὶ δ' ἀμφοτέροισιν ἔοι π. τ. μ. τ. ("Zu den bruchstücken der homerischen dichter," 747) and Köchly's εἴη δ' ἀμφοτέροισιν ἀεὶ π. τ. μ. τ. (*Coniectaneorum Epicorum fasc.* I [1851] p. 10 = *Opuscula Philologica* 1.230) and other emendations in seeking to introduce an imprecatory optative that would be idiomatic in a curse: see e.g. the funerary inscription from Asia Minor cited by J. H. M.Strubbe in Faraone and Obbink, eds., *Magika Hiera* (Oxford 1991) 39: ἐξωλεία καὶ πανωλεία εἴη αὐτῶι πάντων. But a corresponding verb with πολεμοί τε μαχαί τε as its subject can well have stood in the verse that originally followed line 10 (since Athenaeus is usually a careful and conscientious quoter [cf. K. Zepernich, "Die Exzerpte des Athenaeus in den Dipnosophisten und ihre Glaubwürdigkeit," *Philologus* 77 (1921): 324–363 (esp. 362–363)], the omission of the line will be a transmissional error). Without emending we still have an irrevocable prayer for hateful things which supplies a positive equivalent of e.g. μηδέποτε in curses (see Strubbe 56n106) used of benefits *not* to be enjoyed. For "always" in curses see, e.g., Tibullus I 5.51–52 *hanc volitent animae circum sua fata querentes* | *semper,* Propertius IV 5.39 *semper habe morsus circa tua colla recentes,* Genesis 3:14 and 17 (God's curse on the serpent and Adam) "all the days of thy life." **πόλεμοί τε μάχαι τε** |: same phrase at line-end in *Iliad* I 177, V 891, Hesiod *Theogony* 926. But there may be a special point to the phrase here. The curse from Asia Minor cited above provides a parallel for the idiomatic (and "strengthening") juxtaposition of nearly synonymous evils prayed for in a curse.

F3 (*see page 138 for text*)

A few introductory remarks on the text of the note that is our source for this fragment: the legion inadequacies of Papageorgiou's edition of the Sophoclean scholia can from time to time be remedied by consulting V. de Marco's work *De Scholiis in Sophoclis Tragoedias Veteribus* (Reale Accademia Nazionale dei Lincei 6 [Rome 1937]), which handily corrects and amplifies Papageorgiou's information, and nowhere to better effect than on p. 111, which deals with the scholion that is the source for our fragment. I have incorporated the Italian scholar's findings in this fragment's text and *app. crit.* They reappear in his full-scale edition of the scholia on the *Oedipus at Colonus* (Rome 1952). Nauck's small but palmary corrections of the scholion's comment on Oedipus' anger were made in his review of Papageorgiou (*Mélanges gréco-romains,* 50).

οἱ περὶ Ἐτεοκλέα καὶ Πολυνείκην = Ἐτεοκλῆς καὶ Πολυνείκης: on the idiom see S. L. Radt, "Noch einmal Aischylos, Niobe Fr. 162N (278M)," *Zeitschrift für Papyrologie und Epigraphik* 38 (1980): 47–56 and "οἱ (αἱ etc.) περὶ + acc. nominis proprii bei Strabon," *Zeitschrift für Papyrologie und Epigraphik* 71 (1988): 35–40 = *Kleine Schriften* 236–246 and 362–374. The criticism implied by the scholion's use of the adverbs μικρο-ψύχως and τελέως ἀγεννῶς was attributed to Didymus by Robert (1.170); cf. Pfeiffer, *History of Classical Scholarship* 1.276–277. As Griffin suggests (*Homer on Life and Death* 14), it may reflect the inability of a later Greek mentality to understand the importance attached to food as a symbol of honor in earlier literature. This brings us to the fragment itself.

Almost immediately after citing our present fragment, the Sophoclean scholion proceeds to quote a further fragment in the form of fifteen iambic trimeters (*TrGF* 2 F458) which appear to presuppose the same state of affairs. Controversy has long raged over the origin, authorship, and genre of this floscule of drama: see especially Robert 1915:2.67–69. Without becoming unnecessarily embroiled in this matter, we may safely make the following comments on this other fragment's version of events. The speaker of the fifteen verses would seem to be either Eteocles or Polyneices, for he describes how he and at least one other had been accustomed to send to the blind Oedipus a portion of the sacrifice (lines 2–3 θυσίας {γὰρ} ἀπαρχὴν γέρας ἐπέμπομεν πατρί | περισσὸν ἀρνῶν ὦμον, ἔκκριτον γέρας [κρέας *coni.* Methner]). But on one occasion a lapse of memory led to their sending something else (lines 5–6: ἀντὶ τοῦ κεκομμένου | ἐπέμψαμεν βόειον) and the irate old man, interpreting the change as a deliberate insult intended to escape his attention, invokes a curse upon his sons that is remarkably similar to what we find at the close of the epic fragment (lines 14–15: χαλκῶι δὲ μαρμαίροντες ἀλλήλων χρόα | σφάζοιεν ἀμφὶ κτήμασι βασιλικοῖς).

Now even if this dramatic excerpt had suffered less corruption than it has and we felt far more confident as to its source and genre, there would still be danger in resorting to it automatically in order to supplement or clarify our own particular fragment. Let us start then by approaching the epic lines in isolation to see what they will yield us independently.

Our fragment's mention of an ἰσχίον seems to imply (see *ad loc.*) a sacrifice as background to the insult (so e.g. Bethe 1891:102–103). Oedipus does not participate directly as a king normally would (cf. Aristotle *Politics* 1285ᴮ10), perhaps because his hands are polluted by his crime. Clearly his sons have, in practice, taken over the duties of kingship (see Wolff in Roscher 3.2663.39–49). Teiresias in Euripides *Phoenician Women* 875–876 describes how Oedipus' two sons ἄνδρα δυστυχῆ | ἐξηγρίωσαν. In the *Thebais* was the insult intentional or deliberate? The actual fragment represents Oedipus as exclaiming παῖδες μέγ' ὀνείδειον τόδ' ἔπεμψαν, but the words of a proud and angry old man are not perhaps the most reliable testimony or the most objective. The quoter of the epic ascribes the offense to forgetfulness (ἐκλαθόμενοί ποτε) and this corresponds with the explanation given in line 4 of the iambic trimeters treating of the same subject (οὐ μεμνημένοι). Here, certainly, Oedipus' complaint about filial malice seems at odds with the reality. The same picture is implied by Plato's remarks on the malicious nature of Oedipus' curse (*Alcibiades* [2] 138ᶜ and 141ᴬ, *Laws* 931ᴮ). See too Aeschylus *Seven Against Thebes* 780–781 (ἐπ' ἄλγει δυσφορῶν | μαινομέναι κραδίαι), Euripides *Phoenician Women* 66 and 877 (νοσῶν). The idea that an unintentional insult, one occasioned by oversight, is as deserving of punishment as a deliberate crime accords perfectly with archaic Greek morality: see Davies and Finglass on Stesichorus fr. 85.2.

1. ἰσχίου: Evelyn-White, in his Loeb text of Hesiod, the *Homeric Hymns*, and *Homerica* (London 1914) 485n1, explained Oedipus' anger on the ground that the haunch was "regarded as a dishonourable portion." A more accurate way to put this would be to say that Oedipus was expecting a more honorable portion. This is the inference most scholars have drawn, from Welcker (1865:2.336) down to Griffin (*Homer on Life and Death* 14: "the less honourable cut of meat"). It seems borne out by studies of the activities that accompanied sacrifice. So F. Puttkamer, *Quo modo Graeci victimarum carnes distribuerint* (diss. Königsberg 1912) 41: "privatos quoque homines si sacrificabant viris quibus honores debebant eximiam partem misisse verisimile est ex fabula Oedipodea"; Meuli, "*Griechische Opferbräuche*" (*Phyllobolia* [von der Mühll Festschr. (1945)] 219 = *Gesammelte Schriften* 2.943): Oedipus is vexed at not having received the particular γέρας of the shoulder-blade, "der geziemende Anteil für einen Ehrengast." This interpretation seems best to square with Aeschylus *Seven Against Thebes* 786 on τροφή as the cause of Oedipus' curse (presumably the passage referred to by our scholion as similar to this fragment),[21] and with Euripides *Phoenician Women* 874–875: οὔτε ... γέρα πατρί |... διδόντες. For "the motif of food ... to make effects of will and symbolism" in the epics of Homer and other European poets see Griffin as cited 14–15. For "the idea of more honourable cuts of meat" he quotes *Iliad* VII 321–322 (νώτοισιν δ' Αἴαντα διηνεκέεσσι γέραιρεν | ἥρως Ἀτρεΐδης), *Odyssey* viii 474–478 (δὴ τότε κήρυκα προσέφη πολύμητις Ὀδυσσεύς, | νώτου ἀποπροταμών, ἐπὶ δὲ πλεῖον ἐλέλειπτο, | ἀργιόδοντος ὑός, θαλερὴ δ' ἦν ἀμφὶς ἀλοιφή | 'κῆρυξ, τῇ δή, τοῦτο πόρε κρέας, ὄφρα φάγῃσι, | Δημοδόκωι' κτλ.), ix 159–160 and 550–551. Also (15n36) an interesting Irish parallel. See too Puttkamer as cited 39–41 ("distributiones honoris causa factae") and

---

[21] Whether rightly, or (as Hutchinson thinks, pp. xxv–xxvi of his commentary on Aeschylus *Seven Against Thebes*) wrongly.

Burkert *Homo Necans* p. 47 = Engl. trans. 37n12.[22] Simon's alternative interpretation (1981:10 and n13) that the ἰσχίον would normally have been burned for the gods, so that Oedipus is being treated as if he were dead, seems very far-fetched. Welcker and Robert (1915:1.185) thought the curse probably as fundamental for the *Thebais* as the μῆνις for the *Iliad*. Griffin thinks "the Homeric poets would have been reluctant to make such a point the fulcrum for a great movement of the plot." Certainly, as Σ *Iliad* IV 343 (1.510 Erbse) says of a like scene, οὐ περὶ βρωμάτων, ἀλλὰ περὶ τιμῆς ὁ λόγος.

ἐνόησε: at first this verb may seem incompatible with the hypothesis (see page 60 below) that the *Thebais* portrayed Oedipus as self-blinded in the manner familiar from Sophocles' *Oedipus Rex* and elsewhere. After all, LSJ *s.v.* νοέω (I.1) gives "perceive by the eyes, observe" as the word's primary meaning, and Snell echoes the view of many scholars when he claims ("Wie die Griechen lernten, was geistige Tätigkeit ist," *Journal of Hellenic Studies* 93 [1973]: 183 = *Der Weg zum Denken und zur Wahrheit* [*Hypomnemata* 57 (1978)] 41) that the verb is "eng mit dem Sehen verbunden." However, such an approach is misleading, for its present occurrence is perfectly consistent with the results of the painstaking researches of K. von Fritz in his article "Noῦς and voεῖν in the Homeric Poems," *Classical Philology* 38 (1943): 79–93 = *Um die Begriffswelt der Vorsokratiker* (*Wege der Forschung* 9 [1968]) 246–276. Note in particular his conclusion (85 = 260) that "there are two basic meanings of the word voεῖν: to realise a situation and to plan or to have an intention." The first of these obviously fits the present instance of the verb, and von Fritz's general interpretation of the word's history and its application to our passage would become even more convincing if we could be sure that he is right (92–93 = 273) to approve the etymological derivation of voεῖν from the root *snu* "to sniff or smell." The verb would then have had no original association with sight at all. But in fact such a derivation is extremely controversial (for criticism and a list of other suggested etymologies see Fisk and Chantraine *s.v.* in their etymological dictionaries). On the basic meaning of voεῖν see further T. Krischer, "Noos, noein, noēma," *Glotta* 62 (1984): 141–149. Incidentally, one would like to know how the author of these lines visualized Oedipus' perception of the insult (if visualize it he did). Our dramatic fragment tells us that he *felt* the difference (lines 6–7 ὁ δὲ λαβὼν χερί | ἔγνω 'παφήσας). Perhaps so specific and detailed an explanation is beneath epic dignity. Whatever the truth in that area, there is no doubt that the present epic instance fully fits another generalization formulated by von Fritz (84 = 257) in connection with Homer's use of the word: "without exception, in all those cases in which the verb voεῖν has a direct and concrete object, violent emotion is caused by the voεῖν."

| ‿◡ ὡς ἐνόησε: the same phrase in the same metrical position at *Iliad* XV 422, *Odyssey* x 375, etc. χαμαὶ βάλε εἶπέ τε μῦθον: cf. *Iliad* VII 190 (Ajax recognizes his κλῆρός and as a sign of his joy) [τὸν μὲν πὰρ πόδ' ἑόν] χαμάδις βάλε φώνησέν τε. Similar phrasing, very dissimilar content. χαμαὶ βάλε: the same phrase in the same metrical position at *Iliad* XXI 51, *Odyssey* xvii 490, *Homeric Hymn to Hermes* 118 and 298; and (with βάλον for βάλε) *Iliad* V 588 and *Odyssey* xxii 188. But in these instances the phrase has a different meaning from the present occurrence. A closer parallel

---

[22] Comparing Xenophon *Agesilaus* 5.1 (διμοιρία ἐν ταῖς θοίναις) for the Spartan kings, and 1 Samuel 1.5 (double portion for Hanna). On honorable cuts and their withholding see further E. Cingano, "The Sacrificial Cut and the Sense of Honour Wronged in Greek Epic Poetry: *Thebais*, frgs. 2–3 D," in C. Grottanelli and L. Milano, eds., *Food and Identity in the Ancient World* (Padua 2004) 57–67.

for anger expressed by the flinging to ground of an object is *Iliad* I 245–246 ὣς φάτο Πηλεΐδης, ποτὶ δὲ σκῆπτρον βάλε γαίηι | χρυσείοις ἥλοισι πεπαρμένον, though that action has a symbolic dimension (see Griffin, *Homer on Life and Death* 11–12) lacking here. **βάλε εἶπε**: the evidence of so corrupt a fragment is hardly sufficient to allow us to decide whether the poet gave εἶπε a digamma or intended βάλεν. **εἶπέ τε μῦθον**: the same formula ends a hexameter at *Iliad* VII 277, XI 647, XVIII 391, XXIII 204, *Odyssey* viii 302, xiv 494, *Homeric Hymn to Aphrodite* 256, 286, *Homeric Hymn to Hermes* 154, 218, 306, *HH* 7.54 (cf. *Odyssey* v 338: εἶπέ τε μῦθον|: ἔειπε | U⁸ : πρὸς μῦθον ἔειπε | *rell.*). As here, it is directly followed by a speech in *oratio recta* in all these instances except *Iliad* VII 277 (where a line supplying the subject of the verb intervenes) and *Odyssey* viii 302 (where no speech follows). See further R Führer, *Formproblem-Untersuchungen zu den Reden in der frühgr. Lyrik* (*Zetemata* 44 [1967]) 17–19.

2–3: a large number of scholars have wished to posit a lacuna between these two verses (e.g. Ribbeck ["Zu den Fragmenten" (as in F2.9n], 457], who thoughtfully appends his version of the missing line). The reasons for agreeing with them may be grouped and listed as follows:

A
    a) The eccentric μέν *solitarium* in line 2
    b) The lack of any object for ἔπεμψαν in the same line
    c) The extremely abrupt nature of the asyndeton at the start of line 3

B
    d) The excessive brevity of Oedipus' speech as transmitted
    e) The presence of a marginal sign opposite line 2

As regards the oddities collected under heading A, they are all removable by simple emendations (see *ad loc.* for details), the majority of which also recommend themselves on grounds quite independent of the presence or absence of a lacuna. Three emendations within two lines: this is not excessive for a quotation fragment, given the extreme susceptibility to corruption of such texts. Of B we may observe that we have no right to demand a Homeric plenitude from the speeches in later epic; on the contrary, Griffin (1977:49–50), who accepts the notion of a lacuna, nevertheless refers to the "dry manner of indirect reporting" here exhibited and "the indirect and summary manner" in which the curse is reported. Certainly, the presence of the word μῦθος in the introduction to Oedipus' direct speech implies nothing about its length: the self-same formula εἶπέ τε μῦθον heralds a one-line speech at *Iliad* XVIII 391–392.

2.| ὤμοι ἐγώ: the phrase opens a line at *Iliad* XXII 99. For the form of the exclamation see R. Renehan, *Greek Lexicographical Notes* (*Hypomnemata* 45 [1975]) 148. **παῖδες μέν'**: none of the examples of μέν without a following δέ assembled by Denniston, *GP²* 377–380 is really parallel to the μέν offered by the paradosis (the passage is indeed absent from Denniston's collection). The so-called μέν *solitarium* is supposed to convey an unexpressed and contrasting idea (see *GP²* 380–384), but it is hard to see what that could be here. If resort to emendation were forbidden, we might acquiesce in the forced interpretation "My sons *on the one hand* have insulted me (I *on the other hand* will make them rue the day they ever conceived such a plan)," though this surely entails at the very least εὖκτο δέ at the start of the next line. How much more convincing is the sense produced by even Hermann's παῖδές μοι (*De Aeschyli Trilogiis Thebanis* [Leipzig 1835] 11 = *Opuscula* 7.200 is where he justifies the emendation already printed in the note on *Oedipus at Colonus* 1377 in his 1827 revision of Erfurdt [2.435]). Simpler and better, though, is Schneidewin's παῖδες μέγ' (published in *Exercitationum Criticarum in Poetas Graecos Minores capita quinque* [Braunschweig 1836] 29–30). Schneidewin resolutely declined to combine his emendation μέγ' with the ὀνείδειον τόδ' of P. C. Buttmann (see on line 3 below). I find the temptation to do so overwhelming. The paradosis is surely indefensible: in the first place, as we have already seen, ἔπεμψαν at the end of the line is desperately in need of an object, and this can hardly be squeezed in at any other part of the verse but here. Second, ὀνειδείοντες is a highly vulnerable ἅπαξ, a supposedly poetical alternative form for ὀνειδίζω, as LSJ claim.[23]

3. εὖκτο: cf. Aeschylus *Seven Against Thebes* 721 πατρὸς εὐκταίαν ἐρινύν. The verb here is an intriguing form which *prima facie* could be interpreted either as a genuine archaism or a late neologism. Each possibility could be paralleled from other forms in early epic, and each has its scholarly support. The majority of critics have preferred to take it as an archaism, the (unaugmented) athematic imperfect of εὔχεσθαι, what the Homeric epics represent thematically as εὔχετο: so, for instance, Wackernagel 1916: 173 ("ein altes Erbwort" belonging to the "Vorstufen unserer beiden homerischen Epen"); F. Specht, "Griechische Mizellen," *Zeitschrift für vergleichende Sprachforschung auf dem Gebiete der indogermanischen Sprachen* 63 (1936): 212 ("altes sakrales idg. Sprachgut"); Schwyzer, *Gr. Gr.* 1.679 and n6;[24] Frisk, *Griechisches etymologisches Worterbuch* (Heidelberg 1960–1972) 1.586 ("alte Ausdruck ... der religiöse Sprache"). For further bibliography[25] (and useful summary of evidence) see R. Schmitt, *Dichtung and Dichtersprache in indogermanischer Zeit* (Wiesbaden 1967) 261–262. For another specimen of "alte Sprachgut" in cyclic epic see *Ilias Parva* F6.4 and my note *ad loc.* On the other hand, it might be alleged that the form is some sort of neologism, an artificial imperfect[26] or aorist (so, in particular, O. Szemerényi, *Syncope in Greek and Indo-European and the Nature of Indo-European Accent* [Naples 1964] 176 and n4, citing as anologies δέκτο as aorist of δέκομαι, λέκτο as that of λέκομαι).[27] This would be paralleled by the many "late" forms that our early epic fragments in general and the *Thebais* in particular display. Note, indeed, the following pair of nouns. It may be argued that the issue can be decided in favor of the oldness of our form by the analogy with Avestan cited by Wackernagel and those scholars who support his view. For Avestan displays two forms of the corresponding verb,[28] the third-person singular preterite *aogədā* from **eugh+to*

---

[23] Burkert (1981:37–38 = 2001:156) compares τέλος → τελείω for the formation ὄνειδος → ὀνειδείω, and suggests a "transformation" of ὀνειδείοις (ϝ) ἐπέεσιν | to ὀνειδείοντες ἔπεμψαν |. But the verb still stands in great need of the object provided by Buttmann.

[24] Schwyzer's suggestion that εὖκτο for εὔχετο may be paralleled by γεύμεθα for γευόμεθα at Theocritus *Idyll* XIV 51 is dubious: see Dover *ad loc.* for an explanation of the latter which would rule out Schwyzer's idea.

[25] To which add A. Citron, *Semantische Untersuchung zu σπένδεσθαι, σπένδειν, εὔχεσθαι* (Winterthur 1965) 73; J.-L. Perpillou, "Signification de εὔχομαι dans l'épopée," in *Mélanges de linguistique et de philologie grecques offerts à Pierre Chantraine* (Paris 1972) 169–182; L. C. Muellner, *The Meaning of Homeric εὔχομαι through Its Formulas* (Innsbruck 1976) 114n21, etc.

[26] That εὖκτο could be "künstliche für εὔχετο" was specifically denied by Schwyzer.

[27] Szemerényi is surely wrong to insist that the sense of our passage requires the aorist (which is how Jebb on Sophocles *Trachiniae* 610 also took it): clearly Oedipus could have repeated his curse on several occasions.

[28] On the general issues involved here see M. Mayrhofer, *Kurzgefasstes etymologisches Wörterbuch des Altindoarischen* (Heidelberg 1953–1955) fasc. 26, Nachträge p. 658 (*s.v. ćhate*); and C. Watkins,

in the earlier texts (*gathas*) and *achta* in the later texts (*jung-awestisches*). Since both Sanskrit and Avestan tend to thematize whenever possible, we would seem to have here evidence for an early athematic form of the verb exactly matched by εὖκτο. And this picture of Indo-European athematic forms, replaced by Greek thematic forms with one or two exceptions such as the present,[29] is undeniably simpler than the alternative view of Indo-European athematics replaced by Greek thematics, and then by one or two artificially contrived athematics. According to Dodds (*The Greeks and the Irrational* [Berkeley 1951] 158n10) the "oath-formulae of the *Iliad* preserve a belief which was older than Homer's neutral Hades (for such formulae archaise, they do not innovate)" and a similar consideration might explain an archaic form of the verb of cursing in the present context.[30]

δὲ Δί: on the various cases of Zeus' name see Schwyzer, *Gr. Gr.* 1.576–577. As W. Schulze observed (*Quaestiones Epicae* [Gütersloh 1892] 241n1), no adequate parallel for εὖκτο Διὶ βασιλῆι is provided by *Iliad* II 169 (Διὶ μῆτιν), X 16 (Διὶ μμέγα), or II 781 (Διὶ ϝϝώς): see further P. Maas, *Greek Metre* [Oxford 1962] §131. Schulze himself was reduced to considering the possibility of Διεῖ (cf. *Quaestiones Epicae* 239–241; Schwyzer as cited; Burkert 1981:36 = 2001:155, comparing the epithet διίφιλος) or attributing the oddity to the error of "imitatoris contra Homeri usum parum intellectum inviti peccantis." De Marco's discovery that εὖκτο δὲ Διί stands in R clinches the case for Buttmann's palmary εὖκτο δὲ Δί (proposed in *Gr. Gr.* 2¹ [Berlin 1825] 405 = *Gr. Gr.* 1² [Berlin 1830] 225). The corruption of Δί to Διί can be paralleled time and again from Pindar's manuscripts (e.g. *Olympian* XIII 106), and the omission of ΔΕ before ΔΙΙ in LM through haplography was practically inevitable. It is inconceivable that even the most incompetent of epic poets could ever have commenced a hexameter with εὖκτο Διί, thereby introducing at one and the same time an unbearably harsh asyndeton and an unprecedented lengthening of the final vowel. **Δῖ:** for the contracted form see (apart from the Pindaric examples indicated above) the two Etruscan helmets dedicated to Zeus by Hieron in commemoration of his victory over the Carthaginians at Cyme in 474 (cf. Meiggs–Lewis, *A Selection of Greek Historical Inscriptions* [Oxford 1969] p. 62). This is another un-Homeric feature. **Δὶ βασιλῆι:** the application of βασιλεύς to this or, indeed, any god is un-Homeric and another sign of lateness: see Fraenkel on Aeschylus *Agamemnon* 355, Richardson on *Homeric Hymn to Demeter* 358 for the history and frequency of this and similar designations. The earliest parallels are Hesiod *Theogony* 886 Ζεὺς δὲ θεῶν βασιλεύς (where, however, it possesses a strongly predicative sense, as West *ad loc.* observes), *Works and Days* 668 Ζεὺς ἀθανάτων βασιλεύς, *Theogony* 923 μιχθεῖσ᾽ ἐν φιλότητι θεῶν βασιλῆι καὶ ἀνδρῶν, fr. 308.1 MW αὐτὸς γὰρ πάντων βασιλεὺς καὶ κοίρανός ἐστιν, *Cypria* F7.3 Ζηνὶ θεων βασιλῆι.

Indogermanische Grammatik III.1: Geschichte der Indogermanischen Verbalflexion (Heidelberg 1969), 113.

[29] That εὔχομαι was thematic long before Homer (as Szemerényi stresses) does not alter this picture. For a brief introduction to the question of thematic and athematic see L. R. Palmer, *The Greek Language* (London 1980) 294.

[30] With εὖκτο compare Sophocles *Trachiniae* 610 (ηὔγμην) and *TrGF* 4 F730ᶠ 16 Radt (ηὖκτ᾽). Those forms have been regularly taken to be pluperfect (see my note on the former; both taken thus by e.g. Carden [*The Papyrus Fragments of Sophocles* (Berlin 1974) 111] and Radt [p. 505] *ad loc.*). But LSJ s.v. εὔχομαι IV allows that the former (and the *Thebais*'s εὖκτο) may be "plpf. (or non-thematic preterite)," and all three occurrences are treated as imperfect by Schmitt.

Compare Κρονίδαις βασιλεύς in Alcaeus (frr. 38^9, 387). **καὶ ἄλλοις ἀθανάτοισι|**: the same phrase at line-end in *Iliad* II 49. For its use as a comprehensive prayer formula see Davies and Finglass on Stesichorus fr. 85.2. On the role of the gods in fulfilling curses see on F2.8 above.

4. χερσὶν ὑπ' ἀλλήλων: the motif of fraternal ἀλληλοφονία recurs at Stesichorus fr. 97.21 ὑπ' ἀλλάλοισι δαμέντας; Pindar *Olympian* II 41–42 ἰδοῖσα δ' ὀξεῖ' Ἐρινύς | ἐπεφνέ οἱ σὺν ἀλλαλοφονίαι γένος ἀρήϊον; *TrGF* 2 F458.14–15 χαλκῶι δὲ μαρμαίροντες ἀλλήλων χρόα | σφάζοιεν. Cf. Oedipus' remarks to Polyneices at Sophocles *Oedipus at Colonus* 1373–1374 (αἵματι | πεσῆι μιανθεὶς χὼ ξύναιμος ἐξ ἴσου) and at 1387–1388 (συγγενεῖ χερί | θανεῖν κτανεῖν θ' ὑφ' οὗπερ ἐξελήλασαι). | **χερσὶν ὑπ' ἀλλήλων**: cf. | χερσὶν ὑπ' Ἀργείων (*Iliad* XIII 763, XXIV 168). **καταβήμεναι** ‿‿– –‿|: cf. *Iliad* XII 65, *Odyssey* x 432. **Ἀΐδος εἴσω** |: cf. *Iliad* III 322, *Odyssey* ix 524.

Let us now see what the two foregoing fragments tell us about the Oedipus of the *Thebais*. In the first place, had he blinded himself before he cursed his sons? In spite of 2.5's φράσθη and 3.1's ἐνόησε, Welcker supposed he had (1865:2.337, followed by, for example, Bethe [1891:104–106 and 165]). The self-blinding certainly seems basic to the story and occurs in every version (except, by implication, Homer's, which characteristically tones down the story's horrors [see pages 14–15 above]). Blinding and curse seem linked in the corrupt Aeschylus *Seven Against Thebes* 783–791.

In F2 and F3 of our epic Oedipus curses his sons—for slighting him—*in Thebes*. That he remained in the city after the grim revelations is the usual version, at least until Sophocles' *Oedipus at Colonus*. In *Odyssey* xi 275–276, he continues to *rule* in Thebes: ἀλλ' ὁ μὲν ἐν Θήβηι πολυηράτωι ἄλγεα πάσχων | Καδμείων ἤνασσε θεῶν ὀλοὰς διὰ βουλάς, and Thebes is certainly the place of his death according to the tradition that underlies *Iliad* XXIII 679–680 Θήβασδ' ἦλθε δεδουπότος Οἰδιπόδαο | ἐς τάφον and Σ T *ad loc.* = Hesiod fr. 192 MW βασιλεύοντα ἐν Θήβαις φησίν ἀπολέσθαι, οὐχ ὡς οἱ νεώτεροι· καὶ Ἡσίοδος δέ φησιν ἐν Θήβαις αὐτοῦ ἀποθανόντος κτλ. And δεδουπότος is suggestive of death in battle.[31] At the end of Sophocles' *Oedipus Rex,* Creon orders Oedipus to remain in the palace pending clarification of Apollo's will. It seems likely that the second part of this situation is Sophocles' own invention (cf. Davies, "The End of Sophocles' *OT*," *Hermes* 110 [1982]: 268–277) while the first, as, e.g., Robert (1915:1.172) saw, may well derive from the *Thebais*.[32] A similar state of affairs obtains in Euripides' *Phoe-*

---

[31] See A. R. Dyck, "The Glossographoi," *Harvard Studies in Classical Philology* 91 (1987): 139, though cf. Burkert 1981:33 = 2001:153; E. Cingano, "The Death of Oedipus in the Epic Tradition," *Phoenix* 46 (1992): 1–11.

[32] See further Wolff in Roscher 3.2664–2665 for scholars who suppose the *Thebais*'s Oedipus to have been locked away. Edmunds (1981b:230–231) links the tradition with his hypothetical "revenant" Oedipus. Cf. also Euripides *Phoenician Women* 870–879, on which see Mastronarde *ad loc.* and Ed.

nician Women: cf. verse 66 ζῶν δ' ἔστ' ἐν οἴκοις (compare *Oedipus Rex* 1429 ὡς τάχιστ' ἐς οἶκον ἐσκομίζετε).

The only author cited above who definitely portrays Oedipus as continuing to *rule* over the Thebans is Homer, and it seems safe to conclude that he was in fact the only author who ever presented this version of events. This is a feature of his normalization of the story (see pages 14–15 above) and follows inevitably upon his elimination of offspring and their father's curse on them. In our two fragments, by contrast, he no longer participates in sacrifices, and even lacks control over the disposition of his family's ancestral property. Still more suggestive is his use of a curse (the last resort of the weak and helpless: cf. Watson 1991: 38 and 95) to punish his sons. He presumably lacked more direct means.

That Oedipus survived long enough in Thebes to witness the fulfilment of his curse in the mutual slaughter of his sons is first explicitly suggested by Euripides *Phoenician Women* 66–76, etc. Bethe (1891:105, 165n7) assumed that this, like several other features of the play, derived from the *Thebais*. It is more plausibly attributed to the inventive mind of Euripides himself by Robert (1915:1.415), Stephanopoulos (1980:125), Mastronarde (*ad loc.*), etc. For artists' depictions of Oedipus as present at his sons' ἀλληλοφονία see Krauskopf *LIMC* 54ff. Whether such artists really conceived of Oedipus as literally present or merely a brooding symbol of his curse's fulfilment is a moot point.

Let us now turn to *the quarrel of the sons*. The motif of the brothers' quarrel is widespread.[33] A large number of scholars seem to believe that antiquity knew two versions of the circumstances surrounding Polyneices' departure from Thebes. According to one account, "Polyneices voluntarily left Thebes for the first year of the alternating reign agreed between his brother Eteocles and himself in an attempt to avoid fulfilment of their father's curse" (Collard on Euripides *Suppliant Women* [Groningen 1975] line 150). Under this heading, most scholars, I believe, would now rank the treatment of the tale by Stesichorus (see Davies and Finglass on fr. 97) as well as that by Hellanicus (*FGrHist* 4 F98, using the phrase κατὰ συνθήκην of Polyneices' departure), Euripides *Suppliant Women* 149–154 (ἑκούσιον φυγήν [151]) and 930–930 and *Phoenician Women* 71–72 (φεύγειν ἑκόντα—though this is made permanent by force), and Pausanias IX 5.12. Hesiod fr. 192 MW has been taken as consistent with a peaceful departure. In the other version Eteocles expels Polyneices by force. So Pherecydes *FGrHist*

Fraenkel, "Zu den *Phoenissen* des Euripides," 37–41 esp. 40n2. Note especially verse 875: his sons vex Oedipus οὔτ' ἔξοδον διδόντες. Indeed, it would seem that in the *Thebais* seclusion and curse were inextricably combined. For Oedipus to be provoked into a curse he must remain behind.

[33] See Stith Thompson, *Motif-Index* A 525.1; Fontenrose, *The Cult and Myth of Pyrros at Delphi* (University of California Publications in Classical Archaeology 4 [(1960)] 246–248; T. H. Gaster, *Myth, Legend, and Custom in the Old Testament* (London 1969) 163–164.

3 F96 (ἐκβεβλῆσθαι τὸν Πολυνείκην μετὰ βίας), Aeschylus *Seven Against Thebes* 637–638, and Sophocles *Oedipus at Colonus* 377, 1292–1299.

The general outline so far drawn contains nothing very misleading or complex. Difficulties do arise, however, when we pose the question: "How, in each respective version, do the brothers come to quarrel, thus beginning the fulfilment of their father's curse?" In the latter tradition the answer is clear and straightforward, since the very expulsion of Polyneices is sign and symbol that the brothers have already quarreled and the curse is beginning to take effect. With the other tradition things are by no means so clear. Many scholars suppose that here Polyneices returned to Thebes after the death of his father and was then obliged to leave again, this time under duress imposed by a now-hostile brother. Some scholars even equate this version with that of the *Thebais*.[34] In doing so, they overlook several serious problems.

Let us examine the *ipsissima verba* of one testimony to this sequence of events:

Πολυνείκης δὲ περιόντος μὲν καὶ ἄρχοντος Οἰδίποδος ὑπεξῆλθεν ἐκ Θηβῶν δέει μὴ τελεσθεῖεν ἐπὶ σφίσιν αἱ κατᾶραι τοῦ πατρός ... κατῆλθεν ἐς Θήβας μετάπεμπτος ὑπὸ Ἐτεοκλέους μετὰ τὴν τελευτὴν Οἰδίποδος. κατελθὼν δὲ ἐς διαφορὰν προήχθη τῶι Ἐτεοκλεῖ, καὶ οὕτω τὸ δεύτερον ἔφυγε· δεηθεὶς δὲ Ἀδράστου δοῦναί οἱ δύναμιν κτλ.

Pausanias IX 5.12

Scholars have been surprisingly slow to detect the major incoherence here. And yet if Polyneices quitted Thebes because he (and his brother) feared the fulfilment of their father's curse, why on earth should he return (with his brother's active encouragement) merely because Oedipus had died? Would that death make the father's curse one jot the less likely of fulfilment? Would it not (if anything) bring it closer?

A further difficulty resides in the phrase καὶ οὕτω τὸ δεύτερον ἔφυγε, as if Polyneices' initial departure had likewise been enforced! Jacoby, in his commentary on Hellanicus *FGrHist* 4 F98 (1^A.460), notes that the words are due to contamination with the alternative tradition whereby Polyneices is extruded forcibly and once and for all. But surely the entire passage of Pausanias is a late and incoherent conflation of two originally separate and logical traditions, the forcible and permanent exclusion just mentioned, and the voluntary departure of Polyneices κατὰ συνθήκην, as we find it described by Hellanicus. For here and here alone do we find an uncontaminated explanation of how the brothers'

---

[34] Cf. Welcker 1865:2.340.

peaceful attempt to avoid the curse ended in strife. According to this version, Polyneices chooses to leave the kingdom to Eteocles and departs, taking with him τὸ μέρος τῶν χρημάτων (including the tunic and necklace of Harmonia), to live in another city (Argos). In other words, Polyneices takes with him all the wherewithal for making trouble against his native land. The curse has already started to take effect by determining Polyneices' choice.

This is not to say that Hellanicus preserves the *Thebais*'s version. But he seems likely to preserve Stesichorus' version (see Davies and Finglass on fr. 97). Bethe (1891:106–107) was particularly anxious to know how Polyneices obtained the ὅρμος in the *Thebais*. The answer may lie here.

TYDEUS AND POLYNEICES AT THE COURT OF ADRASTUS

Howald (1939:10) convincingly argues that these two heroes originally stood outside the list of the Seven against Thebes, and belonged together as "ein altes Abenteurerpaar" (in the manner of, e.g., Theseus and Pirithous; see further his *Der Mythos als Dichtung* [Zurich 1937] 74–79): Tydeus a brutal bully (see page 71 below), and Polyneices a cunning rogue (see page 48 above). He further suggests (p. 12) that Polyneices originally had no father and belongs to the folktale type of individuals who are "Bastarde, aus niederem Milieu entstammend."

Tydeus and Polyneices clash outside the palace of Adrastus, wearing skins of, or shields or clothing decorated with, a boar and a lion. Adrastus is put in mind of a prophecy he has received bidding him yoke his daughters in marriage to those very animals, and consequently marries Tydeus to Deipyle and Polyneices to Argeia and makes the fatal promise that he will restore each hero to his native land. For a list of the various ancient sources that tell this tale, see Parke-Wormell, *The Delphic Oracle* (Oxford 1956) 2.80 and 150–151 and Fontenrose, *The Delphic Oracle: Its Responses and Operations* (Berkeley 1978) 366. On the emblems see in particular Robert 1915:1.200–204.[35] As Bond remarks (*Euripides' Hypsipyle* [Oxford 1963] 89n1), "the details differ; no doubt the early tradition was not precise." The allusiveness of the reference to the story at Euripides *Suppliant Women* 131–155 certainly presupposes a more detailed earlier account with which the audience was familiar. This account cannot be Aeschylus'. Is it not likely to have occurred in the *Thebais*? Whatever their precise nature originally, such emblems seem, as Hampe(-Simon) 21 observe, particularly suited to the "Vorstellungswelt" of early epic.[36] A Pontic amphora in Basel has been

---

[35] Their absence from Aeschylus *Seven Against Thebes*, in spite of the abundant opportunities for their mention afforded by the description of the shields at 377–652, is striking, as Bethe (1891: 166–167) observed.

[36] If the lion and boar were designs upon shields compare pages 73–74 below on the "Schildzeichen" of the Seven. If they were animal skins, compare Diomedes' lion-pelt, Menelaus' leopard-skin,

interpreted by R. Hampe as a unique depiction of this episode.[37] Two hoplite warriors duel with spears (the mantled female figure who stands dressed in a chiton behind the warrior on the right is taken to be Athena supporting her favorite, Tydeus [see page 81 below]), while the two daughters of Adrastus, their future wives, rush in from the left to stop them. By and large, scholars have not proved very enthusiastic about this identification, which can only be definitively judged in the context of the vase's other scenes (see page 104 below). The alleged Athena's unmartial garb[38] troubled G. Camporeale ("Saghe greche nell'arte etrusca arcaica," *Parola del Passato* 19 [1964]: 439–440), as it does K. Schefold (*Götter- und Heldensagen der Griechen in der spätarchaischen Kunst* [Munich 1978] 184 = *Gods and Heroes in Late Archaic Greek Art* 202), who prefers to interpret the two warriors as Polyneices and Eteocles, the two female figures dashing in from the left as Antigone and Ismene, and the remaining female figure as symbolizing the city of Argos. But do we need to be so specific? Vase-paintings of the combats between Heracles and Geryon or Cycnus remind us (see Davies and Finglass' commentary on Stesichorus pp. 231 and 461) that such scenes are often enriched by the presence of female onlookers to whom we should not try to attach a specific name or identity. And the possibility that the present scene is really a generic duel (see page 75 below) must not be underestimated.

Another artifact was once upon a time thought to reflect our epic. The famous Chalcidian vase now in Copenhagen[39] shows a securely labeled Adrastus reclining on a κλίνη while two mantled figures sit suppliant before him. One of them is labeled "Tydeus." In the days when it was still supposed that the other seated figure was female, Robert (1915:1.196–198) accepted Heydemann's notion[40] that the painting implies a version whereby Tydeus and Polyneices approached Adrastus separately and independently.[41] He concluded that this version was simpler than the more familiar tradition, therefore earlier than it, and probably derived from the *Thebais*. None of these last three inferences is at all compulsive, and now that we know the other seated figure to be as male as

---

and Dolon's wolf-hide in *Iliad* X. Reinhardt (*Die Ilias und ihr Dichter* [Göttingen 1961] 249–250) detected influence by the *Thebais* here: in that epic: "sind die Tierbekleidungen nicht nur Kostüm sondern Verhängnis, mit ihnen beginnt die Vorgeschichte des Unterganges der Sieben."

[37] *LIMC* VIII.1 *s.v.* "Tydeus" C9: cf. Hampe(–Simon) 18–25, esp. 24, plates 8 and 11; R. Hampe and E. Simon, "Gefälschte etruskische Vasenbilder?," *Jahrbuch des Römisch-Germanischen Zentralmuseum Mainz* 14 (1967): 68–71.

[38] For an analogous depiction of the goddess see Hampe(–Simon) 24, with plate 6.1.

[39] Nat. Mus. Chr. VIII 496: for illustration see Hampe(–Simon) 26; see Krauskopf in *LIMC* I.1, p. 234 (B1); cf. p. 237.

[40] *Archäologische Zeitung* 24 (1866): 130–132.

[41] Rzach (1922:2363–2364) follows Robert in supposing the existence of a simpler tradition; he is more cautious over the notion of the *Thebais* as its source. The truth about the figure's sex was seen as early as Bethe (1891:168n13) etc.

Tydeus,[42] we may safely dismiss Robert's theory. Since two female figures stand behind the two suppliants, the most obvious inference is that they represent the two daughters of Adrastus and that the other seated figure is after all Polyneices.

Largely because his own interpretation of the above artifact was essentially incompatible with them, Robert was cautious (1915:1.204) as to the claims of Bethe and others that the more familiar version outlined above derived from epic: he thought it unlikely that the Delphic oracle would have played so significant a role in Ionian epic. But Fontenrose has pointed out (*Delphic Oracle*, p. 95) the general lack of evidence among the ancient sources for the Delphic origin of the oracle concerning Adrastus' daughters. As he observes, Adrastus might have received it from a μάντις (so Apollodorus III 6.1) or, more directly, from Apollo.

We have seen (page 33 above) that the gods' hostility to the expedition against Thebes is posited as early as the *Iliad*, and is a constant feature of tradition thereafter. μάντεις δ' ἐπῆλθες ἐμπύρων τ' εἶδες φλόγα;, Theseus asks Adrastus at Euripides *Suppliant Women* 155, and when this question elicits a groan, οὐκ ἦλθες, ὡς ἔοικεν, εὐνοίαι θεῶν, he rightly infers (line 157). Compare Aeschylus *Seven Against Thebes* 378–379, where Amphiaraus forbids Tydeus to cross the Ismenus (οὐ γὰρ σφάγια γίγνεται καλά).

The possibility that the motif featured in the *Thebais* might be thought to gain some support from R. Hampe's interpretation of a Berlin skyphos.[43] He reads one side as Ismene's death at the hands of Tydeus on the orders of Athena (see page 96 below). The other scene he takes to be Tydeus' departure to the expedition against Thebes, in the presence of Adrastus and his queen. The hero's newly won wife, Deipyle, weeps and tries to restrain him. The reason for her behavior presumably lies with the adjacent altar, where a sacrifice, one imagines, has revealed unfavorable omens.

Bethe (1891:26) saw a rationalized reworking of the *Thebais*'s catalogue of forces in Pausanias IX 9.2 (3.17 Rocha-Pereira):

ὁ δὲ Ἀργείων στρατὸς ἐς Βοιωτίαν τε μέσην ἀφίκετο ἐκ μέσης Πελοπον-
νήσου καὶ ὁ Ἄδραστος ἐξ Ἀρκαδίας καὶ παρὰ Μεσσηνίων συμμαχικὰ
ἤθροισεν, ὡσαύτως δὲ καὶ τοῖς Θηβαίοις μισθοφορικὰ ἦλθε παρὰ Φωκέ-
ων καὶ ἐκ τῆς Μινυάδος χώρας οἱ Φλεγύαι.

---

[42] See, e.g., Hampe(–Simon) 25–26, Krauskopf (n39 above). A complicating factor is the inscription -ομαχος at the edge of the scene. For attempted explanations see Robert 1915:2.74–75n72, Hampe(–Simon) 25–26. Here we may merely observe that attempts to interpret it as the name of Tydeus' companion as suppliant (thus allowing a revival in slightly different form of Robert's hypothesis) are rendered unattractive by the apparent proximity of the two daughters of Adrastus.

[43] R. Hampe, "Tydeus und Ismene," *Antike Kunst* 18 (1975): 13–15 with plate 1.1. Berlin skyphos inv. 1970.9: *LIMC* V.1 *s.v.* "Ismene" C5.

and IX 9.4:

δῆλοι δέ εἰσι καὶ τούτοις οὐ τὸ Ἀργολικὸν μόνον οὐδὲ οἱ Μεσσήνιοι καὶ Ἀρκάδες ἠκολουθηκότες, ἀλλὰ καὶ ἔτι ἐκ Κορίνθου καὶ Μεγαρέων ἐπικληθέντες ἐς τὴν συμμαχίαν.

He could only identify the Arcadian force with that of Parthenopaeus (see page 72 below) and the Messenian with the Biantids.

THE FOUNDING OF THE NEMEAN GAMES

This detail was attributed to the *Thebais* by Welcker (1865:2.375). Wilamowitz too, was of the opinion "dass die Stiftung der panhellenischen Nemeen auf das damals allbekannte Epos [viz. the *Thebais*] zurückgriff" (*Glaube der Hellenen* 1.392). Stoneman (1981:52–54) reassessed the grounds for this supposition and pronounced them generally good. That the victor list in Apollodorus III 6.4 coincides with the identities of the Seven against Thebes as inferred for the *Thebais* (pages 68–69 below) strengthens the hypothesis, as does the overall similarity between the events mentioned by Apollodorus and those in *Iliad* XXIII's ἆθλα ἐπὶ Πατρόκλωι. Stoneman's further suggestion (1981:53–54) that the death of Opheltes also fell within the *Thebais* gains some color from its position within a general framework of gloomy omens: Apollodorus III 6.4 has Amphiaraus rename the child Archemoros as a token of impending doom. So too Bacchylides IX 14, where the dead infant is a σᾶμα μέλλοντος φόνου. We have already seen (pages 33–35 above) that the gods are likely to have expressed their disapproval of the expedition in the *Thebais* by some such παραίσια σήματα.

The sequence of friendly competition at funeral games followed by deadly serious competition in war totally reverses, of course, the relationship between the two exhibited in the *Iliad*. Vergil is often described as doing precisely that in his *Aeneid*.[44] Perhaps the *Thebais* showed him the way.

SEVEN-GATED THEBES AND THE SEVEN AGAINST THEBES

ἑπτάπυλος Θήβη: were there seven leaders against Thebes because the city had seven gates, or did the tradition as to the number of leaders determine the tradition as to the number of gates? Wilamowitz's pungently framed question is best answered by his own fundamental investigation 1891:191–241 = 1971:26–76 (cf. H. W. Singor, "The Achaean Wall and the Seven Gates of Thebes," *Hermes* 120 [1992]: 401–411, associating the number with the seven gates in the Achaean wall of *Iliad* VII 336–359; Kühr 2006:211n63). Thebes was traditionally pictured

---

[44] See, for instance, Heinze, *Virgils Epische Technik*[3] (Leipzig 1928) 152 = Engl. trans. 125–126.

as seven-gated from earliest literature onwards: she is thus in epic (see Hesiod *Works and Days* 162 with West *ad loc.*; W. D. Meier, *Die Epische Formel im pseudo-hesiodeischen Frauenkatalog* [diss. Zurich 1976) 176] and in poets influenced by epic, even Pindar (see Slater's *Lexicon s.v.*), whose own experience of his native city could have given the epithet the lie. For, as Wilamowitz observed (1891:224–225 = 1971:59), seven gates constitute a paradoxically large number of points of attack for the aspiring enemy, and the historical Thebes at the relevant time can never have possessed more than three or four (cf. Wilamowitz 1891:193–196 = 1971:28–30; Howald 1939:3n2; Burkert 1981:39–40 = 2001:157 on the unhistorical nature of "seven-gated Thebes"). Robert (1915:1.120–121) assumed an Ionian author ignorant of the real city.

Wilamowitz's solution (1891:228–229 = 1971:62–64) was that the author of the *Thebais* made Thebes seven-gated because of the Seven against Thebes. The difficulty an epic poet would find in relating the numerous simultaneous events thrown up by the attack on the city would be minimized if the leaders and their troops could each be assigned to one gate. An effective climax would also be provided with the combat of the two brothers at the last remaining gate. A more than convenient structural device, in other words. For such allotting of warriors in battle see West, *Indo-European Poetry and Myth* (Oxford 2007) 472. To this the real construction of the contemporary city would be an irrelevance even if the *Thebais'* author had any knowledge of it. On the basis of this hypothetical device alone, Wilamowitz was prepared to accord our poet the proud title of a "wirkliche Dichter" (1891:229 = 1971:63) and rank him with Dante and the composers of the *Iliad* and the *Odyssey*. This is going a bit foo far, though Wilamowitz's solution is surely more convincing than Friedländer's tentative restatement of the alternative (1914:323–324 = 1969:38–39), or his idea that the seven gates do not particularly represent a specific number, but rather symbolize in a general way the power of the city (cf. LSJ *s.v.* ἑπτά 1; Roscher, "*Sieben- und Neunzahl im Kultus und Mythus der Griechen*" [*Abhandlungen der Philologisch-Historischen Klasse der Königlich Sächsischen Gesellschaft der Wissenschaften* 24.1 (1904)] esp. 115–118; Stith Thompson, *Motif-Index* 6 D 1273.1.3 ["Seven as magic number"], etc.).[45]

Seven operates as "eine alte Märchenzahl" on other levels as well (Seven Thieves, Seven Brides for Seven Brothers; see, in general, Stith Thompson's *Motif-Index* 6 *s.v.* "Seven" [pp. 658–659]; Dirlmeier 1954:154–156 = 1970:51–54; Burkert 1981:44 = 2001:161; Kühr 2006:211–212; M. Davies, "From Rags to Riches:

---

[45] Such considerations tell against Grote's notion (*History of Greece* 1.266), already amply refuted by Pearson (*Euripides* Phoenissae pp. xxii–xxiii), that the number of leaders against Thebes was much more numerous in the *Thebais* and reduced to seven by Attic tragedy. For the various lists of the Seven given by antiquity and for scholars who attribute invention of the number to a source other than the *Thebais* see further Kühr 2006:137nn15 and 17.

Democedes of Croton and the Credibility of Herodotus," *Bulletin of the Institute of Classical Studies* 53.2 [2010]: 35n55, etc.). It was this realization that inspired Ernst Howald's ingenious hypothesis that the Seven under the leadership of Adrastus were originally conceived as seven demons of the Netherworld commanded by their king, the ruler of the Dead (1939:16–17). In a sort of reversal of the motif of the hero's κατάβασις, or descent to the Underworld, these seven demons broke loose and assaulted a city in the upper world of the living, before being despatched, together with their lord, back to their usual abode. Such a theory would explain the unusual brutality that characterizes most of the Seven (see page 70 below) as well as the story's radical transformation of other familiar motifs (see Howald 1939:14), which substitutes villains defeated in an enterprise involving a real city in the midst of the known world for the more orthodox picture of heroes victorious in some remote and otherworldly locale (be it Troy, Colchis, or the like). Howald's case is strengthened by Burkert (1981:40–41 = 2001:158–159), who cites the parallel Babylonian epic of Erra (ninth–seventh century), wherein the god of war and pestilence and seven "matchless warriors" set out to destroy mankind.

Authors variously name the seven gates of Thebes (see Wilamowitz's list and discussion: 1891:210–218 = 45–53; cf. Kühr 2006:212). We have no evidence as to which, if any, of the nomenclature derives from the *Thebais*, though, as Wilamowitz (1891:224 = 59n2) saw, the tragedians' repeated use of Ὁμὄλωΐδὲς, in spite of the metrical difficulties it posed them, is suggestive.

Jetzt erst fühlt man, dass die Siebenzahl wichtiger ist als die einzelnen Helden, dass sie sozusagen vor den Einzelnen da war.

Howald 1939:12

Dass die Sieben gegen Theben ein geschlossener Kreis von Helden, ein Eigenname geworden sind, ist das Verdienst ... des Dichters der *Thebais*.

Wilamowitz 1891:227 = 1971:62

The earliest list of which we have direct knowledge is Aeschylus' (*Seven Against Thebes* 375–652):

> Tydeus
> Capaneus
> Eteoclus
> Hippomedon
> Parthenopaeus
> Amphiaraus
> Polyneices

This is almost identical with the list on an Argive inscription at Delphi (Pausanias X 10.3), datable 464–451.[46] Robert (1915:1.240–241), citing Pausanias II 20.5 (ἐπηκολουθήκασι γὰρ Ἀργεῖοι τῆι Αἰσχύλου ποιήσει), implausibly claimed that the dedication based its list on the recently produced drama (in 469) and that it merely modified its source by replacing the "foreigner" Parthenopaeus (originally Arcadian according to Robert [238–239]: see page 72 below) with Halitherses.[47] Aeschylus' list is followed unchanged by Sophocles *Oedipus at Colonus* 1311–1325,[48] Euripides *Suppliant Women* 857–917, and (with Adrastus ousting Eteoclus)[49] *Phoenician Women* 1104–1144 (cf. Mastronarde *ad. loc.* and Stephanopoulos 1980:124–125). The list as thus modified is reproduced by Apollodorus III 6.3, Hyginus *Fabulae* 70, Diodorus Siculus IV 65.7. Cf. Fowler 2013:413.

See in particular Robert 1915:1.237–244, Fraenkel 1957 = 1964:273–324, for some pertinent remarks on the fluctuations of identity within the number seven which Howald found so significant. Wilamowitz[50] (1891:228–230 = 1971: 62–64, cf. 1914:97–103) assumed that Aeschylus derived the number and names of the Seven from the *Thebais*,[51] an assumption which he supposed to entail the dismissal of Pausanias' claim (II 20.5) that τούτους τοὺς ἄνδρας ἐς μόνων ἑπτὰ ἀριθμὸν κατήγαγεν Αἰσχύλος. Robert (1915:1.237) was perfectly prepared to countenance this dismissal, but supposed the relationship between epic and dramatist to be a little more complex. He attributed to the *Thebais*'s list the Mecisteus mentioned by Apollodorus III 6.3 as one of two variants to the Aeschylean roll call: τινὲς δὲ Τυδέα μὲν καὶ Πολυνείκην οὐ καταριθμοῦσι, συγ-

---

46   Cf. L. H. Jeffery, "The Battle of Oenoe in the the Stoa Poikile: A Problem in Greek Art and History," *Annals of the British School at Athens* 60 (1965): 48–50: A. F. Garvie, *Dionysiaca* (Page Festschrift [1978]) 84n28. For further discussion, cf. E. Cingano, "I nomi dei Sette a Tebe e degli Epigoni nella tradizione epica, tragica e iconografica," in *I Sette a Tebe: Dal mito alla letteratura* (Bologna 2002) 27–62.

47   Not to be equated with the Halimedon depicted on the Amphiaraus vase (page 104 below): see Robert 1915:1.237–238.

48   1313–1325 *del.* Reeve, "Some Interpolations in Sophocles," *Greek, Roman, and Byzantine Studies* 11 (1970): 291–293, *def.* H. Lloyd-Jones and N. G. Wilson, *Sophoclea* (Oxford 1990) 255.

49   "To avoid confusion with Eteocles," according to Collard on Euripides *Suppliant Women* 857–917. The change also restores the *Thebais*'s version, according to Robert (1915:1.243) and Stephanopoulos (1980:124). But since Aeschylus courts precisely the same confusion, Beazley ("Some Inscriptions on Vases: V," *American Journal of Archaeology* 54 [1950]: 313n5) inferred he must have inherited Eteoclus from an earlier tradition (*contra* Garvie [*Dionysiaca* (Page Festschrift 1978) 72–73], who suggests that he is Aeschylus' invention; see further below, page 70). The two heroes were probably one originally: see Howald 1939:13–14.

50   Especially 1891:228n2 = 63n1: "Niemand bezweifelt heute, dass die *Thebais* die sieben Helden gehabt hat, und Pindar allein würde solchen Zweifel verbieten." Pausanias' statement to the contrary (II 20.5) is taken as merely further evidence that he had not actually read the *Thebais*.

51   Bethe backed up this hypothesis (1891:84–85) by observing that the minor figures among the Seven (e.g. Mecisteus) are totally irrelevant to the plot of the play.

καταλέγουσι δὲ τοῖς ἑπτὰ Ἐτέοκλον Ἴφιος καὶ Μηκιστέα. This context as a whole cannot reproduce the *Thebais*'s version—which could never have omitted two such crucial figures as Polyneices and Tydeus—but Mecisteus plays an important part in early presentations of the Theban saga: cf. *Iliad* XXIII 678, considered page 38 above and Herodotus V 67. Furthermore, it is very striking that Mecisteus and, together with him, Adrastus feature as two of the Seven *by implication* in the list of the Epigoni *and their fathers* at Apollodorus III 7.2: Αἰγιαλεὺς Ἀδράστου ... Εὐρύαλος Μηκιστέως. An identical list (though without the fathers) is cited from the Argive dedication at Delphi by Pausanias (X 10.2). By similar implication, Aeschylus' Hippomedon and Eteoclus (or, rather, their sons) are absent from these lists, which Robert (1915:1.243) would have ultimately to descend from the *Thebais*, especially since what they imply about the identity of the Seven is inconsistent with the lists of Aeschylus and the other tragedians as outlined page 68 above.

Robert concludes that the *Thebais*'s Adrastus and Mecisteus were replaced in the Aeschylean catalogue by the colorless Eteoclus (cf. Fraenkel 1957:25 = 1964:294) and Hippomedon. The reason for the elimination of Adrastus is obvious (*sec.* Robert): since Aeschylus' seven champions are each listed to be killed by a corresponding Theban hero, and since Adrastus survives the battle, he cannot be fitted into the schema. Why Mecisteus should have been ousted is less obvious, and even Eteoclus may have been pre-Aeschylean (see page 69n49 above).

We saw earlier (page 68 above) how Howald explained what he called the "furchtbare Gesellen" (1939:13) the Seven constitute. By an exploitation of the few fragments at our disposal, the list of Argive heroes as reconstituted above, and the numerous traces which the *Thebais* has left in later poets such as Aeschylus and Sophocles, Karl Reinhardt[52] ingeniously contrasted the *Iliad*'s complex sympathy for Greeks and Trojans alike with our epic's black-and-white presentation of invaders[53] and defenders. Though no less Greek than the Thebans, the seven chieftains seem to have been presented as monsters of a totally un-Homeric kind: "schon ihre Namen ein Katalog der Arten der Gewalt, der Prahlerei, der Hybris, der Brutalität" (That many of the Seven bear "redende Namen" was already observed by, for instance, Wilamowitz [1891:240 = 75] and Friedländer [1914:325 = 1969:39] and partly anticipated by Bethe [1891:175] on

---

[52] "Tradition und Geist im homerischen Epos," *Studium Generale* 4 (1951): 339 = *Tradition und Geist* (Göttingen 1960) 14–15.

[53] Note especially Aeschylus *Seven Against Thebes* 170: ἑτεροφώνωι στρατῶι (cf. Lloyd-Jones, "The End of the *Seven Against Thebes*," *Classical Quarterly* 9 [1959]: 85n3; G. Zuntz, "Notes on Some Passages in Aeschylus' *Septem*," *Proceedings of the Cambridge Philological Society* 27 [1981]: 90; and Hutchinson *ad loc.*).

"die wilden und starken Argiver"). Contrast (cf. Kühr 2006:141) the shadowy nature of their opponents in Thebes or, indeed, of the Epigoni (page 108 below). For the whole principle of significant names in early epic see page 35 above.

What is meant by "the numerous traces which the *Thebais* has left in" Attic tragedy may be seen by glancing at Bethe's list (1891:83–84) of details about the Seven which are common to Aeschylus *Seven Against Thebes*, Sophocles *Oedipus at Colonus*, and Euripides *Suppliant Women* and *Phoenician Women*. Their consistency in characterization and other respects is such that influence by the *Thebais* becomes the only satisfactory explanation. In the case of Amphiaraus we may regard the hypothesis as proved, since the stress on his double rôles of seer and warrior which we find in *Seven Against Thebes* 569 and *Oedipus at Colonus* 1314–1315 certainly did occur in the *Thebais* (F7: see page 92 below). Elsewhere we lack this kind of confirmation. But when all three tragedians agree in as many as eight places on the nature of Capaneus' death (see page 72 below), it is hard not to divine an epic, and specifically the *Thebais*, as their common source.

TYDEUS

On this hero in general see Robert, *Heldensage* 3.1.924–926; Nilsson, *The Mycenaean Origin of Greek Mythology* (Berkeley 1932) 116–117 ("his character shows traces of a high and crude antiquity which was detested by the Homeric age": for the most extreme instance see page 81 below); and Dirlmeier 1954:157 = 1970:53 on this and other names of the Seven ending in *-eus*. Aeschylus *Seven Against Thebes* 424–425 hints at the tradition as to Tydeus' small stature which we find in the *Iliad* (V 801 μικρὸς μὲν ἔην δέμας, ἀλλὰ μαχητής), and Fraenkel (1957:16 = 1964:285) suggests this may have occured in the *Thebais*. The *Seven Against Thebes* also reveals a state of hostility between this hero and Amphiaraus: Tydeus upbraids the seer for cowardice (lines 382–383); Amphiaraus denounces the blood-lust and bad counsel of Tydeus (lines 570–575). Bethe (1891:82–83) supposed this enmity to derive from the *Thebais*, a suggestion approved by Wecklein (1901:663–664). For ἔρις as an important motif in epic see e.g. D. L. Cairns, "Affronts and Quarrels in the *Iliad*," *Papers of the Leeds International Latin Seminar* 7 (1983): 155–167 = *Oxford Readings in Homer's* Iliad (2001) 203–219, and "Ethics, Ethnicity, Terminology: Iliadic Anger and the Cross-Cultural Study of Emotion," *Yale Classical Studies* 31 (2003): 11–49.

CAPANEUS

Robert (*Heldensage* 3.1.937–940) gives a general survey of traditions on this hero; cf. Hutchinson's note on Aeschylus *Seven Against Thebes* 422–456. "Schon der Dichter der alten *Thebais* muss ihn in grossartiger Kühnheit mit den Zügen ausgestattet haben, die ihn für alle Zeiten zum gewaltigsten *contemptor divum* machen sollten": Fraenkel (1957:15 = 1964:285) is surely right, and the deduction is all the more interesting when we realize (see Griffin 1977:46–47 = 2001:380) how totally un-Iliadic is the conception of this arrogant blasphemer, whose very name is derived from σκάπτειν (see Wilamowitz 1891:226n2 = 61n1; cf. Dirlmeier 1954:157 =1970:53). The strikingly un-Homeric figure of Mezentius in Vergil's *Aeneid* may have owed something to the *Thebais*'s Capaneus, and Statius' Capaneus is often described as indebted to Mezentius: see e.g. Helm, *RE* 18.3 (1949): 994.62–65. Capaneus' blasting by Zeus' thunderbolt as he tries to scale the walls of Thebes is so constant a feature of tradition likewise[54] that scholars are doubtless right to attribute it to the *Thebais*; this, then, is another un-Iliadic feature.[55] ("Kein Held der *Ilias* wird vom Blitz getroffen ... denn das ginge, könnte man sagen, gegen den Geschmack" [Reinhardt, "Tradition und Geist im homerischen Epos," 339 = *Tradition und Geist* 15]).[56] For the Iliadic restriction of Zeus' thunderbolt to a warning sign see Nilsson, "Der Flammentod des Herakles auf dem Oite," *Archiv für Religionswissenschaft* 22 (1923): 366 = *Opuscula Selecta* 1.359; Griffin 1977:47 = 2001:380. Even in the description of Ajax the Locrian's death at *Odyssey* iv 499–511, nothing is said of a thunderbolt (contrast later accounts as cited by Tarrant on Seneca *Agamemnon* [Cambridge 2004] 528–529). Idas is blasted by a thunderbolt in Pindar *Nemean* X 71 (probably from the *Cypria*: see e.g. West 2013:94–97).

PARTHENOPAEUS

On this figure see in general Hutchinson on Aeschylus *Seven Against Thebes* 526–567 and Fowler 2013:411. "P's Arcadian birth and early metoecism to Argos is a constant detail, whether original to *Seven Against Thebes* 547–548 or not" (Collard on Euripides *Suppliant Women* 888–891 [2.331]). See Fraenkel 1957:37–38 = 1964:306. The hero's status as Arcadian and a son of Atalanta was confidently attributed to the *Thebais* by Bethe (1891:86n11). More cautious are Jacoby on Hellanicus *FGrHist* 1 F32 (p. 328) and Fraenkel as cited. Howald (1939:12–13) sees the association of this hero (and, indeed, the Seven at large) with Argos as the product of a late tendency to locate saga in specific contexts (cf. Kühr

---

54 See Collard on Euripides *Suppliant Women* 496–497 (2.242); on the evidence of art, see page 76 below.

55 When Collard writes, "Epic, however, ignores the episode, dignifying C. as ἀγακλειτός *Iliad* II 564 and κυδάλιμος IV 403," he means "Homer" not "Epic."

56 According to Σ Euripides *Phoenician Women* 1173 (1.374 Schwartz) ὁ Καπανεὺς θέλων μιμήσασθαι τὸν Δία ἀνῆλθεν εἰς κλίμακα ἔχων δύο λαμπάδας. τὴν μίαν κεραυνὸν ἔλεγεν εἶναι καὶ τὴν μίαν ἀστραπήν. ἐπὶ τούτοις ὀργισθεὶς ὁ Ζεὺς ἐκεραύνωσεν αὐτόν. In his note on Aeschylus *Seven Against Thebes* 422–456, Hutchinson suggests this version is early and presupposed by the Aeschylean passage.

2006:138n26), and attributes it to epic. On the likely original form of the name see Beazley, "Some Inscriptions on Vases: V" (as in 69n49), 313–314.

Wilamowitz (1914:99n1) and Fraenkel (1957:32 = 1964:301) suppose he featured in epic, while Bethe (1891:87n13) specifically assigned him to the *Thebais*'s list of the Seven. Against this latter supposition see page 70 above.

In Aeschylus, of course, each of the Seven Argive commanders is allotted a Theban warrior as opponent. *Prima facie* we would expect this to be Aeschylus' own invention, one demanded, as Robert (1915:1.246) puts it, by the play's dramatic framework. Besides, as Wilamowitz (1891:225 = 60) and Robert saw, the *Thebais* seems to have made Periclymenus the opponent of both Amphiaraus and Parthenopaeus (see pages 78–79 and 90 below). Aeschylus fails to mention him at all. Polyneices must have been matched with Eteocles, of course, from the very first; and Aeschylus' ranking of Melanippus against Tydeus also prob-ably derives from the *Thebais*, where the enmity of the two reached a grisly climax (see pages 80–81 below), though in fact it was Amphiaraus who finally despatched Melanippus. On Melanippus' presumed importance in the *Thebais* see Fraenkel 1957:14 and n1 = 1964:283 and n4.

Friedländer prefers to suppose that Πολυφόντης, Μεγαρεύς, Ὑπέρβιος, and Οἶνοπος were also taken over from epic by Aeschylus, who merely invented the figure of Λασθένης in order to provide a potential opponent for Amphiaraus (1914:325n1 = 1969:39n54). Since Amphiaraus actually sinks below the earth before he can encounter this opponent, Lasthenes, as Wilamowitz too observed (1914:75), has nothing to do. The form of his name (Λᾱσθένης rather than Λαοσθ-) also tells against epic origin. Megareus is certainly an obscure non-entity. Polyphontes is a name that appears elsewhere in connection with the Seven's expedition against Thebes (see page 35 above). Like Hyperbius, it is a significant and therefore invented name, though this fact tells us nothing about who invented it.[57]

Wilamowitz (1914:78) assumed that the "Schildzeichen" were Aeschylus' own invention. T. G. Tucker, in his commentary on Aeschylus' *Seven Against Thebes* (Cambridge 1908) p. LIII, took it for granted that the *Thebais* supplied Aeschylus with the basic idea of a description of the shield devices of the Argive leaders. The idea was cautiously approved by Fraenkel (1957:9–10 = 1964:279–280), who

---

[57] Bethe was certainly wrong (1891:88) to lump him with others as "keine berühmten Namen." But one should not follow Wilamowitz (1914:102) in supposing that Herodotus V 67 is testimony to Megareus' importance: see page 30 above.

compared the famous "Schildbeschreibung" in the *Iliad* and the *Aethiopis* (cf. West 2013:144), while reserving for Aeschylus' invention the symbolic overtones in, for instance, the account of Tydeus' emblem. Archaeological evidence seems to reinforce the views of Tucker and Fraenkel as against the position of Wilamowitz.[58] Thus, on the general level, by the time of Aeschylus shield emblems and decorations had lost the imaginative vivacity that characterized them in the Archaic age.

More specifically, the Basel amphora perhaps depicting the setting out of Amphiaraus[59] also shows a number of warriors with variously emblazoned shields, including one that displays a crescent moon and stars. This unusual device has reminded several scholars of Tydeus' similar emblem in *Seven Against Thebes* 387–390 ἔχει δὲ ὑπέρφρον σῆμ' ἐπ' ἀσπίδος τόδε, | φλέγονθ' ὑπ' ἄστροις οὐρανὸν τετυγμένον | λαμπρὰ δὲ πανσέληνος ἐν μέσωι σάκει, | πρέσβιστον ἄστρων, νυκτὸς ὀφθαλμός, πρέπει. The discrepancy between full and crescent moon is easily explained, since an artist would soonest choose the latter as a less ambiguous sign for a shield (Hampe[-Simon] 27; Krauskopf 68n74, etc.). However, the number of warriors depicted easily exceeds seven (the famous Seven each with a companion, Hampe[-Simon] would assure us), and "if the ... painter knew that Tydeus' blazon was the moon and stars and intended Tydeus for one of the combatants in the larger and more important scene on the shoulder [see above page 64], why did he not put the correct blazon there?" (R. M. Cook, "Greek Rhapsodes in Etruria?," *Classical Review* 15 [1965]: 98). Hampe and Simon's retort in "Gefälschte etruskische Vasenbilder?," *Jahrbuch des Römisch-Germanischen Zentralmuseums Mainz* 14 (1967): 85 (two different blazons for two different stages of the story—at Argos and before Thebes) does not convince, and I concur with Brommer's *Vasenlisten*[3]: "Deutung nicht sicher."

For handy surveys of vases that possibly depict the Seven commanders see Small, pp. 135–138 and M. Tiverios, "Sieben gegen Theben," *Mitteilungen des Deutschen Archäologischen Instituts, Athenische Abteilung* 96 (1981): 145–161. The likeliest candidates (*LIMC* VII.1 *s.v.* "Sieben" 730ff.) are the cup by Macron (Louvre G271: *ARV²* 461.33), ca. 490/80; a hydria in Basel (the Borowski Collection), ca. 470/60; a lekythos by the Terpaulus Painter (Agrigentum Mus. Civ. 23: *ARV²* 308.5, *Paralip.* 357), first decade of the fifth century; and the cup by the Kleophrades Painter (Aths. Nat. Mus. Acrop. 336 [B 87]: *ARV²* 192.105), ca. 480 (for illustrations see Tiverios, plates 43–45). Each vase presents a similar scene.

---

[58] See, for instance, Hampe(-Simon) 27: "die reichen und vielfältigen Schildembleme der archaischen Zeit verschwinden in der frühen Klassik fast ganz und verlieren Kraft und Ausdrucksfülle"; cf. Beazley and Caskey, *Attic Vase Paintings in Boston*, vol. 2 (Boston 1954) 79.

[59] *LIMC* I.1 *s.v.* "Amphiaraos" E161: plate 8 in Hampe(-Simon); see page 104 below.

Thanks to the relative inexplicitness of this type of representation, we could not be sure, even if we knew for certain that the figures involved were the Seven, how precisely to interpret their activities. Tiverios supposes they are preparing for battle by arming themselves; but other scholars (see Small as cited on page 40 above) have taken them to be leaving home for the war.

Tiverios' hypothesis of a literary source (our *Thebais*) is perfectly arbitrary and leads him into unconvincing stratagems like his attempt (p. 147) to produce a single unitary figure from the warrior holding a helmet in his hand (Terpaulus Painter and Kleophrades Painter), the warrior holding a greave (Macron), and the warrior holding a sword (Basel hydria). Parthenopaeus and Adrastus seem safely identified on these vases. As for the rest of the figures, one may more safely generalize Small's conclusion vis-à-vis the Basel hydria (p. 176): "the other warriors take genre poses and must remain nameless."

Those who are reluctant to accept that Onasias' painting derives (see page 24 above) from the *Oedipodeia* have sometimes wondered whether the *Thebais* may not in fact be the inspiration behind this artifact (cf. Robert 1915:1.180). The obstacle to this is roughly the same as before: why does Pausanias fail to add the *Thebais*'s name? Why, indeed, does he mention Onasias at all?

The brothers' conflict was also depicted on the Chest of Cypselus (Pausanias V 19.6: *LIMC* V s.v. "Eteokles" Aa4): Πολυνείκει πεπτωκότι ἐς γόνυ ἔπεισιν Ἐτεο-κλῆς)[60] and described at Euripides *Phoenician Women* 1414–1417:

ὁμοῦ δὲ κάμψας πλευρὰ καὶ νηδὺν τάλας
σὺν αἱματηραῖς σταγόσι Πολυνείκης πίτνει,
ὃ δ᾽ ὡς κρατῶν δὴ καὶ νενικηκὼς μάχηι,
ξίφος δικὼν ἐς γαῖαν ἐσκύλευέ νιν.

The similarities between the two passages have led various scholars[61] to posit the *Thebais* as the common source.

For a useful survey of the numerous artifacts that have been thought to display the duel of the brothers see Small (104–108), who stresses the frequency with which the cautious scholar must abandon the combatants as unidentifiable or anonymous participators in a generic duel, and shows that numerous Etruscan urns are likelier interpreted as revealing the duel of Aeneas and Turnus, or Arruns and Brutus, or Romulus and Remus.

---

[60] Such a scheme only appears in extant artifacts from the fourth century, and Krauskopf (16) derives these from the *Phoenician Women*. For bibliography on reconstructions of this scene of the Chest see Small 104n12.

[61] For instance, Robert 1915:1.224–225; Rzach 1922:2369.40–42; Krauskopf 69n80.

From the beginning of the fifth century a large number of Etruscan scarabs depict the overthrow of Capaneus.[62] Perhaps, as Krauskopf (p. 41) suggests, the importance of Zeus' lightning in Etruscan cult sharpened interest in the story. But by nature of their restricted size these scarabs add nothing to our knowledge. The types vary somewhat: Capaneus' scaling-ladder is but rarely shown, even the lightning-bolt is no necessary ingredient, and often it is only the inscription that reveals the warrior's identity at all. Even if, as Krauskopf supposes, these artifacts presuppose a market acquainted with a literary source for the tale (to wit, the *Thebais*), we learn nothing at all about that poem from these gems.

Similarly uninformative as to details are those Etruscan scarabs showing Tydeus in various warlike poses.[63] Indeed, there is even less in the way of characterizing features than with Capaneus and his lightning. And when we are, for once, offered by some gems an otherwise unattested detail (an arrow wound in Tydeus' shin bone from which Krauskopf [43 and 84n287] infers a literary tradition of a nonfatal hurt in that region as opposed to the mortal stomach wound testified by Apollodorus III 6.8), we should pause long before accepting it. Cautious scholars will be led to nothing more specific than to Small's unambitious conclusion (p. 147): "the gems prove that the Etruscans knew the stories related to the Theban Cycle at least as early as the fifth century B.C. and that the Seven were popular enough heroes to be used in genre scenes."

Further depictions of Capaneus striving to storm Thebes are not very informative from our point of view. As with Tydeus, the few novel details we encounter are productive of complication rather than enlightenment. Thus, on an urn relief now in the Museo Civico at Chiusi,[64] we see Capaneus climbing his regular ladder and grasping his regular shield with his left hand. But over his left shoulder slumps an inert (and presumably dead) body. What are we to make of this? A literal interpretation would be too absurd: it is difficult enough to climb a ladder while burdening one hand with a shield. Not even Capaneus would have wished to render the task near impossible by draping himself with a cadaver besides! The urn dates from the second half of the second century BC. Scholars (e.g. Robert and Krauskopf) usually cite the scene in Statius' *Thebaid* (VIII 745–750) where Capaneus lifts the dying Melanippus and bears him on his left shoulder to Tydeus (see page 81 below). Brunn and Körte (*Rilievi delle*

---

[62] See *LIMC* V.1 *s.v.* "Kapaneus" D (Krauskopf), 41–42 (discussion) and 957–959 (lists) with plate 18; cf. Small 146–147.

[63] See *LIMC* VIII.1 (Krauskopf), 142–143 (discussion) and 102–103 (lists), with plate 19; cf. Small 145–146.

[64] 215: *LIMC* V.1 *s.v.* "Kapaneus" III C318; Small, cat. 15, plate 9; see in particular Robert 1915:1.227–231; Krauskopf p. 57 (and plate 23.2); a full description of contents in Small 122–123.

Urne etrusche 2.1.68–71) go further in suggesting that the common source for the Roman poet and the Etruscan artifact was the epic *Thebais*. Such a theory presupposes that the urn presents us with a typical artistic combination of two separate scenes, a possibility that is accepted by Krauskopf. Robert (1915:1.229) objects that the urn's corpse is still trailing its shield, inconsistently with the situation outlined by Statius. This is a trivial complaint. More significant for the hypothesis of our epic as a common source is his observation (1915:1.228–229) that Statius "die *Thebais* notorisch nicht gelesen hat": see page 40 above.

Since other reliefs represent Capaneus' ascent of his ladder without the troublesome corpse,[65] and since the relief which does include the corpse is unlikely to derive that detail from the work which is usually taken to be the original of these and similar reliefs,[66] there is much to be said for Robert's conclusion (1915:1.233) that the modification in question may be the artist's own idea and need not reflect anything in the *Thebais* (cf. Krauskopf p. 57: "[man sollte] die Zeugnis der Chiusiner Urnen nicht zu hoch bewerten"). Small's analysis (152–154) arrives at much the same verdict. Note in particular the assertion that "it is extraordinary how much the figure of Capaneus with the dead man resembles Ajax carrying Achilles. ... The Etruscan artisan knew that Capaneus climbed a ladder to take Thebes single-handedly, but, since he had no readily available type for this figure, he took another figure and plugged him into Capaneus' position. That this particular figure, who could fit so easily on a ladder, happened also to be carrying the body of a dead warrior did not concern the artisan. He just inserted the group intact. Consequently, there is no specific name for the figure carried by Capaneus. That the ladder climber is indeed Capaneus is probable because of his association with the ladder. But the identification should not be pressed further" (153–154). Other Etruscan urns,[67] which show a warrior plunging from a ladder, need not be depictions of Capaneus in particular: see Small 155–164 (esp. 155: "The figure could just as well represent some Etruscan hero in an attack on an Etruscan town as well as any other Greek myth").

On *the defeat of the Seven*, the Attic tragedians have a simple tale to tell: the Argive army besieges Thebes, and their chieftains try to storm its walls. They fail, and when Capaneus is killed in the attempt, the Argive army turns to flight. A rather more complex account is given by Pausanias IX 9.1–3. The Argives win a preliminary victory over the Thebans in a hand-to-hand battle at the river Ismenus. The Thebans are driven back to their city and escape to its walls. When

---

[65] E.g. the Roman sarcophagus in the Villa Pamphili: *LIMC* V.1 *s.v.* "Kapaneus" C2.17: Krauskopf plate 23.3.

[66] Cf. O.-W. von Vacano, "Die Figurenanordnung im Giebelrelief von Telamon," *Mitteilungen des Deutschen Archäologischen Instituts, Römische Abteilung* 76 (1969): 154.

[67] Cf. *LIMC* V.1 *s.v.* "Kapaneus" D10 (p. 959).

the Argives try to scale the latter they are massacred by Thebans shooting from the walls. These Thebans then sally out and defeat the remainder. A similar tale, partly obscured by contamination with an account derived from Euripides' *Phoenician Women*, is to be found in Apollodorus III 6.7 (μάχης δὲ γενομένης οἱ Καδμεῖοι μέχρι τῶν τειχῶν συνεδιώχθησαν κτλ.).[68] Capaneus' overthrow is the turning point in these accounts too.

I am sympathetic to the idea that this latter version of events stems from the *Thebais* (Bethe 1891:123–126; cf. Wilamowitz 1891:225 = 1971:60; Stoneman 1981:49 etc.), not so much for the reasons alleged by Bethe as because it is hard to conceive of any other source for an account that survives into such late authors and yet is at odds with the tragic vulgate. The motif of the victorious battle followed by the unsuccessful assault on the walls is certainly both Homeric and epic, as Bethe observed. Likewise, the striking down of the triumphant hero from the walls he seems set to scale and the routing of his side, with the sallying forth of the besieged in consequence, also have numerous analogies in epic, the *Aethiopis'* Achilles in particular (cf. West 2013:149).

Apollodorus III 6.8 places Ismarus' killing of Hippomedon, Leades' killing of Eteoclus, Asphodicus'[69] killing of Parthenopaeus, and Melanippus' fatal wounding of Tydeus amid the Argive rout that follows Capaneus' overthrow. This passage too Bethe (1891:125) would derive from the *Thebais*, but his conviction that Hippomedon appeared in that epic is to be treated with caution: see page 73 above.

F6 on Adrastus' escape need not imply that the *Thebais* envisaged the Argive army as fighting on horseback in a strikingly un-Homeric manner. Lloyd-Jones[70] observes that "the Argives may well have been imagined as using chariots to bring them up to or away from the scene of battle, but as doing the actual fighting on foot. This seems to be how Aeschylus conceived the battle."

F4 *(see page 139 for text)*

For the mode of reference to this episode (τὰ ἐν Θηβαΐδι ἔπη τὰ ἐς τὴν Παρθενοπαῖον τελευτὴν) Rzach (1922:2361.52–57) compares ἐν Διομήδεος ἀριστείηι (Herodotus II 116) or Plato's Λιταί (*Cratylus* 428ᶜ)[71] and infers (2369.26–27) "eine ausführliche Behandlung." Periclymenus, son of Poseidon, also features as

---

[68] For the self-sacrifice of Menoeceus, here interpolated, as a Euripidean invention, see Stephanopoulos 1980:115–118,

[69] See page 79 below.

[70] "Notes on Sophocles' *Antigone*," *Classical Quarterly* 7 (1957): 15n1 = *Academic Papers* [I] 372n7.

[71] For further parallels see Schmid, *GGL* 1.1.128n1; S. West, *The Ptolemaic Papyri of Homer* (Cologne 1967) 20–35.

Parthenopaeus' slayer in the messenger speech at Euripides *Phoenician Women* 1153–1162:

ὁ δ' Ἀρκάς, οὐκ Ἀργεῖος, Ἀταλάντης γόνος,
τυφὼς πύλαισιν ὥς τις ἐμπεσὼν βοᾶι
πῦρ καὶ δικέλλας, ὡς κατασκάψων πόλιν.
ἀλλ' ἔσχε μαργῶντ' αὐτὸν ἐναλίου θεοῦ
Περικλύμενος παῖς, λᾶαν ἐμβαλὼν κάραι
ἀμαξοπληθῆ, γεῖσ' ἐπάλξεων ἄπο
ξανθὸν δὲ κρᾶτα διεπάλυνε καὶ ῥαφάς
ἔρρηξεν ὀστέων, ἄρτι δ' οἰνωπὸν γένυν
καθηιμάτωσεν οὐδ' ἀποίσεται βίον
τῆι καλλιτόξωι μητρὶ Μαινάλου κόρηι.

See too Apollodorus III 6.8: Ἀσφόδικος (Wilamowitz: Ἀμφίδικος codd.)[72] δὲ Παρθενοπαῖον (*scil.* ἀπέκτεινεν). ὡς δὲ Εὐριπίδης φησί, Παρθενοπαῖον ὁ Ποσειδῶνος παῖς Περικλύμενος ἀπέκτεινε. Euripides' lines here replace the *Thebais*, as the later and more familiar author so often ousts the earlier and less read in the texts of mythographers and scholia: see page 80 below.

In Euripides' account, Parthenopaeus is thrown from the wall like Capaneus. In Apollodorus, by implication, he is killed in the hand-to-hand fighting that accompanies the Argive retreat caused by Capaneus' death. Bethe (1891:125) thinks this latter context more appropriate both for the kind of battle we expect in an epic and for the mighty son of Poseidon. The *Thebais* certainly seems to have had Periclymenus attack Amphiaraus at this stage of the conflict: see page 90 below.

Why Aeschylus should have chosen to omit Periclymenus is, as Bethe says (1891:88), a mystery: see page 68 above.

F5 *(see page 140 for text)*

On "Die Genfer Iliasscholien," our source for this fragment, see Erbse, "Die Genfer Iliasscholien," *Rheinisches Museum* 95 (1952): 170–191.[73] The passage in Σ Gen., with its reference to ἡ ἱστορία παρὰ τοῖς Κυκλικοῖς, was first published by J. Nicole, *Les scolies genévoises de l'Iliade 2* (Geneva 1891) 63–64. The same tale occurs, without the attribution to the cyclic poets, in Σ Ab T *Iliad* V 126 (2.22 Erbse):

---

[72] See Wilamowitz 1891:225 = 60n2.
[73] This is summarized in his preface to the reprint of Nicole's edition (Hildesheim 1966).

φασίν ἐν τῶι Θηβαϊκῶι πολέμωι Τυδέα τρωθέντα ὑπὸ Μελανίππου τοῦ Ἀστακοῦ σφόδρα ἀγανακτῆσαι. Ἀμφιάρεων δὲ κτείναντα τὸν Μελάνιππον δοῦναι τὴν κεφαλὴν Τυδεῖ. τὸν δὲ δίκην θηρὸς ἀναπτύξαντα ῥοφᾶν τὸν ἐγκέφαλον ἀπὸ θυμοῦ. κατ᾽ ἐκεῖνο δὲ καιροῦ παρεῖναι Ἀθηνᾶν ἀθανασίαν αὐτῶι φέρουσαν ἐξ οὐρανοῦ καὶ διὰ τὸ μύσος ἀπεστράφθαι. τὸν δὲ θεασάμενον παρακαλέσαι κἂν τῶι παιδὶ αὐτοῦ χαρίσασθαι τὴν ἀθανασίαν. ἱστορεῖ Φερεκύδης.

FGrHist 3 F97

That in our fragment οἱ κυκλικοί = ἡ Θηβαΐς was first seen by Robert.[74] Compare the phrase ἡ κυκλικὴ Θηβαΐς in F2 and F3. The identification of our fragment's resting place with the *Thebais* has been accepted by most scholars.[75] The only serious dissent comes from Van der Valk,[76] who argues that Σ Gen.'s reference to the Cycle may be a mere elaboration built upon Pherecydes' name, a plausible guess based on the assumption that Tydeus' death must have been mentioned in the *Thebais* (compare the similar deductions of the more recent scholars listed above) and one calculated to give a pleasingly (and misleadingly) learned impression. That Pausanias indulged in this kind of pretense to wide reading is itself by no means certain (see West 2013:49). In the present case, when we do not even know the identity of the individual responsible for the statement, the explanation is bound to strike us as arbitrary. The process of substituting a more familiar and later name for an earlier, less read author is very familiar (cf. Severyns 1928:75–79, esp. 77–78). And since Van der Valk himself allows (334n220) that Pherecydes may have followed the *Thebais*'s version of events, his argument has little to commend it.

"Aus wiederholten Hinweisen älterer Lyriker ... und Dramatiker ... darf geschlossen werden dass jene schaurige Szene des alten Heldenliedes mächtigen Eindruck übte" (Rzach 1922:2368.54–61). The story falls into two inseparable parts.[77] As Beazley observes (p. 4), those authors who only mention Tydeus' singular meal cannot have been ignorant of the loss of immortality which forms its inevitable sequel: "The legend ... is a unity and cannot be split into two. In oral tradition, or in the rude narrative of a primitive bard, the trespass might have been described by itself; but to the high poetry of mature Greek

---

[74] 1915:1.195 (the story of Tydeus' cannibalism "kann ... in der *Thebais* kaum gefehlt haben") and 205; see too Rzach 1922:2368.42–43, A. Severyns, "Le cycle épique et l'épisode d'Io," *Musée Belge* 30 (1926): 122 and n1, repeated in 1928:77–78, 219–220, etc.

[75] E.g. Pearson, *Fragments of Sophocles* 3.39; Griffin 1977:42 and 46 = 2001:372 and 380; Stoneman 1981:57.

[76] *Researches on the Text and Scholia of the Iliad* (Leiden 1963) 1.333–334.

[77] On which see Robert 1915:1.131–134 and 2.48–49 and Beazley, "The Rosi Krater," *Journal of Hellenic Studies* 67 (1947): 1–9 (with bibliography in 3n4 and 5n5).

epic it would have seemed a pointless brutality unless followed by a terrible punishment." Athena obviously featured in the *Thebais* no less than the *Iliad* (see page 34 above) as Tydeus' protectress.

The idea of a drug (or something similar) of immortality is widespread throughout the world from the epic of Gilgamesh[78] onward.[79] It is usually an integral part of the motif that the mortal involved comes close to immortality and then forfeits it (like Gilgamesh and Tydeus) through some deficiency basic to humanity. A heartening pair of counterexamples from Greek legend is provided by Glaucus[80] and Tydeus' own son (see page 84 below). According to Fontenrose, in the present case "the herb is no more than a refined version of the head, which is the means of immortality in the primitive tale" (p. 125) and "the herb which restores the Champion is a recurring feature of the combat myth" (125n42 with examples), as examined exhaustively in the same scholar's *Python: A Study of a Delphic Myth and Its Origins* (Berkeley 1959).

The intensely un-Homeric nature of the whole picture is stressed by Reinhardt and Griffin.[81] So easy a prospect of immortality would be unthinkable in the *Iliad* or even the *Odyssey*. Again, in the former poem, wishes to feast on the enemy's flesh are expressed but never fulfilled (*Iliad* IV 35, XXII 346, XXIV 212), and in the latter cannibalism is the prerogative of monsters like the Cyclops. Furthermore, Tydeus is very favorably presented in the *Iliad* (see page 37 above). Possible precedents or analogies for Tydeus' horrific act are considered by Dirlmeier and Delcourt.[82] See further page 82 below.

In saying that Amphiaraus slew Melanippus and cut off his head and brought it to Tydeus, Σ Gen. is in agreement with all our sources save Apollodorus III 6.3 (see Davies and Finglass on Stesichorus fr. 92); Statius (*Thebaid* VIII 739–750), who, having already despatched Amphiaraus to subterranean gloom, appropriately transfers the action to the hateful Capaneus (see page 76 above); and Libanius (*Progymnasmata* R 4.1100 [8.40 Förster]), who assigns the task to a nameless companion of Tydeus. On Melanippus' function in the *Thebais* see further

---

[78] Cf. G. S. Kirk, *Myth: Its Meaning and Functions in Ancient and Other Cultures* (Cambridge 1971) 140, 144–145.

[79] See J. Bauer's article *s.v.* "Lebenskraut" in *EM* 8.836–838; T. H. Gaster, *Myth, Legend, and Custom in the Old Testament* (London 1968) 29–30; cf. T. Karadagli, *Fabel und Ainos: Studien zur griechischen Fabel* (*Beiträge zur klassischen Philologie* 135 [1981]) 145–148; M. Davies, "The Ancient Greeks on Why Mankind Does Not Live Forever," *Museum Helveticum* 44 (1987): 69, and " 'Unpromising' Heroes and Heroes as Helpers in Greek Myth," *Prometheus* 37 (2011): 125.

[80] Cf. Frazer, Loeb Apollodorus 2, appendix 7; J. Fontenrose, "The Cult and Myth of Pyrros at Delphi," *California Studies in Classical Antiquity* 2 (1969): 127–128.

[81] Reinhardt, *Studium Generale* 4 (1951): 339 = *Tradition und Geist* 15; Griffin 1977:42 and 46 = 2001:372 and 380.

[82] Dirlmeier 1954:152–153 = pp. 49–50. M. Delcourt, "Tydée et Mélanippe," *Studi e Materiali di Storia delle Religioni* 37 (1966): 139–188; cf. Vicaire (as cited below page 90), p. 7n5.

page 78 above. The fight between him and Tydeus is traced back to the widespread motif of the Combat Myth (the Champion against the dark Antagonist) by Fontenrose as cited, 124–126 and n42.

Nothing is said in any of the Iliadic scholia regarding the motive behind the parting of Melanippus' head from its owner and the bringing of it to Tydeus. There are, in fact, two divergent explanations of this. According to Σ Pindar *Nemean* X 12^b (3.168 Dr.), Statius, and Libanius, Tydeus had asked for the head. Apollodorus III 6.8, however, gives a more devious account: Amphiaraus, hating Tydeus for having persuaded the Argives into the attack on Thebes, and aware, by virtue of his mantic powers, that Athena intended to make Tydeus immortal, brought the head in the fully justified hope that Tydeus would act true to type and throw away his unique opportunity rather than forego revenge.[83] For comparable bloody acts of vengeful savagery see West, *Indo-European Poetry and Myth* 492–493; cf. Fowler 2013:412n44. Bethe (1891:76–77) supposed that the simpler version which we have mentioned first actually developed first, and that Apollodorus' more complex and sophisticated account suggests a later elaboration: this he identified with the *Thebais*.

As for the exact form in which Athena brought the immortality, most of our sources regard it (either explicitly or by implication) as a drug or potion (e.g. Apollodorus' φάρμακον δι' οὗ ποιεῖν ἔμελλεν ἀθάνατον αὐτόν), and this fits well with the motif-parallels mentioned above page 81. Two vase-paintings[84] certainly and one Etruscan mirror[85] probably depict Ἀθανασία as a young girl whom Athena leads by the wrist.

We have here, then, a nice example of the different approaches of art and literature. For I agree with Beazley (p. 7) when he suggests that "the complete personification of Athanasia may be due to a painter, who from the nature of his

---

[83] It may well be—as suggested by J. G. Frazer, Loeb Apollodorus 1.369n4 and 2.70–71n2; also *The Golden Bough: Spirits of the Corn and of the Wild* (London 1912) 138–168 (the same idea in, for instance, Radermacher, *Mythos und Sage bei den Griechen* [Leipzig 1939] 37; D. S. Robertson, "The Food of Achilles," *Classical Review* 54 [1940]: 178; Griffin, *Homer on Life and Death* 20; Vicaire [as cited below page 90], 7–8n5; *contra* Wilamowitz, *Glaube der Hellenen* 1.287n3)—that Tydeus' act was originally connected with the primitive belief that eating raw flesh transfers to the eater the qualities of the eaten. But in the story as it now stands this motivation is impossible, and a new psychological twist is given to the motif. Compare Homer's revision of the significance of burned clothing and human sacrifice in *Iliad* XXII 508, XXIII 22 (cf. Griffin as cited, 3 and n7: "psychological motives replace superstition").

[84] "The Rosi Crater" (no longer extant): *LIMC* VIII.1 s.v. "Tydeus" F17 (Beazley fig. 1); a fragmentary bell-krater in New York: 12.229.14: *LIMC* F17a (Beazley fig. 2): full descriptions and discussion in Beazley.

[85] Cab. Méd. 1289: cf. I. Mayer-Prokop, *Die Gravierten etruskischen Griffspiegel* (*Mitteilungen des Deutschen Archäologischen Instituts, Römische Abteilung*, Ergänzungsheft 13 [1967]) 70–72 and plate 15: the interpretation is Beazley's (p. 7) followed by e.g. Mayer-Prokop, Krauskopf 45, Small 158: Tydeus himself is not shown.

art, had to choose, and could not sit on the fence between person and thing." He is clearly right to observe that none of the literary allusions to the incident need imply personification, not even Σ Pindar *Nemean* X 12, cited above, which tells how ἡ Ἀθηνᾶ τὴν ἀθανασίαν παρήγαγε but proceeds to describe immortality as a "gift" (δωρεά, δῶρον).

Two other artifacts have been supposed to deal with the story of Tydeus' death in a way that is revealing as to the differing operations of literature and art. The Etruscan relief from temple A at Pyrgi now in the Villa Giulia at Rome[86] brings out the full horror of Tydeus' deed, in a manner presumably gratifying to Etruscan taste, by having him gnaw at the head of Melanippus while it is still attached to the very much living body of its owner. In other words the artist seems to have telescoped the two separate incidents just as he further combines the story of Tydeus with that of Capaneus, whom Zeus smites with a thunder-bolt at the back of the two struggling enemies. Athena comes up behind Tydeus carrying a vessel presumably filled with immortality. Dohrn (as cited page 40 above) explains this unorthodox representation as a repetition of the schema that conveys the death-locked Eteocles and Polyneices, and, in spite of the skepticism of Small (p. 160: "there is a great difference between swallowing the brains of a severed head and biting the head of your opponent in self-defence"), it still seems to me that the likeliest interpretation of the artifact sees it in terms of a concentrated depiction of the story's two consecutive stages.

An analogous telescoping of events has been thought by some to underlie several Etruscan urns, especially two in Volterra and one in Florence,[87] which have been popularly taken to depict Tydeus and other Argive warriors seeking to storm the walls of Thebes. In his right hand the alleged Tydeus is holding a severed head which he seems ready to hurl up at the wall's defenders as if it were a stone. If this had to be interpreted as Melanippus' head, the likeliest explanation would be that the detail was meant to identify the head's holder as Tydeus without making a literal statement about the weapons Tydeus actual-ly brandished against Thebes, or about the precise point in the battle at which Melanippus was slain. Robert (1915:1.235) believed that this "extraordinarily effective artistic motif" could still be compatible with a fairly strict representa-tion of the *Thebais*'s contents. Rzach (1922:2368.61–62) referred to "eine freie künstlerische Verwendung." Small (157–160), however, is right to be skeptical about this identification and prefers to regard the urns in question as depicting an attack upon an unidentified city whose name could be left to the viewer

---

[86] *LIMC* VIII.1 *s.v.* "Tydeus" D.f. 16: cf. Krauskopf p. 144 and plate 17; Small 159–160; T. Dohrn, *Die etruskische Kunst im Zeitalter der griechischen Klassik* (Mainz 1982) 24.

[87] Volterra: inv. 370: Small, cat. 87, plate 39a; inv. 436: Small, cat. 89, plate 40a. Florence: inv. 78483: Small, cat. 90, plate 40b. For a full description of their appearance and contents see Small 67–76.

to supply. Since the figure holding the head is not "on the point of imminent collapse ... but is not even wounded. He is, in fact, the robust leader of the attackers," Small (p. 159) concludes that "there is no particular reason for a severed head to be connected immutably with Tydeus," particularly when we bear in mind the number of Greek and Roman legends of battle (e.g. Nisus and Euryalus in *Aeneid* IX) that exploit severed heads in a way that will have excited Etruscan taste.

We may close with a few points of detail. The word Ἀθανασία cannot have occurred in the *Thebais*, since, as Beazley reminds us (7; cf. R. Renehan, "A New Lexicon of Classical Greek," *Greek, Roman, and Byzantine Studies* 24 [1983]: 13), it will not fit into a hexameter and is not securely attested until the fourth century. Apollodorus' picture of Athena παρὰ Δίος αἰτησαμένη ... φάρμακον ... δι' οὗ ποιεῖν ἔμελλεν ἀθάνατον αὐτόν [*scil.* Τύδεα] is strongly reminiscent of a scene in the *Aethiopis* as summarized by Proclus where we have Ἠὼς παρὰ Διός αἰτησαμένη ἀθανασίαν and presenting it to her son Memnon (cf. West 2013:148–149).

It is striking that Σ Gen.'s ἀνοίξας αὐτὴν [*scil.* τὴν κεφαλήν] ὁ Τυδεὺς τὸν ἐγκέφαλον ἐρρόφει ἀπὸ θυμοῦ has a much more colorful and poetic counterpart in the other Iliadic scholia: τὸν δὲ δίκην θηρὸς ἀναπτύξαντα κτλ. One cannot be surprised that Robert (1915:2.49) suggested the relevant phrase "wohl auf das Epos zurückgehen könnte." Finally, the tale of Tydeus' frustrated immortality is obviously connected with the story of his son's successful attainment of that state (Ibycus 294 *PMGF*, Pindar *Nemean* X 7, *carmen conviviale* 894.4 *PMG*, etc.) at the hands of the same goddess. But how connected: which inspired which? Wilamowitz (1891:239 = 1971:74) thought it inconceivable that the poet who described Tydeus' death at Thebes could have had any knowledge of a tradition whereby that death was avenged by a son who helped sack the city his father had failed to destroy. In taking up what was a diametrically opposed position, Friedländer (1914:328 = 1969:42) went so far as to assert that the successful immortalization must be primary, the unsuccessful attempt secondary and derivative (a schema he proceeded to adapt to the larger question as to the priority between the Seven and their offspring [see page 109 below]). A similar principle has been applied to the parallel stories of Tithonus and Memnon, and Eos' bungled attempt at winning immortality for her paramour, and her successful attainment of life everlasting for their son.[88] Of course, even if this principle fits the present case (which most scholars have doubted), Friedländer will not have proved that Diomedes was immortalized because of his exploits at Thebes rather than at Troy. Besides, as we saw (page 81 above), narrow failure

---

[88] Cf. J. Th. Kakridis, "ΤΙΘΩΝΟΣ," *Wiener Studien* 48 (1930): 36–37.

to gain proffered immortality exists as an independent motif in its own right. In view of this important consideration, I prefer to follow Andersen (1978:30n6; cf. Fontenrose as cited, 126) in seeing transference of the immortality motif from father to son.

That Tydeus died and was buried at Thebes is implied by *Iliad* XIV 114 (Τυδέος, ὃν Θήβῃσι χυτὴ κατὰ γαῖα κάλυψεν): cf. Σ Gen. *ad loc.* (2.135 Nicole): ὃς ἐν Θήβαις ἐτελεύτησεν, ἐν Θηβαικῶι πολέμωι. Zenodotus athetized and Aristophanes deleted the line (see Σ A *ad loc.* [3.583 Erbse] and Erbse's note *ad loc.* for a bibliography of attempts to understand this odd attitude). Σ T *ad loc.* (3.584 Erbse) explains the Homeric verse ὅτι οὐ κατὰ τοὺς τραγικοὺς ἐν Ἐλευσῖνι μετηνέχθησαν οἱ περὶ τὸν Καπανέα, which looks, as Severyns saw (1928:224), to be a relic of the usual Aristarchean contrast between Homer's version and that of οἱ νεώτεροι. On the *Thebais*'s version of the fates of the defeated Argive corpses see further page 93 below.

F6 (*see page 140 for text*)

ARION

For the horse Arion see e.g. Matthews' commentary on Antimachus (1996) general index *s.v.* In our fragment Bethe (1891:90) equated (b)'s οἱ ἐν τῶι Κύκλωι and (c)'s οἱ Κυκλικοί with ἡ κυκλικὴ Θηβαίς of F2 and F3.[89] If we accept that the reference is to the *Thebais*, how much of the scholion's ἱστορία are we to attribute to that epic? All of it, including the list of Arion's previous owners and the detail of Heracles' killing of Cycnus at Pegasae? Or should it be the list without the latter detail? Or merely the parentage of Adrastus' horse? Since some scholars have gone even further and deny that (b–c) add anything in effect to the line (a) quotes, we had better begin with their extreme case. For bibliographies of supporters and opponents of the fragment's authenticity see R. Janko, "The *Shield of Heracles* and the Legend of Cycnus," *Classical Quarterly* 36 (1986): 52nn76–77. On the text of part (c) of the fragment see 51–52 and nn74–75.

Pausanias records the fact that several people in antiquity inferred from the phrase Ἀρίονι κυανοχαίτῃ Poseidon's paternity as regards the famous horse. Schwartz ("De scholiis Homericis ad historiam fabularem pertinentibus," *Jahrbücher für classische Philologie,* Supplementband 12 [1881]: 426–427) therefore concluded that (b)'s words οἱ δὲ ἐν τῶι Κύκλωι Ποσειδῶνος καὶ Ἐρινύος involve no independent information, indeed do no more than represent the ancient inference alluded to by Pausanias (p. 427: "de Arionis origine in *Thebaide* nihil certi traditum erat, sed ex epitheto κυανοχαίτης absurda coniciebantur"). A

---

[89] The same line is taken by Rzach (1922:2370.35–38), Malten (as cited page 86 below, 201), etc.

similar skepticism is displayed by Van der Valk (*Researches on the Text and Scholia of the* Iliad, 367–368), and (by implication) in Pfeiffer's note on Callimachus fr. 652 (1.434: "fort. iam in *Thebaide* cycl. ...?"). But although the epithet in question might (reasonably or not) be taken as evidence for Poseidon's status as Arion's father, it is hard to see how anyone could deduce anything about Arion's mother from this adjective, much less come to the conclusion that she was an Erinys. And yet this latter tradition is precisely what (b) and (c) appear to attest for our poem. οἱ ἐν τῶι Κύκλωι must, therefore, at the very least be cited for the picture of Arion as offspring of Poseidon and an Erinys.[90]

Severyns (1928:222) thought (a) an important document for Pausanias' ignorance of the Epic Cycle: "visiblement, il n'a pas connu, par une lecture personelle, le passage ... auquel il fait allusion," for he automatically reproduces a verse which is not very explicit on Poseidon's alleged parentage. In fact the alleged oral tradition of the priests is very dubious (Severyns takes it too seriously) and may be a supposititiously circumstantial and "historical" way of conveying (*more Herodoteo*) an Alexandrian dispute over the significance of κυανοχαίτης. At any rate, Severyns' skepticism will neatly dispose of Van der Valk's: the latter says that if the *Thebais had* really related Arion's filial relationship to Poseidon, Pausanias would have adduced it. But if Pausanias' knowledge was indirect this line of argument must fall.

Van der Valk's attempts to discredit the testimony of (c) are no more fortunate. It is arbitrary of him to suppose that because (b) is shorter than (c) it represents a "correction" of (c)'s error in attributing too much to our epic. And his customary explanation of the contents of the relevant scholion as a "guess" (this time based on the common knowledge that the *Thebais* named Adrastus as Arion's owner) is as unconvincing as usual. Further arguments in favor of (c) as an integral part of our fragment are to be found in Janko 51–55.

A description of Arion's passage through the hands of successive owners would be quite in keeping with early poetry (see, for instance, the account of Agamemnon's scepter in *Iliad* II 101–105), as Severyns (1928:221) saw. For the significance of the mention of Cycnus see Janko 51–55. On Arion and his role in saving Adrastus' life see in general L. Malten, "Das Pferd im Totenglauben," *Jahrbuch des Kaiserlich Deutschen Archäologischen Instituts* 29 (1914): 201–208. Building on foundations laid by Wilamowitz ("Lesefrüchte," *Hermes* 35 [1900]: 563–564 = *Kleine Schriften* 4.140), Malten ingeniously inferred from passages such as Propertius II 34.37 (*vocalis Arion*), Statius *Thebaid* VI 424 (*praesagus Arion*), and *ibid.* XI 442–443 (*fata monentem* | ... *Ariona*) that the horse could speak in a

---

[90] That they are cited only for this detail is suggested by Jacoby on Ar(i)aethus of Tegea *FGrHist* 316 F5 (3[b] text p. 70).

human voice, not only in the context indicated by these passages (the Nemean funeral games for Archemorus), but as a warning to his master Adrastus of the impending catastrophe at Thebes. This warning he attributed (p. 205) to our epic, comparing the prophecy of Achilles' horse at *Iliad* XIX 400–418. A similar picture, with Arion and Adrastus as the models for the Homeric Achilles and Xanthus, was drawn by E. Heden, *Homerische Götterstudien* (diss. Upsala 1912) 136–138; cf. B. C. Dietrich, *Death, Fate and the Gods* (London 1965) 237. For artifacts that depict Adrastus' escape with his horse (including the famous relief from Gjölbaschi-Trysa) see Krauskopf in *LIMC* I.1 H1 (pp. 235–236).

The tradition that Arion was the offspring of Poseidon and an Erinys may also be found in Hesychius α7267 (1.246 Latte): Ἀρίων· ὁ ἵππος, Ποσειδῶνος υἱὸς καὶ μιᾶς τῶν Ἐρινύων. It is readily explicable, since both Poseidon and the Erinyes were originally conceived of as horse-shaped: see, for instance, the two articles of E. Wüst in *RE* (22.1 [1953]: 482–484 and 499 [Poseidon]; *Suppl.* 8 [1956] 92.3–30 [Erinys]); B. C. Dietrich, "Demeter, Erinys, Artemis," *Hermes* 90 (1962): 129–134 = *Death, Fate and the Gods* 118–132; Richardson on *Homeric Hymn to Demeter* 18. The alternative spelling of Arion's name as Ἐρίων is suggestive of Ἐρινύς.[91] For full bibliography and discussion see Dietrich as cited, 140n8 = 136–137n7; cf. Janko 54n90. For Poseidon as a begetter of horses compare Hesiod *Theogony* 276–281, where the god sleeps with Medusa and when Perseus later cuts her head off out jump Chrysaor and Pegasus. Medusa was originally identified with Demeter-Erinys (see Richardson on *Homeric Hymn to Demeter* 4 [p. 140]) and the deity on whom Poseidon fathers Arion is sometimes said to be Demeter-Erinys or Demeter in horse-shape: cf. Pausanias VIII 25.4–8 and 42.1–6; also Apollodorus III 6.8. On Demeter-Erinys see Wilamowitz, *Glaube der Hellenen* 1.398–403; Dietrich as cited; Burkert, *Structure and History in Greek Mythology and Ritual* (Berkeley 1979) 125–129; A. Schachter, *Cults of Boeotia* 1 (*BICS* suppl. 38.1 [1984]): 164. For the un-Homeric nature of such animal metamorphoses see Griffin 1977:41 = 2001:369.

Arion's begetting was sometimes located in Arcadia and sometimes in Boeotia. For the details see Pfeiffer on Callimachus fr. 652 and Fontenrose, *Python* 367–371; for discussion see Wilamowitz, Dietrich, and Fontenrose as cited. Bethe (1891:92–93) infers that the Boeotian version is the earlier (because that land, unlike Arcadia, is suited for the breeding of horses and because Copreus in [b] can be linked to Boeotia [cf. Σ T *Iliad* XV 639 (4.133 Erbse): Κοπρεύς … ἄλλος Βοιώτιος, Ἁλιάρτου παῖς]), and equates this older form with the *Thebais*'. Wilamowitz

---

[91] See in particular Bethe 1891:89n17; Wilamowitz 1891:225 = 60n1 and "Excurse zum *Oedipus des Sophokles*," *Hermes* 34 (1899): 71 and n1 = *Kleine Schriften* 6.224 and n1; *Pindaros* (Berlin 1922) 40n2; *Glaube der Hellenen* 1.393.

(1891:225n1 = 60n1) took the reverse view on account of the Arcadian spelling Ἐρίων (see page 87 above). For further bibliography and discussion see Dietrich as cited (126n2).

ADRASTUS

On Adrastus in myth see in general H. Usener, "Der Stoff des griechischen Epos," *Sitzungsberichte der Philosophisch-philologischen und der Historischen Classe des Königlich Bayerische Akademie der Wissenschaften* 137 (1897): 37–42 = *Kleine Schriften* 4.234–239; Malten 202–208, esp. 207; Howald 1939:15–16; Braswell's commentary on Pindar *Nemean* IX (Berlin 1998) and Matthews' on Antimachus (Leiden 1996), general index s.v. He is connected with Arion as early as *Iliad* XXIII 345–347 in a quasi-proverbial remark[92] (οὐδὲ παρέλθοι, | οὐδ' εἴ κεν μετόπισθεν Ἀρίονα δῖον ἐλαύνοι, | Ἀδρήστου ταχὺν ἵππον, ὃς ἐκ θεόφιν γένος ἦεν) which already implies considerable acquaintance with the tradition. It is thanks to this unusual horse that Adrastus emerges as the sole survivor of the disastrous expedition, a fact allusively indicated by Aeschylus *Seven Against Thebes* 49–50 (cf. Σ *ad loc.* [2.2.35–36 O. L. Smith]). The present hexameter was presumably part of a wider description of his flight back to his native city, the only conceivable place of refuge, as Bethe (1891:93–94) saw, for a general who has lost his entire army.[93]

Adrastus is represented as the expedition's leader by Aeschylus *Seven Against Thebes* 575, Euripides *Suppliant Women* 105, and *Phoenician Women* 1187 (which includes him in the Seven—uniquely). This special position may be explained in the light of Howald's theory that Adrastus was originally a god of the Underworld (cf. the supposed etymology of Ἄδραστος as "the unescapable": see H. von Kamptz, *Homerische Personennamen* [Berlin 1982] 83)[94] and that of his horse Arion, as discussed page 87 above), who led seven demons from the nether regions in an assault upon the upper world.

εἵματα λυγρά: Welcker (1865:2.369) ludicrously supposed these to be garments of mourning ("Trauergewand": the rendering was still taken seriously by Wecklein [1901: 685]), an idea rightly scotched by Bethe (1891:93n25): as if a defeated general fleeing for his life from the battlefield will have time to slip into something appropriately gloomy! We should follow Bethe in turning first to those Odyssean passages where similar phrases are used (λυγρὰ δὲ εἵματα ἕσσε περὶ χροΐ [xvi 457] and τὰ δὲ λυγρὰ περὶ χροΐ εἵματα ἕστο [xvii 203, 338; xxiv 158]) of Odysseus' disguise as a decrepit old

---

92 Which Wilamowitz (*Glaube der Hellenen* 1.399) took as a reference to the *Thebais* (see too Malten p. 203 etc.). The mythological exemplum is of the type discussed by Arnott on Alexis fr. 306 KA and Zagagi, *Tradition and Originality in Plautus* (*Hypomnemata* 62 [1980]) 19.

93 For the further significance of Argos (Ἄργος ἵππιον in the account of Pindar *Isthmian* VII 11) as the place to which Arion brings Adrastus see Malten 203. Howald (1939) supposes he originally returned to the appropriate abode for a god of the Underworld.

94 Who points out the actual implausibility of the derivation.

beggar. "Dirty, tattered" is the meaning suggested by the context of all these passages, and a very similar meaning seems required in our own line. *Iliad* XVIII 538, from the battle scene on the Shield of Achilles (εἷμα δ' ἔχ' ἀμφ' ὤμοισι δαφοινεὸν αἵματι φωτῶν), conveniently reminds us of the way in which εἷμα in the singular can be used of a warrior's armor and suggests the nature of the grime in the present passage. For a comparable exploitation of tattered clothing in elevated poetry we may cite Xerxes' rags in Aeschylus' *Persae*. On the meaning of λυγρός see further I. Anastassiou, *Zum Wortfeld "Trauer" in der Sprache Homers* (diss. Hamburg 1973), esp. 154–155. For the possibility that the noun is corrupt see the following note.

φέρων: previously rendered as "wearing" (Evelyn-White in his Loeb text of Hesiod, the *Homeric Hymns* and *Homerica* [London 1914] 485, Huxley 1969:44 etc.; Krauskopf, *LIMC* 1.1.232, etc.). But the verb does not mean this anywhere else in Greek: φορῶν is what this translation requires, and the two verbs are often interchanged in MSS (see Barrett on Euripides *Hippolytus* [Oxford 1964] line 316). Perhaps the poet intended this here: for the Attic contraction in epic see φοροῦσ' (*Cypria* F 4.3). Synezesis (φορέων) is another possibility. εἵματα λυγρὰ φέρων could hardly mean "enduring filthy garments" (*Odyssey* xviii 134–135 ἀλλ' ὅτε δὴ καὶ λυγρὰ θεοὶ μάκαρες τελέσωσι, | καὶ τὰ φέρει ἀεκαζόμενος τετληότι θυμῷ is a merely formal parallel), or "bringing" them "with him" (Grote, *History of Greece* 1.268–269). But we cannot absolutely exclude the possibility of the "weak" meaning "with" here, which φέρων, like ἄγων, ἔχων, and λαβών, can exhibit in tragedy (see Stinton, "Agamemnon 1127 and the Limits of Hyperbaton," *Proceedings of the Cambridge Philological Society* 21 [1975]: 85 = *Collected Papers on Greek Tragedy* 101). Compare West's translation 2003:55. Alternatively, we may follow W. Beck, "*Thebais* Fr. 6ᴬ Davies (Pausanias 8.25.8)," *Museum Helveticum* 38 (2001): 137–139 in emending the first word of our fragment to σήματα (an easy change), with reference to the tokens attached by the Seven to Adrastus' chariot at the start of their expedition, as keepsakes for their heirs should they fail to return (cf. Aeschylus *Seven Against Thebes* 49–51). **σὺν Ἀρίονι**: "with the help of" A.: cf. *Iliad* V 219–220 σὺν ἵπποισιν καὶ ὄχεσφιν | ἀντιβίην ἐλθόντε. Other epic instances of σύν with this nuance in Chantraine, *Gramm. hom.* 2.135. **Ἀρίονι**: this (not -είονι) is the right spelling: see *LfrgE s.v.* (1. col. 1304), Pfeiffer on Callimachus fr. 223. **Ἀρίονι κυανοχαίτηι** |: cf. [Hesiod] *Shield of Heracles* 120 ὡς καὶ νῦν μέγαν ἵππον Ἀρίονα κυανοχαίτην |. The epithet is also associated with horses in *Iliad* XX 224 (Boreas) ἵππωι δ' εἰσάμενος παρελέξατο κυανοχαίτηι |, Hesiod *Theogony* 278 τῆι δὲ μιῆι παρελέξατο Κυανοχαίτης | (of Poseidon's intercourse with Medea, from whose severed head Pegasus later springs), Antimachus fr. 50 Matthews πατρί τε κυανοχαῖτα Ποσειδάωνι πεποιθώς (probably referring to Arion: see Matthews *ad loc.*). But of course it is most often employed in Homer of Poseidon (*Iliad* XIII 563, *Odyssey* ix 528, etc.), to whom it is so often applied that it can be used as a substitute for his actual name (*Iliad* XX 144, *Odyssey* ix 536, Hesiod *Theogony* 278). μελαγχαίτης is used of centaurs in [Hesiod] *Shield of Heracles* 186 and on the François Vase.

Adrastus had a son called Κυάνιππος (Apollodorus I 9.13). If Adrastus was originally the leader of a host of underworld demons, as Howald supposed (see above page 68), the epithet becomes even more significant (cf. *Homeric Hymn to Demeter* 347 Ἅιδη κυανοχαῖτα, Euripides *Alcestis* 439 ἅιδας ὁ μελαγχαίτας θεός). On Tydeus' opponent Melanippus see page 73 above.

Chapter 2

AMPHIARAUS

On Amphiaraus in myth see Robert 1915:1.205–214; Howald 1939:13–14; Usener, "Der Stoff des griechischen Epos," 37–39 = *Kleine Schriften* 4.234–239; F. Bener, *Die Amphiaraossage in der griechischen Dichtung* (diss. Zurich 1945); P. Vicaire, "Images d'Amphiaraos dans la Grèce archaïque et classique," *Bulletin de l'Association Guillaume Budé* 1 (1979): 2–45; Braswell's commentary on Pindar *Nemean* XI (Berlin 1998); and Matthews' on Antimachus, general index *s.v.*; *LIMC* I.1 *s.v.* "Amphiaraos" E (pp. 694–697). On the connection between horse and chariot, underworld and death which the manner of Amphiaraus' end implies see (apart from Usener) Malten (as cited page 86 above); Dietrich, *Death, Fate, and the Gods*, 131–132; Richardson on *Homeric Hymn to Demeter* 18. For Baton and Amphiaraus in the Underworld in art see *LIMC* I.1 E 20 (p. 85); S. I. Johnston and T. J. McNiven, "Dionysus and the Underworld in Toledo," *Museum Helveticum* 83 (1996): 29. Howald (1939:14) assumes that the hero's relatively merciful fate was a later modification induced by reluctance to accept a collective retribution suffered by every one of the seven commanders. The fullest surviving literary treatment of his disappearance is Pindar *Nemean* IX 24–27:

> ὁ δ' Ἀμφιαρεῖ σχίσσεν κεραυνῶι παμβίαι
> Ζεὺς τὰν βαθύστερνον χθόνα, κρύψεν δ' ἄμ' ἵπποις
> δουρὶ Περικλυμένου πρὶν νῶτα τυπέντα μαχατάν
> θυμὸν αἰσχυνθῆμεν. ἐν γὰρ δαιμονίοισι φόβοις φεύγοντι καὶ παῖδες
> θεῶν.

That this description derives from the *Thebais* was suggested by Welcker (1865: 2.366) and approved by such scholars as Wilamowitz (1891:225 = 1971:60 and n3), Robert (1915:1.246), Stoneman (1981:49), and Braswell *ad loc.*

The role accorded to Periclymenus in this account is noteworthy. It recurs in Apollodorus III 6.8: Ἀμφιαράωι δὲ φεύγοντι παρὰ ποταμὸν Ἰσμηνόν, πρὶν ὑπὸ Περικλυμένου τὰ νῶτα τρωθῆι, Ζεὺς κεραυνὸν βαλὼν τὴν γῆν διέστησεν. It is further implied by a black-figure lekythos[95] showing Amphiaraus in a four-horse chariot expressing lively discomfort at the presence of a spear in his back (two eagles carrying respectively a garland and a snake symbolize Zeus' intervention). For another possible depiction of Amphiaraus' disappearance (on a volute krater in Ferrara: *ARV²* 612.1 [1]) see Small 143–144. We should also note two Etruscan urn-reliefs from Volterra dating to the second century BC which come from a larger group that depicts Amphiaraus' disap-

---

[95] Athens, Nat. Mus. 1125 (cc 960): *LIMC* I.1 *s.v.* "Amphiaraos" L37; Haspels, *Attic Black-Figured Lekythoi*, plate 50, fig. 3.

pearance (see Krauskopf 98; Small 143–150). The pair we are concerned with go further in providing an enemy to assail Amphiaraus as he sinks from sight. One is a fairly normal presentation of this scene,[96] while the other[97] places the assailing warrior in front of Amphiaraus so that he must turn around (as he does) to strike at him. Robert (1915:2.89n163) explained this arrangement on grounds of symmetry. However that may be, it seems likely that the warrior is Periclymenus, an identification that is accepted in Small's discussion (149–156) of these and related works. From the role thus inferred for Periclymenus in the *Thebais*, Wilamowitz and Robert as cited above concluded that the epic did not anticipate Aeschylus' balanced allotment of a single Theban defender to a single Argive chieftain (see page 73 above): for F4 of our poem informs us that Periclymenus also killed Parthenopaeus.

Apollodorus III 6.8 continues the narrative quoted above with the following: ὁ δὲ σὺν τῶι ἅρματι καὶ τῶι ἡνιόχωι Βάτωνι, ὡς δὲ ἔνιοι Ἐλάτωνι, ἐκρύφθη. Amphiaraus' charioteer appears on the above vases and on two Volterran urns (Small, cat. 13 and 14, pp. 20–21 and 150–151). He is also given some prominence in depictions of Amphiaraus' departure from home and family (see page 104 below); scholars have generally inferred that he was mentioned in the *Thebais*. Amphiaraus' chariot is specified as a *quadriga* by Hyginus *Fabulae* 250 and Propertius II 34.39 (compare the two vases mentioned above): see page 90 above.

F7 *(see page 142 for text)*

"Die übrigenzitate eines A[sclepiades] in den Pindarscholien gehören sicher einem kommentator, d.h. doch wohl dem Myrleane" (Jacoby, *FGrHist* 1ᴬ.487.39–40, citing A. Adler, "Die Commentare des Asklepiades von Myrlea," *Hermes* 49 [1914]: 39–46). Thanks to the Pindaric scholion *ad loc.* we know that the relevant portion of the sixth *Olympian* exemplifies a common practice in early Greek poetry (see R. Kassel in that part of his article "Dichterspiele" which deals with Metaphrasis [*Zeitschrift für Papyrologie und Epigraphik* 42 (1981): 11–17 = *Kleine Schriften* 121–128]), whereby phrases or lines from epic were re-cast in similar metres by later poets. But how far does Pindar's indebtedness to the author of the *Thebais* extend? The question must be answered by examining first of all the individual line and then the general context.

---

[96] Volterra 186: *LIMC* L41 = Small, cat. 12, plate 7b; see in particular O.-W. von Vacano, "Studien an Volterraner Urnenreliefs," *Mitteilungen des Deutschen Archäologischen Instituts, Römische Abteilung* 87 (1960): 57–62, with plate 22.1; full description in Small 19–20.

[97] Volterra 185: *LIMC* L40 = Small, cat. 11, plate 7a; Vacano pp. 62–64, with plate 22.2 (also illustrated in Robert 1915:2.89); full description in Small 18–19; the object is rather fragmentary.

(i) As Leutsch saw (Thebaidis *cycl. Reliquiae* [Göttingen 1830] p. 63), Pindar's dactylo-epitrite line ἀμφότερον μάντιν τ' ἀγαθὸν καὶ δουρὶ μάρνασθαι can easily be converted to an epic hexameter[98] by substituting as the final word μάχεσθαι, a verb conveniently analogous in appearance and sense. This solution has been accepted by numerous scholars (e.g. Bethe [1891:58 and 96], Rzach [1922:2371.1–4], Fraenkel [1957:42n1 = 1964:310n4]).

(ii) Wilamowitz preferred to suppose that Pindar's reworking was a little more extensive and, comparing *Iliad* III 179 (ἀμφότερον βασιλεύς τ' ἀγαθὸς κρατερός τ' αἰχμητής), he reconstituted the original verse of the *Thebais* thus:

ἀμφότερον μάντιν τ' ἀγαθὸν κρατερόν τ' αἰχμητήν[99]

This approach was approved by Robert (1915:1.248, 2.90n170) and is considered with some sympathy by Fraenkel. But it is rejected by Bethe (1891:58–59n19) and Rzach (1922:2371.4–10). Burkert's citation (1981:48 = 2001:164) of *SEG* 16.193.2 (370 BC) ἀμφότερον μάντιν τ' ἀγαθὸν καὶ δορὶ μα[χήτην *vel* μα[χέσθαι and Stoneman's (1981:51n41) of Hesiod fr. 25.37 MW (ὅς ῥ' ἀγαθὸς μὲν ἔην ἀγορῆι, ἀγαθὸς δὲ μάχεσθαι) remind us that there are other possibilites to hand. For the allusion to Amphiaraus' twin rôles as warrior and seer cf. Pindar *Nemean* X 9 μάντιν Οἰκλείδαν, πολέμοιο νέφος (compared by Rzach [1922:2370n]) and Aeschylus *Seven Against Thebes* 569 ἀλκήν τ' ἄριστον μάντιν, Ἀμφιάρεω βίαν, whose dependence upon our fragment was seen by e.g. Verrall (*ad loc.*) and Fraenkel. See too Sophocles *Oedipus at Colonus* 1313–1314 οἷος δορυσσοῦς Ἀμφιάρεως, τὰ πρῶτα μὲν | δόρει κρατύνων, πρῶτα δ' οἰωνῶν ὁδοῖς (cited by Bethe [1891:59 and 86]).

(iii) That the allusion to the *Thebais* is confined to verse 17 of Pindar's sixth *Olympian* was argued by Wilamowitz (*Isyllos von Epidauros* 163n4) and Robert (1915:1.248). For more generous interpretations of ταῦτα εἰληφέναι see Rzach 1922:2371.30–31. If we wish to decide whether the *Thebais*'s influence extends further than the words just considered, we would do well to start by examining the first part of Adrastus' speech as reported by Pindar: ποθέω στρατιᾶς ὀφθαλμὸν | ἐμᾶς. Many scholars have automatically assumed that this too derives from the Theban epic (Ribbeck ["Zu den Fragmenten der griechischen Epiker," *Rheinisches Museum* 33 (1878): 458] restored the noble hexameter ὀφθαλμὸν ποθέω στρατιῆς

---

[98] *Ol.* VI 17 = epode 3, where (quite uniquely in Pindaric dactylo-epitrite) we find the repetition d¹–d¹.

[99] In *Isyllos von Epidauros* (Berlin 1884) 163n4; "Hieron und Pindaros," *Sitzungsberichte der Königlich Preussischen Akademie der Wissenschaften zu Berlin* (1901): 1285n1 = *Kleine Schriften* 6.247n3; and *Pindaros* 310n3. In the former book he supposed the Iliadic verse to be modeled on the *Thebais*; in the latter he reversed the relationship.

ἐὺν Ἀμφιάρηον and *alii aliter finxerunt*). As Bethe observes (1891:58–59), no very staggering implications for the history of the myth would follow if this assumption could be proved correct. "This means that in the *Thebais* too, after the battle was over, Amphiaraus was not to be found among either the fallen or the survivors—was in fact translated." So writes Rohde (1.114n2 = Engl. trans. 103n2), one of the most enthusiastic supporters of a generous interpretation of the Greek phrase ταῦτα εἴληφεν. But since the mysterious disappearance of Amphiaraus must be basic to any version of the story, Rohde's enthusiasm is here perhaps misplaced.

Is there any good reason why this part of the speech too should not emanate from the *Thebais*? The only objection with which I am acquainted is Robert's (1915:1.248): that ὀφθαλμός is unlikely to have possessed the required metaphorical sense in early epic. Certainly, whether we take the metaphor to be one where "ὀφθαλμός is ... used metaphorically of anything precious" (Stevens on Euripides *Andromache* 406; cf. W. Schadewaldt, "Experimentelle Philologie," *Wiener Studien* 79 [1966]: 75–76 = *Hellas und Hesperia*, 2nd ed., 1.491–492) or (with D. Bremer, *Licht und Dunkel in der frühgriechischen Dichtung* [Bonn 1976] 239) detect an allusion to the motif "des leitenden Blickes," the closest analogies are provided from tragedy and elsewhere in Pindar, and early epic has nothing comparable. However, in view of the numerous un-Homeric features of the few surviving fragments of the latter, this argument cannot be pressed.

But what of the area over which Bethe and Rohde do disagree—as violently as possible? I mean the latter's intuition that "Pindar must have taken over not merely the words of the lament of Adrastus but the whole situation that led up to these words, as he described it, from the *Thebais*." Welcker (1865:2.324, 367) had certainly taken for granted that the *Thebais*'s framework for the mention of Amphiaraus' prowess as seer and warrior was, as with Pindar, a speech by Adrastus at the funeral of the Greeks who perished at Thebes. See Bethe 1891:94n27 for a bibliography of those who take this view. Bethe himself (58–59, 94–96) thought otherwise. His primary objection was to the whole idea of the cremation of the dead, which he believed alien to early epic. Homeric analogies, he argued, would lead us to expect the abandonment of the defeated army's corpses to the open air and the tender mercies of birds and beasts of prey. And such a fate is precisely what befalls the body of Capaneus in Aeschylus fr. 17 Radt (from the Ἀργεῖοι), the body of Polyneices in Sophocles' *Antigone*, and the bodies of the invading army in general at verses 1080–1083 of the same play. Only when the burial of the dead becomes widely regarded as a sacred duty does literature turn its attention to the fate of the corpses of the Argive expedition. Then it is that plays such as Aeschylus' Ἐλευσίνιοι (*TrGF* 3 pp. 175–176 Radt) and Euripides *Suppliant Women* are written, and Pindar (on Bethe's interpretation) revises the earlier myth at verses 15–18 of *Olympian* VI to bring it into conformity with contemporary religious beliefs concerning the dead.

How then did the *Thebais*'s Adrastus praise Amphiaraus (for Bethe rather eccentrically retains from the theory he is criticizing this particular feature) and lament his loss? Bethe, who on page 95 of his book sneers at Welcker over "einer neuen Bethätigung seines erfinderischen Geistes," proceeds, on page 96, to a display of his own inventive spirit by conjuring up the following vivid context for the encomium of Amphiaraus: speeding over the battlefield in wild flight from his pursuers, Adrastus suddenly sees the noble seer sink from sight and with him the last vestige of hope. An immeasurably more exciting and logical framework for Adrastus' speech of praise (Bethe finds) than the comparatively feeble and banal adaptation of the motif by Pindar, whose wording first leads us to expect precisely the same picture (lines 12–14 αἶνος ... ὃν ἐνδίκας | ἀπὸ γλώσσας Ἄδραστος μάντιν Οἰκλείδαν ποτ' ἐς Ἀμφιάρηον | φθέγξατ' ἐπεὶ κατὰ γαῖ' αὐτόν τέ νιν καὶ φαιδίμας ἵππους ἔμαρψεν) and then oddly and awkwardly postpones the speech (and with it Adrastus' realization of the significance of his loss) until some unspecifically later occasion when the dead were buried at Thebes (lines 15–16: ἑπτὰ δ' ἔπειτα πυρᾶν κτλ.).

Few scholars have been convinced by all this. Even Robert (1915:1.248), who for once found much of Bethe's argument "irrefutable," thought its reconstruction of the *Thebais* implausible,[100] and suggested that Bethe would have been well advised to jettison his belief in the epic origin of ποθέω στρατιᾶς ὀφθαλμὸν ἐμᾶς (see page 93 above). One would indeed expect Amphiaraus' disappearance beneath the earth to have been no less veiled to mortal eyes than Oedipus' at Colonus (Robert 1915:1.250), and Bethe's claim that his reconstruction of the epic scene is supported by Pindar's own narrative at verses 12–16[101] is based on a misunderstanding of Pindar's ring-composition technique, a misinterpretation of ἐπεί (line 14) and ἔπειτα (line 15), and a quite fantastic literary misjudgment. Among the numerous other objections[102] that might be raised, one should not forget the strong possibility that the unburied corpses of the assailants against Thebes may be an invention of the Attic tragedians in whom they are first

---

[100] "Wie matt!" he cries, the very exclamation which Pindar's narrative at 15–18 evoked from Bethe (1892:96).

[101] In Ἀρίσταρχός φησι ὅτι ἰδιάζει καὶ ἐν τούτοις ὁ Πίνδαρος (Σ Pindar *Olympian* VI 23ᴬ [1.158 Dr.]) the scope of the reference is quite uncertain.

[102] Some of Bethe's argumentation takes strict logic to such absurd extremes—Pindar's Adrastus (see above) should have noted Amphiaraus' absence earlier, Pindar should not allow Amphiaraus to be called στρατιᾶς ὀφθαλμὸν ἐμᾶς when that army no longer exists (1891:96n30)—that one is glad to see such logic used against Bethe himself in P. Corssen's protest (*Die Antigone des Sophokles* [Berlin 1898] 26) that the fleeing Adrastus would have no time or inclination to deliver even "eine kleine Lobrede."

attested, or of a local Attic tradition upon which they drew. The corpses had to be left uncared for in order that the noble city of Athens might force Thebes to afford them burial. For the possible origins of this edifying tale and for the Athenian authors who exploit it for patriotic purposes see Collard's introduction to his commentary on Euripides' *Suppliant Women* (1.3–6).[103]

The absence of burial might, then, be relatively late. And automatic cremation might be relatively early. Collard may be right, indeed (2.344), to assert that "warriors slain on the Epic battlefield were burned and their ashes buried there," and it does indeed seem that *when it matters* (e.g. *Iliad* VII 327–343: cf. Proclus' summary of the *Cypria*: τοὺς νεκροὺς ἀναιροῦνται [*scil.* οἱ Ἀχαιοί]), corpses in epic can be recovered from the enemy and cremated. See my remarks in "Nestor's Advice in *Iliad* 7," *Eranos* 84 (1986): 69–75. Following Boeckh on Pindar *Olympian* VI (p. 155), Welcker (1865:2.367–368), and Wecklein (1901:677), Rzach (1922:2371–2372) reminds us of one way (involving Adrastus' legendary eloquence)[104] in which the recovery of the dead might have been negotiated and their funeral performed by that hero.

Of course, if we derive the *whole* of Pindar's context from the *Thebais*, we shall have to extend to that epic the question raised by the relevant lyric narrative: why are there seven pyres if Amphiaraus has disappeared and Adrastus has survived? But those of us who are satisfied by the explanation preserved in one of the Pindaric scholia[105] will find no difficulty in supposing a similar state of affairs in the alleged epic source. Besides, we must bear in mind Howald's insistence (see page 68 above) that in this legend the number seven was always of primary importance, and was far more significant than such merely realistic questions as the actual identity of the commanders.

F8 (*see page 143 for text*)

As Rzach observes (1922:2367–2368), this fragment may derive from an account of Tydeus' genealogy.

---

[103] F. Legras, *Les légendes thébaines dans l'epopée et la tragédie grecque* (Paris 1905) 80–82, followed by Severyns (1928:222), thought the motif of prevented burial originated in the *Epigoni* or *Alcmaeonis* to explain the need for a second expedition.

[104] This does not entail that the actual phrase Ἄδρηστον μειλιχόγηρυν *vel sim.* should be excogitated as a fragment of the *Thebais* from Plato *Phaedrus* 269^A 5 and Tyrtaeus fr. 12.8 W (γλῶσσαν δ' Ἀδρήστου μειλιχόγηρυν), as advocated by Merkelbach, *Kritische Beiträge zu antiken Autoren* (*Beiträge zur Klassischen Philologie* 47 [1974]) 2–3, followed by Burkert (1981:29 = 2001:150n4) and (West 2003:41). See my remarks in "Poetry in Plato: A New Epic Fragment?," *Museum Helveticum* 37 (1980): 131–132.

[105] 23^D (1.159 Dr.): seven pyres for the seven divisions of the army (so e.g. Barrett, *Euripides Hippolytus*, p. 367; Braswell on Pindar *Nemean* IX 24; *contra* Stoneman 1981:50n38, Fowler 2013:413–414).

Loose Ends

At the start of his somber catalogue of things we do not know about the *Thebais*, Robert (1915:1.180–182) gave pride of place to Oedipus' wife, what her name was, and whether she was alive or dead by the time her sons clashed for the last and fatal time. His suggestion that, as in the *Oedipodeia*, she went by the name of Euryganeia (1.180–181) is a rather misleading guess, which is best ignored.

Ismene and Antigone seem attested for the *Oedipodeia* (see page 26 above) and may well have featured in our epic too. Indeed, we may well feel happier about the notion, since the plot of the *Thebais* supplies, *prima facie*, more potential opportunities for significant activity on their part. The first attested mention of both sisters is Pherecydes *FGrHist* 3 F95: see Fowler *ad loc.* (2013:407).[106] Mimnermus fr. 21 W, however, has Ismene killed by Tydeus, and this detail was once attributed to the *Thebais* by Robert (*Bild und Lied: Archäologische Beiträge zur Geschichte der griechischen Heldensage* [Berlin 1881] 20–21n19, approved by Bethe 1891:166)[107] in connection with the Corinthian neck amphora[108] showing Tydeus stabbing a reclining and naked Ismene in the breast with a sword, while an equally naked Periclymenus runs off discomforted. Robert supposed that Mimnermus referred to the same event and therefore corrected the wording of this fragment to M. φησι τὴν μὲν Ἰσμήνην προσομιλοῦσαν Περικλυμένωι [Θεοκλυμένωι cod.][109] ὑπὸ Τυδέως κατὰ Ἀθηνᾶς ἐγκέλευσιν τελευτῆσαι. Periclymenus is certainly at home in the *Thebais* (see page 90 above). In his later and more cautious and detailed treatment of the relevant texts and artifacts (1915:1.121–124; cf. E. Pfuhl, "Der Tod der Ismene," *Hermes* 50 (1915): 468–479 for modifications), Robert restated this part of his theory confidently, but jettisoned most of the rest, stressing in particular the impossibility of accommodating any reconstruction of the story within the framework of the attack on Thebes.

However, Robert's own interpretation of the available data (an angry Athena—Athena Onca: cf. Aeschylus *Seven Against Thebes* 486–487 and 501–502—demands the punishment of her votaress, who has offended by intercourse with Periclymenus, son of Poseidon and therefore [cf. Robert, *Heldensage* 3.1.924–925] the goddess's enemy) is perfectly compatible with a peacetime visit to Thebes by Tydeus, and this is precisely what Friedländer postulated [see page 34 above]).

---

[106] This is the passage where Tydeus kills Ismene ἐπὶ κρήνης καὶ ἀπ' αὐτῆς ἡ κρήνη Ἰσμήνη καλεῖται. Welcker (1865:2.357) derived this version from the *Thebais*; Bethe (1892:166) from the *Oedipodeia*.

[107] As it is by Wecklein (1901:676), Wilamowitz (1914:93), etc.

[108] Louvre E 640: *LIMC* V.1 *s.v.* "Ismene" C3 (p. 797); cf. R. Hampe, "Tydeus und Ismene," *Antike Kunst* 18 (1975): 11 with plate 1.5; Small 93–94; R. Wachter, *Non-Attic Greek Vase Inscriptions* (Oxford 2001) 299. All the figures are labeled.

[109] The emendation goes unrecorded in the editions of West and Gentili-Prato.

R. Hampe ("Tydeus und Ismene," *Antike Kunst* 18 [1975]: 12–14) detects the same story (with slightly different iconography) on a variously interpreted Berlin skyphos[110] which he takes, together with the Corinthian amphora mentioned above, to derive from the *Thebais*. But he need not have inferred (p. 13) from Tydeus' armor a wartime setting for the scene, and his interpretation of the other scene on this vase as Tydeus' departure for war is no necessary confirmation of a martial setting for the story depicted on the reverse.

For a survey of other artifacts which may depict the same legend see Small 94–95. Our views as to whether Antigone played a part in the *Thebais* will naturally be colored by various preconceptions (cf. Bethe 1891:165 and n9). Did Sophocles invent the famous story of Polyneices' burial at his sister's hands?[111] Such was the assumption of P. Corssen, *Die Antigone des Sophokles* (Berlin 1898), followed at first by Wilamowitz, "Drei Schlussscenen griechischer Dramen, I.–II.," *Sitzungsberichte der Königlich Preussischen Akademie der Wissenschaften zu Berlin* (1903): 438. Wilamowitz later changed his mind (1914:90–92), because he supposed he had detected in Apollodorus III 7.1[112] a pre-Sophoclean tradition wherein Creon punishes Antigone's defiance by burying her alive in the grave she had intended for her brother. This convinced Lloyd-Jones, "The End of the *Seven Against Thebes*," *Classical Quarterly* 9 (1959): 96. Let us examine the relevant words:

Ἀντιγόνη δὲ μία τῶν Οἰδίποδος θυγατέρων κρύφα τὸ Πολυνείκους σῶμα κλέψασα ἔθαψε καὶ φωραθεῖσα ὑπὸ Κρέοντος αὐτὴ ἐν[113] τῶι τάφωι ζῶσα ἐνεκρύφθη.

For our present purposes we should particularly note that to infer the foregoing to be the version of the *Thebais* one must pile hypothesis upon hypothesis: the tradition is un-Sophoclean, therefore pre-Sophoclean, therefore epic, therefore (finally) our own epic. But I should contest the initial premise. Frazer *ad loc.* (1.373n2) assumes that Apollodorus is here following Sophocles' *Antigone*, and this is surely right. Such references in that play as verse 849 (πρὸς ἔργμα τυμβόχωστον ἔρχομαι τάφου ποταινίου), 888 (ζῶσα τυμβεύειν) or 891–892 (ὦ τύμβος, ὦ νυμφεῖον, ὦ κατασκαφὴς | οἴκησις) adequately explain and justify Apollodorus' rather elliptical phraseology. See further Robert 1915:1.367–368,

---

[110] Inv. 1970.9: his plate 1.2; *LIMC* V.1 *s.v.* "Tydeus" C5 (p. 797).

[111] For the general ban on burial of the Argive dead as Attic in origin see page 94 above.

[112] He acknowledges the reference to this passage in Bruhn's tenth edition (1904) of Sophocles' *Antigone*. The passage is also interpreted as pre-Sophoclean and potentially epic in origin by Drachmann ("Zur Composition der Sophokleischen *Antigone*," *Hermes* 43 [1908]: 70–76).

[113] *Sic coni.* Lloyd-Jones p. 96n2; αὐτ' (i.e. the compendium) K, αὐτήν A, αὐτοῦ Wilamowitz 1914:91.

who sees the Apollodorean passage as a mere paraphrase of Sophocles *Antigone* 773–774.

Rzach maintained (1922:2372.44–47) that if the corpses of the Argive chieftains were cremated in the *Thebais* on seven pyres, Polyneices' corpse must have been among them. This is not necessarily the case (see page 94 above).

Whether we are impressed by the appearance of the two sisters at the end of Aeschylus' *Seven Against Thebes* will depend, of course, upon whether we suppose that portion of the play to be genuine or not. I suppose I will not be expected to embark upon that problem.[114]

Did Creon feature in the *Thebais*? We know him to have been named as the father of a victim of the Sphinx in the *Oedipodeia* F1, which only makes sense if (see *ad loc.*) he was also conceived as regent of Thebes. But that does not necessarily guarantee his appearance in our epic.

---

[114] Note, however, that the question can be unexpectedly complicated from our point of view. Thus Robert (1915:1.181), though decidedly of the opinion that most of the end of the drama has been interpolated, took the anapaests at verses 861–874 for genuine, and was therefore impressed by the way in which they presuppose in the audience knowledge about the sisters. Cf. A. L. Brown, "The End of the *Seven Against Thebes*," *Classical Quarterly* 26 (1976): 207n6. A treatment of Antigone's fate was assumed for the *Thebais* by Wecklein (1901:676), as previously by Boeckh (in his translation of the *Antigone* [10 p. 146]). Lloyd-Jones ("The End of the *Seven Against Thebes*," *Classical Quarterly* 9 [1959]: 98–99) once argued that Pausanias IX 25.2 and Philostratus *Imagines* II 29 preserve the *Thebais*'s account of how Antigone buried her brother.

3

Ἀμφιάρεω ἐξελασία[1]

T HE THIRD CHAPTER OF BETHE'S *THEBANISCHE HELDENLIEDER*, bearing
the title "Des Amphiaraos Ausfahrt," is a plump and succulent item which,
like many other reference works and similar studies of the time, gives the
misleading impression that the epic that passed under this title in antiquity is
an oft-attested composition of which numerous fragments survive. Building on
this impression, Bethe developed a picture of an epic that embraced the whole
of the Theban War as its subject matter and thus largely coincided in content
with the *Thebais*.

Handy demolition work was accomplished by Friedländer (1914:332–333 =
1969:45–46), incorporating the skeptical views of Wilamowitz, and by Robert
(1915:1.218–225), at considerably greater length.[2] Robert's book was published
in 1915, and the first volume just cited reached its conclusions independently of
Friedländer's article, which, however, is referred to in Robert's second volume,
containing the notes (2.80). For further bibliographical material see J. U. Powell's
note on what he calls "Ἀμφιαράου Ἐξέλασις, ut videtur" (*Collectanea Alexandrina*
[Oxford 1925] 246). Of the works he cites, O. Immisch, "Klaros," in *Neue Jahrbücher
für klassische Philologie,* suppl. 17 (1890): 171–180 is particularly important.

The starting point of any refutation must be the basic recognition that,
so far from being a frequently attested work, what Bethe calls the Ἀμφιαράου
ἐξέλασις is in fact referred to only once (in the pseudo-Herodotean *Life of Homer;*

---

[1]   The title is more usually given in the form we find in the *Suda*: Ἀμφιαράου Ἐξέλασις. But see
      page 100 below.
[2]   Earlier advocates of the notion that the Ἀμφιαράου Ἐξέλασις was part of, or another name
      for, the *Thebais* include H. Düntzer, *Die Fragmente der epischen Poesie der Griechen* (Cologne 1840)
      5; Grote, *History of Greece* 1.261–262n3, 2.129n2; O. Crusius, "Litterargeschichtliche Parerga,"
      Philologus 54 [1895]: 725n32; Wilamowitz 1914:104 (with a special twist: see below page 100).

see page 143 for text) and then with the phrase Ἀμφιάρεω ἐξέλασίην τὴν ἐς Θήβας.[3] As Robert observes (1915:1.219), the context in which this composition is mentioned suggests that Homer's would-be biographer envisaged it as a juvenile composition of rather short scope (it was recited in one sitting, which may perhaps imply that it occupied about the same length as those Homeric hymns in whose company it is cited). Wilamowitz (1914:104) is also surely right to insist that the phrase Ἀμφιάρεω ... Θήβας "nimmermehr ein Titel sein kann."

There are, then, three possible explanations of the phrase:

(i) It represents a short epic poem independent of the *Thebais*, though sharing (as its name suggests) some of that composition's subject matter.

Robert (1915:1.219–221), following in the footsteps of several scholars (cited by him 1.220–221, cf. 2.81), especially Bergk (see 1915:2.81n114), posited a connection with the two hexameters preserved by Clearchus fr. 75 Wehrli = Athenaeus 7.316[F] ("Homer" F3 [Davies EGF]):

πουλύποδός μοι, τέκνον, ἔχων νόον, Ἀμφίλοχ' ἥρως,
τοῖσιν ἐφαρμόζου, τῶν κεν <κατὰ> δῆμον ἵκηαι.[4]

But in fact the obstacles against identifying the source of these with the Ἀμφιάρεω ἐξελασία are even more intimidating than Robert's admirably cautious exposition allows.

Let us begin with those phenomena which are regularly assumed to support such an identification. Antigonus of Carystus 25 (*Naturalium Rerum Scriptores Graeci* p. 9 Keller) certainly implies an epic origin for the similar one and a half hexameters that he introduces with the phrase ὅθεν καὶ ὁ ποιητὴς τὸ θρυλούμενον ἔγραψεν. Immisch (171n2) and Robert (1915:1.220), for example, rightly see that the words ὁ ποιητής indicate Homer. But the fact remains that the lines that follow this introductory phrase

πουλύποδος ὥς, τέκνον, ἔχων ἐν στήθεσι θυμόν,
τοῖσιν ἐφαρμόζειν

---

[3] Both Friedländer (1914:332 = 1969:45) and Robert (1915:2.80n109) are aware that the *Suda*'s mention of the poem derives from the pseudo-Herodotean *Life of Homer*. The latter allows the possibility of Welcker's hypothesis (1849:1.187–188) that Σ Sophocles *Electra* 836 (p. 213 Xenis) χρυσοῦ ... τοῦ δοθέντος Ἐριφύληι διὰ τὴν Ἀμφιαράου ἔξοδον alludes to this epic.

[4] Bergk (in a note on Theognis 215 in his edition of the elegiac poets [*PLG*[4] 2.139]) was the first to add to these two lines a third (ἄλλοτε δ' ἀλλοῖος τελέθειν καὶ χώρηι ἕπεσθαι), which we find cited in isolation by Zenobius (1.7 Leutsch–Schneidewin) and Diogenian (1.184 L.–S.). He is followed by, for instance, Nauck, *Mélanges gréco-romains*, 382; Immisch; Powell in *Collectanea Alexandrina* (Oxford 1925); and West 2003:50.

are not identical with those cited by Clearchus. In particular the all-important apostrophe to Amphilochus is missing. So far, then, we have no evidence at all for the existence in antiquity of an *epic* in which someone addressed gnomic advice to Amphiaraus' younger son.[5]

Nor can the undeniable popularity of one of the sets of hexameters be used as a substitute for this missing evidence. Numerous passages from Greek literature exhibit close verbal affinities; see, for instance, Theognis 215–216 πολύπου ὀργὴν ἴσχε πολυπλόκου, ὃς ποτὶ πέτρηι | τῆι προσομιλήσηι, τοῖος ἰδεῖν ἐφάνη with the parallels cited *ad loc.* in Douglas Young's Teubner edition. Of these, Pindar fr. 43 Sn. ('ὦ τέκνον, ποντίου θηρὸς πετραίου | χρωτὶ μάλιστα νόον | προσφέρων πάσαις πολίεσσιν ὁμίλει. | τῶι παρεόντι δ' ἐπαινήσαις ἑκών | ἄλλοτ' ἀλλοῖα φρόνει') is particularly interesting, since we are told that it was delivered by its speaker παραινῶν Ἀμφιλόχωι τῶι παιδί. But again, such popularity in itself does nothing to establish the source of Clearchus' hexameters as epic, let alone the Ἀμφιάρεω ἐξελασία. And the Pindaric fragment, rather than disposing of the problems that throng about us, adds one more to their number.

Most scholars, like Snell, have mentally supplied ⟨Ἀμφιάραος⟩ before παραινῶν Ἀμφιλόχωι τῶι παιδί in the phrase that introduces Pindar fr. 43. Immisch demurs (p. 172), and maintains that the advice contained in the lyric verses would come very well from an Alcmaeon advising his young brother. Such an attitude may seem to take caution to incautious extremes, but it cannot be refuted, and it serves as appropriate proem to Immisch's caveat on the speaker of Clearchus' hexameters. This, too, is usually assumed to be Amphiaraus, because of the vocatival phrase τέκνον ... Ἀμφίλοχ' ἥρως, but, as Immisch observes, it is precisely this phrase which ought to give proponents of this thesis pause. The evidence of art (see pages 103–106 below) suggests that Amphilochus was a mere child when his father departed for the Theban Wars.[6]

---

[5] Pindar *Nemean* IX 9–22 deals with the myth of Adrastus and Amphiaraus in a manner that might derive from epic (see page 92 above), and Σ *Nemean* IX 30 (3.153 Dr.) cites in connection with Eriphyle's marriage to Amphiaraus the hexameter ending μέγ' ἔρισμα μετ' ἀμφοτέροισι γένηται (*Iliad* IV 38). But again it would be rash and unrealistic to restrict one's views on the inspiration of both general context and specific line to an epic entitled the Ἀμφιάρεω ἐξελασία. Robert rightly stresses (1915:1.222) the multiplicity of potential sources for this particular myth of Pindar's: not all are epic. He further observes (222–223) how many different epics might have had cause to treat of the quarrel between Adrastus and Amphiaraus in the terms suggested by μέγ' ἔρισμα μετ' ἀμφοτέροισι γένηται.

[6] Immisch also cites Euripides *Suppliant Women* 100–103 (γυναῖκες αἵδε μητέρες τέκνων | τῶν κατθανόντων ἀμφὶ Καδμείας πύλας | ἑπτὰ στρατηγῶν) and 1213 (παισὶ δ' Ἀργείων λέγω). Collard *ad loc.* regards the second phrase as a mere "epic periphrasis," but this fails to take into account the following two lines (πορθήσεθ' ἡβήσαντες Ἰσμηνοῦ πόλιν | πατέρων θανόντων ἐκδικάζοντες φόνον).

In such circumstances, would Amphiaraus have addressed him as ἥρως? In such circumstances would he have addressed him at all in the terms of Clearchus' hexameters? Art again represents Amphiaraus as leaping with impetuous anger and haste onto his chariot (see page 104 below): the speed of his departure is emphasized by both Welcker (2.324n8) and Immisch.

Euripides fr. 69 Kannicht (from the *Alcmaeon in Psophis*) is sometimes cited as support for the picture of an Amphiaraus delivering himself of gnomic saws and sententiae on the point of departure for Thebes (μάλιστα μέν μ' ἐπῆρ' ἐπισκήψας πατήρ | ὅθ' ἅρματ' εἰσέβαινεν ἐς Θήβας ἰών), but once again it rather seems to refute any such thesis. The advice which his elder son received from Amphiaraus could hardly be more different from the devious moral Machiavellianism supposedly heard by the younger. Alcmaeon was given instructions on matricide, as emerges from Anon. in Aristotle *Nicomachean Ethics* III.1.1110^A28 (*Commentaria in Aristotelem graeca* 20 p. 142.27 Heylbut): τοῦ πατρὸς ἐντειλαμένου ἀποκτεῖναι τὴν μητέρα καὶ καταρασαμένου [Nauck: -σομένου] αὐτῶι εἰ μὴ ἀποκτείνηι ἀκαρπίαν γῆς καὶ ἀτεκνίαν. Such terse injunctions, grim and to the point, differ *toto caelo* from the cautious sagacity of the saws examined above.

It becomes difficult, in the light of these considerations, to avoid the conclusion that a short, or indeed any, epic source for the moralizing is out of the question. As Wehrli comments on the relevant fragment of Clearchus (p. 72): "dass es sich um eine selbständige Spruchsammlung mit heroischem Rahmen handelt, ist mir wahrscheinlicher als ein erzählendes Epos." The Χείρωνος Ὑποθῆκαι have long been claimed as a potentially comparable source for the above γνώμη. If one believed that the artifacts mentioned above derive from the *Thebais*, and if one had to accept that the gnomic hexameters derived from a poem that associated them with Amphiaraus' departure, it would be impossible to dissent from Immisch's conclusion (p. 172) that that poem presented "eine von der *Thebais* verschiedene Behandlung des Amphiaraos' Abschiedes" in which the hero's farewell was "freundlich und ohne groll."

(ii) It represents an alternative title for the *Thebais*.

This was Welcker's solution (1865:2.371), developed by Wilamowitz (1914: 104), who supposed that it was specifically used to distinguish that part of the epic attributed to Homer from the section later combined with the *Epigoni* (whose Homeric status was early denied: see T1, page 144 below). The hypothesis is attractive to scholars like Wilamowitz and Friedländer as explaining the *Thebais*'s absence from that *Vita Homeri* which alone mentions the ἐξελασία. But we have already seen (page 100 above: compare [iii] below) how Robert (1915:2.80n110) removed the grounds for perturbation by reminding us that neither *Iliad* nor *Odyssey* finds any mention either. Besides, although the alternate title was a common phenomenon in antiquity (see Davies and Finglass' commentary on Stesichorus' *Iliupersis* fr. 99), there is no just parallel for an alternative title derived from so tangential and uncentral an area of the poem's concern as Amphiaraus' departure would be to a work otherwise entitled the *Thebais*.

(iii) It represents a section or episode from the *Thebais*.

This is virtually the interpretation devised by E. Hiller ("Beiträge zur griechischen Litteraturgeschichte," *Rheinisches Museum* 42 [1887]: 341–342), and Robert (1915:1.219) rightly prefers it to (ii). I rather prefer it to (i) as well. Again, the phenomenon is a familiar one: the Iliadic Διομήδεος ἀριστείη, the Odyssean Ἀλκινόου ἀπόλογος. See further S. West, *The Ptolemaic Papyri of Homer* (Cologne 1967) 20n35. Bergk (*Griechische Literaturgeschichte* [Berlin 1883]2.41n31), renouncing his earlier ideas (see above under [i]), suggested a more specific hypothesis ("vielleicht ursprünglich Name des ersten Buches"). The Τηλεμαχεία would be an approximate parallel for that. But since we are under no obligation to believe in either of these hypotheses, the range of possibilities surrounding the source of Clearchus' gnomic hexameters becomes almost infinite.

Robert notes that the choice of a section of the *Thebais* rather than the *Iliad* on the part of the pseudo-Herodotean *Vita* would be explained by its composer's wish to indicate that the *Thebais* is earlier than the *Iliad*.

The Evidence of Art

The departure of a hero for war was a popular subject in art (*LIMC* I.I s.v. "Amphiaraos" E [pp. 694–697]; see, for instance, Beazley and Caskey, *Vase Paintings in Boston* 2 [Boston 1954] 10; A. Yalouri, "A Hero's Departure," *American Journal of Archaeology* 75 [1971]: 271), and the departure of Amphiaraus especially so. That this hero is specifically intended can be conveyed, for instance, by the labeling of Amphiaraus or Eriphyle (see Yalouri) or by the employment of recurrent motifs (the hero's angry glare, his naked sword, the presence of the fatal necklace). On the numerous relevant artifacts see Hampe(–Simon) 19–22 (esp. 20n11), Krauskopf 16–17 (discussion) and 97 (list), Beazley and Caskey, *Vase-Paintings in Boston* 1 (Boston 1951) 51 (on examples from red-figure vases), Krauskopf (2) (= *Tainia* [*Hampe Festschrift* (Mainz 1980)] 105–108 [on examples from Tyrrhenian amphorae), and (3) (= *LIMC* 1.694–697 [a general survey]).

A particularly memorable example was the Corinthian crater once in Berlin and dated ca. 570 (F 1655: Krauskopf *LIMC* E1.7), for whose similarity to the Chest of Cypselus described by Pausanias V 17.4, see Krauskopf *LIMC* E1.15, Davies and Finglass on Stesichorus' *Eriphyle* frr. 92–93. As observed there, the possibility of that work's influence upon the two artifacts has to accept an equal place in our considerations with the possibility that the epic *Thebais* is the poem from which they took their inspiration. We must now consider that latter possibility in the more general context of a survey of the whole range of relevant artifacts. Let me first hail as salutary the skepticism encapsulated in the following quotation from Krauskopf 1980:112: "Auch die ausführlichste Darstellung, der Amphiaraos Krater, gibt ja keine sklavisch getreue Illustration einer bestimmten Szene, etwa der *Thebais*."

Of the supernumerary figures variously presented by vase-painters I would judge it is the individuals and not their actions that are likelier to derive from an epic source. If this formulation seems unduly paradoxical or obscure, an examination of Eriphyle's role will instantly clarify matters. On the Chest of Cypselus and the Corinthian krater, Eriphyle stands in Amphiaraus' presence holding the necklace with which she has been bribed to send him to certain death. We do not instantly conclude that these artifacts are evidence for a version in which Eriphyle actually added insult to injury in this drastic manner by flaunting the evidence of her wickedness. Still less do we infer that such a version stood in the *Thebais*. Rather we recognize that Eriphyle holds her necklace, as Hampe puts it (Hampe[-Simon] 20), "in naiver Darstellungsweise dem Betrachter des Bildes zur Schau geboten."

Again, the grim glare which the hero often directs at his wife (particularly well conveyed on the Basel amphora [Krauskopf *LIMC* E1.10: discussed by Hampe(-Simon) 19–22, with plates 8–11] through the artist's use of white paint) is probably the vase-painter's shorthand. Epic is fully capable of describing eyes flashing in anger, of course, but perhaps it is rather the relevant epic's lengthy narrative of Amphiaraus' grounds for anger that is here, as it were, concisely summarized. Likewise, it would be rash to infer (with Bethe 1891:127) from those vase-paintings that display Amphiaraus drawing his sword as he leaps onto his chariot, an epic scene in which the hero thus openly threatened his wife. To quote Krauskopf again (1980:112): "das motiv des Schwertziehens kann auch eine Erfindung der Bildkunst sein um die innere Verfassung des Amphiaraos, seinen Zorn auf die verräterische Gattin, äusserlich sichtbar zu machen"; cf. Krauskopf *LIMC* p. 707 (col. 1). Conversely, we are not to deduce anything as to literary treatments from such vases as appear to depict a peaceful farewell to wife and sons: cf. Stoneman 1981:47–48.

Turning, then, to the slightly safer ground of identifiable characters, one might select as likeliest candidate for derivation from an epic source Amphiaraus' charioteer Baton: the figure of the ἡνίοχος is a familiar one in epic, and this particular man is depicted on a large number of artifacts, securely labeled as Baton on several (e.g. the Corinthian krater and the Chest of Cypselus mentioned above; or the Tyrrhenian amphora in Basel dating from the second quarter of the sixth century: Krauskopf *LIMC* E1.10). He is also mentioned in the Argive dedication at Delphi (Pausanias X 10.3: see page 69 above) and further attested by the evidence of literature and art as involved in Amphiaraus' descent into the earth (see page 90 above).

But we do not advance very far before learning that in this area too there are uncertainties attaching all too readily to various figures. A nurse can be seen on several vases; thus on a Boston vase of 440–430 (03.798: *ARV²* 1011.16 = Krauskopf *LIMC* E3.25) this woman is, in Beazley and Caskey's words (1.51), "stretching out her right hand and holding the child, Amphilochus, on her left arm." Are we to attribute to the *Thebais* a scene featuring an individual comparable to the anonymous figure who holds Astyanax in *Iliad* VI 467 before Hector's departure? Certainly Amphilochus was similarly held on the Chest of Cypselus by πρεσβῦτις ἥτις δή. But other vases show Eriphyle herself carrying the child, and the child is sometimes identifiable as Alcmeon rather than Amphilochus (so, for instance, on an amphora of ca. 520: Chiusi 1794: *ABV* 330.1 = Krauskopf *LIMC* E1.13, a labeled Eriphyle bears in her arms a labeled [Al]cmeon).[7]

This last example neatly brings us to the next stage of the discussion. For while assessing the possibility of detecting a change in the identity of the work of literature supposed to inspire these artifacts, Stoneman (1981:48) alleges a tendency for the figure of Alcmaeon to gain importance at the expense of Amphilochus (note, for instance, his prominence on the bell-krater at Syracuse [18421: *ARV²* 1075.7: Krauskopf *LIMC* E4.26], ca. 440). Such a rise in significance might ultimately derive from literature, but the latter's influence upon the trend may well have been of the most general type. A later artist's general awareness that Alcmaeon's act of matricide was now being described in the *Epigoni*, the *Alcmaeonis*, or in Stesichorus' *Eriphyle* (leaving aside tragedy, in particular Euripides [see page 102 above]), is far likelier than that the aforesaid artist had read any of these texts and was deliberately reproducing their version, as against earlier works of art, based on a reading of the *Thebais*. We should also bear in mind the tendency (noted by W. Wrede, "Kriegers Ausfahrt in der archaisch-griechischen Kunst," *Mitteilungen des Deutschen Archäologischen Instituts, Athenische Abteilung* 41 (1916): 270–272; cf. Krauskopf *LIMC* p. 707 [col. 2]) for vase-depictions of this story to become progressively simplified and

---

[7] A further example of problematic identity: an old man of sorrowful aspect squats in front of the horses of Amphiaraus' chariot on the Corinthian vase and several others besides. He is often taken to be a seer (on such figures in literature see Fraenkel on Aeschylus *Agamemnon* 409 [2.214]). Robert (1915:1.224) preferred to see him as Alcmaeon's *paidagogos*. But a similar old man positioned behind the horses on the Tyrrhenian amphora mentioned above (Krauskopf, *LIMC* E1.10) is identified by his label as Oecles, the father of Amphiaraus.

to shed the large cast of characters exhibited by, for instance, the Corinthian krater. This movement is marked in the second half of the sixth century but has nothing to do with literary influences.

4

Epigoni

The Relationship of the *Epigoni* to the *Thebais*

Just as several scholars have supposed the *Iliupersis* to be part of a larger epic called the *Ilias Parva* and have sought thereby to resolve a number of apparent anomalies, so some critics would have the *Epigoni* be the latter portion of a more general work entitled the *Thebais*.[1]

Leutsch in particular among earlier scholars expressed with an economic clarity his view that "unum carmen et *Thebaidem* et *Epigoni* complexum esse" (*Thebaidis cyclicae reliquiae* [Göttingen 1830] 12), a view which he later expanded and elaborated thus: "*Thebais* cyclica prius Argivorum bellum contra Thebanos complexa est: postea vero a Grammaticis cum *Epigonis* coniuncta est. Hinc explicandi Herodotus 4.32, Pausanias 9.9, Schol. Apoll. [Rhod.] 1.308" (*Theses Sexaginta* [Göttingen 1833] n150).[2] But of the three passages thus listed, Herodotus IV 32 needs no such explanation, for it is perfectly intelligible without recourse to the hypothesis here advanced by Leutsch. Pausanias too, as we have already seen (page 31 above), can be explained in terms of two separate epics. Σ Apollonius of Rhodes certainly requires some solution for its undeniable difficulties, and here the hypothesis of a single unifying epic is at its most attractive.

The last two passages, together with Σ Aristophanes *Peace* 1270's attribution of *Epigoni* F1 to an Antimachus, have led more recent scholars (Bethe 1891:36–38; cf. Robert 1915:1.183–184) to very much the same conclusion as Leutsch. Since a "cyclicus poeta" called Antimachus is elsewhere credited with a poem embracing the expedition of the Seven against Thebes (Porphyrio on

---

[1] K. O. Müller, *GGL* 1⁴ p. 117 = Engl. trans. 1.96; Bethe 1891:89n16, 122, etc.
[2] Similarly Wilamowitz 1914:104.

Horace's *Ars Poetica* 146: see page 111 below), Bethe infers (1891:37) "dass es ein dem Homer ebenso wie dem Kykliker Antimachos von Teos zugeschriebenes Epos gab, welches sowohl den Zug der Sieben gegen Theben, als auch den der Epigonen besang, und dass dasselbe zwei Titel führte Θηβαίς und Ἐπίγονοι." But again, the phenomena (in particular the attribution to Antimachus) are capable of a different explanation (see page 111 below).

Not only are F1 and F2 of the *Epigoni* not particularly suggestive of the unitary hypothesis, but they are positively incompatible with it in several vital respects. F1 contains several formal features which are characteristic of an epic's opening line (see my comments *ad loc.*). F2 (= T1), with its revelation of Herodotus' skepticism as to the Homeric authorship of the work, surely constitutes valuable early evidence that it must be segregated from the *Thebais*, which passed as Homeric until long after Herodotus.[3]

The most reasonable account of the relationship between the two epics explains the *Epigoni* as a sort of *sequel* to the *Thebais*. Hesiodic analogies can be cited for "epic poems apparently composed in continuation of existing poems": see West's commentary on Hesiod's *Theogony* p. 49 and n4. Wilamowitz expressed the relationship in characteristically extreme terms: "der Epigonenzug ist ein ziemlich ärmlich erfundenes Nachspiel zur *Thebais* ohne jeden echten Inhalt" (1891:240 = 1971:74).[4] It may, indeed, be alleged that the tradition of the Epigoni was so weak and colorless that Attic tragedians felt free to omit it[5] when convenient (cf. Andersen 1978:16).

Finally, it is hard to see how anything is solved by M. B. Sakellariou's notion (*La migration grecque en Ionie* [Athens 1958] 157–158) that our fragment derives from the *Thebais* of Antimachus of Colophon: as Wyss in his edition (p. XI) sees, there is no cause to suppose this poem extended to the exploits of the *Epigoni* (so too Prinz [1979:171]: pages 110–111 below). The safest conclusion (though even this is by no means certain) would seem to be that, to the individual responsible for the contents of the present note, the *Thebais* and the *Epigoni* were so closely connected that the former's name was used by him to refer to an event in the latter. Whether he possessed any formal justification for this or whether pure and simple error is to be blamed we cannot tell; but it would be rash to infer any

---

3   See page 29 above. I can detect no merit or plausibility in Wecklein's attempt at a compromise, which presents us with a composition "… teils gesondert, teils in Verbindung mit der *Thebais* verbreitet" (*Sitzungsberichte der Philosophisch-philologischen und der Historischen Classe des Königlich Bayerische Akademie der Wissenschaften* 5 [1901]: 678).

4   Cf. Wilamowitz 1914:104: "es gab eine Forsetzung, die *Epigonen*…"

5   E.g. Aeschylus in his *Seven Against Thebes* (cf. Dawe, "The End of *Seven Against Thebes*," *Classical Quarterly* 17 [1967]: 19–21; Lloyd-Jones, *Justice of Zeus* p. 214 [n. on p. 90], and Hutchinson on Aeschylus *Seven Against Thebes* [Oxford 1985] 749 and 903).

far-reaching deductions about the relationship between the two epics on the evidence of this baffling testimony.

The question of when the tradition arose of a second avenging and successful expedition against Thebes has been much debated. On a general level, Howald (1939:4) is doubtless right to maintain that "diese Weiterführung nur erdacht werden konnte zu einer Zeit, wo man sich über die Niederlage der Sieben grämte und sie wettmachen wollte; dies kann aber erst erfolgt sein, nachdem die Hauptsage längst ausgebildet war und sich durchgesetzt hatte." Friedländer's paradoxical attempt to argue the exact reverse (1914:328 = 1969:42), on the ground that success must be a primary motif, and defeat secondary and derivative, is refuted by Howald's explanation of the significance of the Seven's defeat (see page 68 above). One passage implies Homer's knowledge of the tradition:

> τὸν δ' υἱὸς Καπανῆος ἀμείψατο κυδαλίμοιο.
> "Ἀτρεΐδη, μὴ ψεύδε' ἐπιστάμενος σάφα εἰπεῖν.
> ἡμεῖς τοι πατέρων μέγ' ἀμείνονες εὐχόμεθ' εἶναι.
> ἡμεῖς καὶ Θήβης ἕδος εἵλομεν ἑπταπύλοιο,
> παυρότερον λαὸν ἀγαγόνθ' ὑπὸ τεῖχος ἄρειον,
> πειθόμενοι τεράεσσι θεῶν καὶ Ζηνὸς ἀρωγῆι.
> κεῖνοι δὲ σφετέρηισιν ἀτασθαλίηισιν ὄλοντο.
> τῶ μή μοι πατέρας ποθ' ὁμοίηι ἔνθεο τιμῆι."

Iliad IV 403–410

Such passages, however, have not always been accepted at their precise face value. Scholars of an analytic frame of mind endeavored to separate and distinguish those strata of the *Iliad* which knew of the second expedition against Thebes, and those which were ignorant of it. Thus Robert, for instance (1915: 1.185–191), could hardly deny that *Iliad* IV 406–410 showed awareness of the Epigoni, but he argued that book V of the poem was perfectly oblivious of them. The terms in which Athena's inspiration of Diomedes is described at the beginning of that book convinced him that the hero was conceived as previously unversed in war. Likewise, he supposed, the prayer-formula in *Iliad* V 116–117 (εἴ ποτέ μοι καὶ πατρὶ φίλα φρονέουσα παρέστης | δηΐωι ἐν πολέμωι, νῦν αὖτ' ἐμὲ φίλαι, Ἀθήνη) would never have been used unless Diomedes himself had no previous martial assistance from Athena by which to appeal. And again (p. 195), would Diomedes have chosen to rally the Greeks at *Iliad* XIV 114–132 by recalling his father Tydeus' exploits had he any of his own to brandish about?

    Such observations reveal an undeniably sharp intelligence, but are in fact as inappropriately applied here as their fellow objections in the *Thebais*. To take them in the reverse order, no one has any right to be surprised at Diomedes' failure to mention his earlier successes before Thebes in view of the emphatic apologia by which the whole speech is prefaced (XIV 111–113): μή τι κότωι ἀγάσησθε ἕκαστος | οὕνεκα δὴ γενεῆφι νεώτατός εἰμι μεθ' ὑμῖν. | πατρὸς δ' ἐξ ἀγαθοῦ καὶ ἐγὼ γένος εὔχομαι εἶναι | κτλ. The reference to Diomedes' father in the prayer at *Iliad* V 116–117 is perfectly in keeping with the whole poem's use of Tydeus as a παράδειγμα οἰκεῖον for his son (on which see Andersen 1976:41). Finally, *Iliad* V 1–8 conveys Athena's intervention on Diomedes' behalf in a way perfectly appropriate for an introduction to the ἀριστεία of a warrior whom we have yet to see engaged in battle in the *Iliad*. But the manner in which Homer shows us the hero busy at war for the first time in the epic must not be taken to imply ignorance of Diomedes' activities before the walls of Thebes, any more than it is meant to indicate that Diomedes spent the first nine years of the Trojan War in total inactivity!

Testimonium

T2 (*see page 144 for text*)

On the alleged reference to the *Epigoni* foisted on the *Tabula Borgiana* by Wilamowitz's supplement see McLeod (as cited on pages 1–2 above) 162: the relevant entry "has the wrong gender or number (masculine singular or neuter plural), the wrong author (an anonymous Milesian), and the wrong length (9,500 lines) to refer to" our poem.

Fragments

F1 (*see page 144 for text*)

ἡ ἀρχὴ τῶν Ἐπιγόνων Ἀντιμάχου: the formula's use by the scholion on Aristophanes' *Peace* is also an ἀρχὴ κακῶν. Several intractable problems have become mixed up here and it is essential to distinguish them:

(i) Who is the Antimachus mentioned by Σ Aristophanes *Peace* 1270 as author of the *Epigoni*? Antiquity knew of two epic poets with this name, one from Colophon and the other from Teios. But the Colophonian of that name is nowhere credited with a poem that included the expedition of the Epigoni. We know too little of the Teian epic poet to be dogmatic as to whether he could be meant; cf. Powell, *Collectanea Alexandrina* (Oxford 1925) 247, Wyss ad Antimachus fr. dub. 150. Kranz ("Sphragis: Ichform und Namensiegel als Eingangs- und Schlussmotiv antiker Dichtung," *Rheinisches Museum* 104 [1961]: 7 = *Studien zur antike Literatur und ihrem Fortwirken* [Heidelberg 1967] 30) automatically concludes that the Teian is referred to here. Note at this stage that, whatever the identity of Antimachus, he is not described, here or anywhere else, as the author of the cyclic epic called the *Thebais*.

(ii) Who is the Antimachus mentioned by various commentators on Horace's *Ars*

Poetica[6] (= Antimachus T12 Matthews) as a "cyclicus poeta" who produced a very lengthy work on the expedition of the Seven against Thebes? For bibliography see Wyss' *Antimachus* (1936) p. VIn1, Matthews pp. 20–21. The usual answer is "the Colophonian" (see esp. Wyss pp. V–VII), which fits well with our other data about this poet (e.g. Cicero *Brutus* 191 = Antimachus T5 Matthews: *magnum ... volumen*). The only difficulty is that this poet has no right to the title "cyclicus." But the term may be being used in a wider, nontechnical sense (so Robert 1915:1.183) in the manner of Callimachus (cf. Pfeiffer, *History of Classical Scholarship* 1.227–230; Cameron, *Callimachus and His Critics* 396). Or, if we prefer to talk in terms of a mistake, we may lay the blame at the doors of pseudo-Acro, who erroneously supposed that *Ars Poetica* 137's quotation from a "scriptor cyclicus" (line 136) stemmed from the Colophonian Antimachus (see Wyss as cited p. VIf.).

This small accommodation seems infinitely preferable to the idea (which we owe in particular to Bethe [1891:36–37], following but going much further than Wilamowitz [1884:345–346n26]) that the cyclic poet of these commentators is Antimachus of Teios. Important consequences would then follow: this man must be credited with the cyclic *Thebais* (and the *Epigoni*, of course, which must be interpreted as a part of that larger whole: see page 108 above), an immense work which covered twenty-four books before reaching the Seven's arrival at Thebes!

The difficulties of reconciling this hypothesis with the number of lines variously attested for *Thebais* and *Epigoni* (seven thousand a piece) are well brought out by Robert (1915:1.183), closely followed by Wyss (p. VI). Besides, it cannot be stressed too much that the cyclic *Thebais* (as opposed to the *Epigoni*) is nowhere attributed to the poet of Teios.

The ἡ ἀρχή + genitive formula (on which see Davies and Finglass on Stesichorus fr. 90.8) tells against Bethe's vision of a single epic embracing *Thebais* and *Epigoni*, as O. Crusius ("Ansichten über die Echtheit homerischer Dichtungen," *Philologus* 54 (1895): 724n31) saw.

νῦν: for the word's use "in passing to new subjects" see West on Hesiod *Theogony* 963. This feature is not, of course, an argument against our line's presumed position at the start of its poem: cf. the proem to the Σίλλοι of Timo Philiasius (fr. 775 *Suppl. Hell.*) ἔσπετε νῦν μοι ὅσοι πολυπράγμονες κτλ. and Cratinus fr. 237 KA (*PCG* 4.242) ἔγειρε δὴ νῦν Μοῦσα, Κρητικὸν μέλος (cf. Apollonius of Rhodes 1.20 νῦν δ᾽ ἂν ἐγὼ γενεήν τε καὶ οὔνομα μυθησαίμην). See further Davies and Finglass on Stesichorus fr. 100.9. **αὖθ᾽**: this word is a regular component of initial invocations to the Muse(s): see Davies and Finglass on Stesichorus fr. 90.9. Its appearance here, then, does not indicate that several verses originally preceded the present as Bethe (1891:38) presumes in keeping with his theory that the *Epigoni* was merely the concluding portion of the *Thebais* (see page 108 above). Nor does it even necessarily "imply another poem preceding" (West, *OCD*[2] p. 389), or serve to prepare the reader "ad brevem et concisam orationem" as Wyss (*Antimachus* p. VI) seems to infer. **ὁπλοτέρων ἀνδρῶν ἀρχώμεθα**: for a poem's subject-matter expressed in a genitive dependent upon ἄρχεσθαι at the start of the given poem see West's note on Hesiod *Theogony* 1. The significance of ὁπλότεροι might have been clarified (as Bethe 1891:38 is obliged to admit) in the following lines:

---

[6] Dreadful confusion in J. A. Scott, "Homer as the Poet of the *Thebais*," *Classical Philology* 16 (1921): 21: "Horace [sic] refers to [Antimachus of Colophon] as *scriptor cyclicus* in *Ars Poet.* 142."

compare Sthenelus' remarks at *Iliad* IV 405–409 ἡμεῖς τοι πατέρων μέγ' ἀμείνονες εὐχόμεθ' εἶναι. | ἡμεῖς καὶ Θήβης ἕδος εἵλομεν ἑπταπύλοιο |...|...| κεῖνοι δὲ σφετέρῃσιν ἀτασθαλίῃσιν ὄλοντο.

ἀρχώμεθα: such a subjunctive expresses resolve: compare Hesiod *Theogony* 1 and West's note *ad loc.* (p. 152). The same note gives examples of first-person plurals for singulars, but it is impossible to tell whether our own specimen is an instance of this, or is meant to include the poet and the Muses together, as Kranz ("Sphragis," 7 = *Studien zur antike Literatur und ihrem Fortwirken* 30) assumes.

Μοῦσαι: on the variation between one and a plurality of Muses in such invocations see West on Hesiod *Theogony* 60.

Kranz, as cited above, ingeniously supposes that the next line began οἳ τότε κτλ. The relative would certainly be most idiomatic (see on ἔνθεν in *Thebais* F1).

F2 *(see page 145 for text)*

On references to the Hyperboreans in these two and other passages in Greek literature see J. D. P. Bolton, *Aristeas of Proconnesus* (Oxford 1962) 22–26 and subject index *s.v.*; J. Romm, *The Edges of the Earth in Ancient Thought* (Princeton 1992).

Huxley (1969:47) ingeniously reminds us that according to Herodotus V 61.2 ἐπὶ τούτου δὴ τοῦ Λαοδάμαντος τοῦ Ἐτεοκλέος μουναρχέοντος ἐξανιστέαται Καδμεῖοι ὑπ' Ἀργείων καὶ τρέπονται ἐς τοὺς Ἐγχελέας. The reference is to Illyria (see below page 129).

F3 *(see page 145 for text)*

The great difficulty here, of course, lies in the attribution of a story concerning the Epigoni to a work alluded to by the phrase οἱ τὴν Θηβαΐδα γεγραφότες. This is surprising, not because of the plural οἱ ... γεγραφότες (on which see page 1 above). Numerous attempts have been made to remove the inconcinnity. None of them convinces. Thus:

(i) Welcker (1849:1.194) supposed τὴν Θηβαΐδα to be somehow equivalent to τὰ Θηβαϊκά.[7] This is most unlikely.

(ii) Independent considerations have led several scholars to the conclusion that the *Thebais* and the *Epigoni* in some sense formed a single poem (see page 108 above). Wilamowitz 1914:104: "dass beide Gedichte, als sie athetiert waren, auch zusammengefasst wurden und *Thebais* hiessen, zeigt das Scholion Apoll. Rh. 1.308."

(iii) οἱ τὴν Θηβαΐδα γεγραφότες means "the author of the *Thebais*" who is therefore also signified as the author of the *Epigoni*. This would be a most clumsy and incoherent way of expressing any such idea.

---

[7] So too Huxley (1969:47: "this is a loose way [!] of referring to the Theban cycle as a whole").

On Manto as the appropriately named daughter of the seer Teiresias see Sulzberger, "ONOMA et ΠΡΑΓΜΑ" (as cited page 25 above), 394 and 443. For offspring named after their father's qualities cf. *Iliad* VI 402–403 and XXII 506–507 (Hector and Astyanax), Ajax and Eurysaces, Oenomaus and Hippodameia, Ixion and Perithous (see Critias *TrGF* 1.43 F5.20 as supplemented by Housman ["Oxyrhynchus Papyri XVII. 2078," *Classical Review* 12 (1928): 9 = *Classical Papers* 3.1147]); more generally *Iliad* IX 561–564 (daughter called Halcyone because her mother suffered like a halcyon), J. Th. Kakridis, *Homeric Researches* (Lund 1949) 31. The tradition that the victorious Argives sent Manto to Delphi together with a portion of the booty recurs in Apollodorus III 7.4, whose explanation of the action (ηὔξαντο γὰρ αὐτῶι [*scil.* Ἀπόλλωνι] Θήβας ἑλόντες τὸ κάλλιστον τῶν λαφύρων ἀναθήσειν) gives point to our passage's reference to ἀκροθίνιον (for which see Hutchinson on Aeschylus *Seven Against Thebes* 278). It is also to be found in Pausanias IX 33.2 (minus the explanation). The sequel involving Rhacius occurs, with less detail and a different sequence of events, in the same passage (προστάξαντος δὲ τοῦ θεοῦ ναυσὶν ἐς τὴν νῦν Ἰωνίαν καὶ Ἰωνίας ἐς τὴν Κολοφωνίαν περαιωθῆναι. καὶ ἡ μὲν αὐτόθι συνώικησεν ἡ Μαντὼ Ῥακίωι Κρητί) and is presupposed by Pausanias VII 3.2 (Μόψος ὁ Ῥακίου καὶ Μαντοῦς). For a full treatment of the story and its sources see Prinz 1979:18–23.

Our epic seems to have employed two very common motifs, that of the sacrifice, or the similar surrender of the fairest (see my remarks in "'Sins of the Fathers': Omitted Sacrifices and Offended Deities in Greek Literature and the Folk-Tale," *Eikasmos* 21 [2010]: 331–338), and that of the injunction that a princess *vel sim.* must marry the first man she meets (see e.g. Stith Thompson, *Motif-Index* T 62 ["princess to marry first man who asks father"] and the analogous motifs cited *ad loc.* [3.343]). The way in which our scholion postpones mention of this latter injunction reminds one of the technique discussed by Fraenkel on Aeschylus *Agamemnon* 59 and in appendix A, "On the Postponement of Certain Important Details in Archaic Narrative" (3.805).

On the significance of the epic's reference to Delphi's oracle see Parke-Wormell, *The Delphic Oracle* 1.51–52. The reply is L2 in Fontenrose's catalogue of responses (*The Delphic Oracle*, 322). As Fontenrose there observes, "the lost epic account of the response must have included a direction to go to Ionia."

Lloyd-Jones (2002:6 = 2003:25n41), in his newly acquired eagerness to learn from "Pisander" about the contents of the *Oedipodeia* (see page 3 above), suggested that Σ Euripides *Phoenician Women* 854 = Peisander *FGrHist* 16 F9, naming the offspring of Tiresias and Xanthe as Phanemus, Pherecydes, Chloris, and Manto, was "more likely to come from epic than from a tragedy, and may well come from" that poem. But the *Epigoni* is another possibility. For other sources that name some of these offspring see Jacoby *ad loc.* p. 495.

Spurium

Kirchoff's attribution of the two hexameters to our epic was approved by Dindorf (*Poetae Scenici Graeci* [London 1830] 5); H. F. Genthe and F. T. Ellendt (*Lexicon Sophocleum* [Berlin 1872]), e.g., *s.v.* ποτιμάστιος (p. 649); and Nauck (*Mélanges gréco-romains* 375), who was, however, perturbed by the disyllabic form κοΐλός, which would be unusual for epic.

5

Alcmaeonis

OUR SOURCES VARIOUSLY REPORT THE EPIC'S TITLE as Ἀλκμαιονίς, Ἀλκμαιωνίς, and Ἀλκμεωνίς. Ἀλκμέων is the Attic form of the hero's name (cf. Radt, *TrGF* 4 p. 149). The briefest comparison of its title with its fragments (especially F1, F5, and F7: see pages 146–148 below for texts) will confirm that the *Alcmaeonis*, in Huxley's words, "was wide in scope and diffuse in content" (1969: 52). Indeed, it is quite impossible to relate any of the directly quoted fragments to the legend that gave the poem its name, and the relevance of the remaining fragments is only marginally more obvious.

Clearly the poem must have covered a great deal of the same ground as that other epic, the *Epigoni*, and several scholars have tried to derive the variant mythographic traditions from the two respective works. We shall cast a skeptical eye upon their efforts in Appendix 1 (pages 123–131 below). Here let it suffice to remind ourselves that Prinz (1979:187) has readvanced the bracing hypothesis that *Alcmaeonis* and *Epigoni* are merely different names for one poem.[1] But this conclusion does not necessarily follow from Prinz's effective demolition of Bethe's idea that our late sources and mythographers preserve traces of two separate epic traditions about the Epigoni's expedition and Alcmaeon's act of matricide. Prinz may well have established that in fact these late authors only convey a single epic tradition on these matters. A second epic may have existed nonetheless, which happens not to have left its trace in later writers.

The epic is generally dated ca. 600 in the wake of Wilamowitz (1884:73n2 and 214n13), who based his conclusion on the evidence of F5 (see page 122). For a bibliography of scholars who subscribe to this see Prinz 1979:39n13.

---

[1] So already H. Düntzer, *Die Fragmente der epischen Poesie der Griechen* (Cologne 1840) 7; Welcker 1865: 2.404–405, etc.

Fragments

F1 *(see page 146 for text)*

We cannot say how the poem came to mention the incident of Phocus' murder by his brothers: but it would be rash, with, for instance, Stoneman (1981:52n50), to suspect misattribution. Such treacherous acts are one of the features which distinguish non-Homeric from Homeric epics: see Griffin 1977:46 = 2001:378–379. On Phocus in general see West's note on Hesiod *Theogony* 1004; J. Fontenrose, "The Cult and Myth of Pyrros at Delphi," *California Studies in Classical Antiquity* 2 (1969): 115–116 and n20. On the story of his murder and Peleus' consequent exile see K. Wesselmann, *Mythische Erzählstrukturen in Herodots "Historien"* (Berlin 2011) 229–230. For similar stories of fratricide see Fontenrose, 247. For the specific pattern of two murderous brothers envious of a third half-brother, who is "different" and often "the child of an alien mother," cf. the fate of Erpr in Norse literature's *Hamðismal*: see U. Dronke, *The Poetic Edda* I (Oxford 1969) 164 (text) and 196–197 (discussion and parallels).

Various versions obtained in antiquity as to the way in which Phocus was killed (see, for instance, Frazer, Loeb Apollodorus 2.57–58n2). Jealousy over his prowess in games was the usual motive. The *Alcmaeonis*'s conviction that both Telamon and Peleus took a part in the crime is shared by Σ Pindar *Nemean* V 25 (3.92 Dr.) and Tzetzes on Lycophron 175 (2.84 Scheer), though these two late sources reverse our epic's distribution of responsibility and give Peleus the quoit and Telamon the axe. Other authors give sole responsibility either to Telamon (Apollodorus III 12.6, "Dorotheus"[2] *ap.* [Plutarch] *Parallel Stories* 25 [311^E]) or (more usually) Peleus (e.g. Pausanias II 29.9–10). Others still (Antoninus Liberalis 38, Hyginus *Fabulae* 14) implicate both heroes without specifying the exact apportionment of guilt. Pindar clearly knew the story, perhaps from the present epic, but in *Nemean* V 14–18 he displays a characteristic reluctance to dwell upon a legend so discreditable to heroes of his beloved Aegina.[3] Diodorus Siculus IV 72.6–7 claims Phocus' death as an accident. Exile (of Peleus to Pthia; of Telamon to Salamis) is the regular sequel to Phocus' death.

[2] Perhaps a "Schwindelautor": for arguments on either side see J. Schlereth, *De Plutarchi quae feruntur Parallelis minoribus* (Freiburg 1931) 114–115; Jacoby, "Die Überlieferung von Ps. Plutarchs Parallela Minora und die Schwindelautoren," *Mnemosyne* 8 (1940): 127 = *Abhandlungen zur griechischen Geschichtsschreibung* 407. On pseudo-Plutarch see now Cameron, *Greek Mythography in the Ancient World* (Oxford 2004) 125.

[3] See, for example, M. C. van der Kolf, *Quaeritur quomodo Pindarus fabulas tractaverit quidque in eis mutaverit* (Rotterdam 1923) 51–52; or G. Huxley, *Pindar's Vision of the Past* (Belfast 1975) 19–20; cf. Lloyd-Jones, "Modern Interpretation of Pindar: The Second Pythian and Seventh Nemean Odes," *Journal of Hellenic Studies* 93 (1973): 137 = *Academic Papers* [I] 152 and n141.

In most accounts (including Pindar's in the fifth *Nemean*: see the family tree printed by Huxley as cited) Telamon and Peleus are both sons of Aeacus by Endäis, while Phocus, begot by Aeacus upon Psamatheia, is their half-brother. A different tale was told by Pherecydes *FGrHist* 3 F60: Φ. δέ φησι Τελαμῶνα φίλον, οὐκ ἀδελφὸν Πηλέως εἶναι, ἀλλ᾽ Ἀκταίου παῖδα καὶ Γλαύκης τῆς Κυχρέως. This obviously represents an attempt to dissociate Telamon from Aegina and to link him instead with Athens: see Jacoby's commentary *ad loc.* (1^A.410).[4]

Jacoby states that our fragment is the earliest literary attestation of the Aeginetan tradition.[5] Of course the actual words that survive from the *Alcmaeonis* contain no mention of a fraternal relationship between Peleus and Telamon. It is merely that we have no grounds whatsoever for supposing that this epic utilized the Athenian version. Similarly Vian, in his note on Quintus Smyrnaeus I 496, where Ajax, contrary to Homeric practice, is dubbed Αἰακίδης, argues that the genealogy thereby implied "remonte soit a *l'Alcméonide,* soit à *l'Éthiopide*" (1.31n3), and Prinz (1979:39) concludes from the narrative that follows our three verses in the Euripidean scholion and from the very similar account in Apollodorus III 12.6 "dürfen wir für das Epos *Alcmaionis* mit Sicherheit Peleus und Telamon als Brüder und Söhne des Aiakos sowie die aus dem Mord am Halbbruder resultierende Flucht annehmen."

1–2: on the phraseology in general see M. Campbell, *Echoes and Imitations of Early Epic in Apollonius Rhodius* (*Mnemosyne* suppl. 72 [1981]) 8.

1. τροχοειδέϊ: this instance of the adj. should be added to LSJ *s.v.* as perhaps the earliest and certainly the only genuinely literal use (elsewhere of Delos' oval lake *vel sim.*).

2. ἀνὰ χεῖρα τανύσσας: Schwartz's correction in his edition of the Euripidean scholia ἐνὶ χεῖρι τινάξας is not necessary, though the instances cited by LSJ *s.v.* ἀνατανύω are late (Callimachus *Hymn* 1.30 ἀντανύσασα θεὴ μέγαν ὑψόθι πῆχυν, *IG* 14.4–5 ὅταν ζωαλ[κέα χεῖρα | ἀντανύσηις; Apollonius of Rhodes I 344 δεξιτερὴν ἀνὰ χεῖρα τανύσσατο; *Anth. Planud.* 101.3 (Ἡρακλῆα) ἀντανύοντα κορύνην). The present instance is absent from both LSJ and *LfrgE s.v.*

3. |ἀξίνηι εὐχάλκωι: cf. *Iliad* XIII 612 | ἀξίνην εὔχαλκον ἐλαΐνωι ἀμφὶ πελέκκωι. **μέσα νῶτα**: μέσα νώτων Kinkel *sine adnotatione.* R. Peppmüller, "Zu den Fragmenten der griechischen Epiker," *Neue Jahrbücher für Philologie und Pädogogik* 133 (1886): 466 noted that we would expect, in the light of *Odyssey* x 161–162 κατ᾽ ἄκνηστιν μέσα νῶτα | πλῆξα, what Schwartz then revealed as the paradosis. (Kinkel's text was still quoted by Renehan, *Greek Lexicographical Notes: Second Series* [*Hypomnemata* 74 (1982)] 99).

---

4 Frazer was wrong, then, to suggest (Loeb Apollodorus, 2.51–52n2) that Pherecydes may preserve an "original tradition" whereby "Peleus, not Telamon, was described as the murderer of Phocus."

5 ἔοικεν ἀγνοεῖν τὰ περὶ Ψαμάθης ὁ ποιητής says Σ T *Iliad* XVIII 432 (4.520 Erbse) of Homer. On Psamathe/Psamatheia see West on Hesiod *Theogony* 260, Kannicht on Euripides *Helen* 6–7.

F2 (see page 146 for text)

Since the fragment which Athenaeus here quotes mentions στέφανοι and ποτήρια, two most un-Homeric entities, his ultimate source may be a note by Aristarchus, stressing Homer's ignorance of garlands.[6] Compare *Cypria* fr. 4, also quoted by Athenaeus and featuring garlands.

The fragment also shows us an attitude to the dead as distant as can be conceived from what prevails in the Homeric epics. There, because, in Jasper Griffin's words (*Homer on Life and Death* 3), the poet is "anxious ... to underline the absolute separation of the world of the dead from that of the living," the ψυχή of the dead warrior flees immediately to Hades and there is no regular communication between the living and the deceased to blur the sharp distinction between their two states. In our fragment, on the contrary, the corpses are treated with care and consideration, and offered food, drink, and garlands.

For introductions to Greek funeral rites see e.g. Boardman and Kurtz, *Greek Burial Customs* (London 1971) esp. 142–162; R. Garland, *The Greek Way of Death* (London 1985); K. Meuli's *Gesammelte Schriften* (Basel 1975) 2 index I *s.v.* "Tod und Trauer" (1240–1242). Cf. Burkert, *Griechische Religion* 293–300 = Engl. trans. 190–193. For analysis of the mental or emotional states that led the Greeks to treat the dead as if they were still alive see, for instance, Dodds, *The Greeks and the Irrational* 136 and 157n6; Nilsson, "Letter to Professor Arthur D. Nock on Some Fundamental Concepts in the Science of Religion," *Harvard Theological Review* 42 (1949): 85–86 = *Opuscula Selecta* 3.359–361 and *GGR* 1³ 40–41 and 182; A. Schnaufer, *Frühgriechischer Totenglaube* (*Spudasmata* 20 [1970]) 8–9, etc.

1. **χαμαιστρώτου ... στιβάδος**: cf. Euripides *Trojan Women* 507 στιβάδα πρὸς χαμαιπετῆ, which confirms Welcker's correction (1865:2.554). LSJ ignores the present (and earliest) attestation of the noun and still interprets the adjective (ἅπ. λεγ.) as applying to νέκυς. στιβάς is not used by Homer. The considerate treatment of the corpses here contrasts strongly with the state of affairs in the *Iliad*, where (see Griffin as cited, index *s.v.* "Corpse, fate of") the mistreatment and mutilation of dead bodies on the battlefield is often described or imagined in order to suggest the antithesis "alive, a hero; dead, a mindless ghost and a corpse not even recognizable, unless the gods will miraculously intervene" (Griffin 138). On the nature of the leaves from which such beds were constructed see J. Köchling, *De coronarum apud antiquos vi atque usu* (Giessen 1914) 49.

2-3. **θάλειαν δαῖτα |**: the same phrase at line-end in *Iliad* VII 475, *Odyssey* iii 420, *Homeric Hymn to Hermes* 480, ἐν δαιτὶ θαλείηι | at *Odyssey* viii 76 (δαιτὶ ... θαλείηι |,

---

[6]   Cf. Severyns 1928:236–237; M. Schmidt, *Die Erklärungen zum Weltbild Homers und zur Kultur der Heroenzeit in den bT-Scholien zur Ilias* (*Zetemata* 62 [1976]) 215–218 (with bibliography in n1); M. Blech, *Studien zum Kranz bei den Griechen* (Berlin 1982) 390–391.

ibid. 99). For the offering of food to the dead see in particular Meuli, *Phyllobolia* (von der Mühll Festschrift [1946]) 189–201 = *Gesammelte Schriften* 2.911–924; R. N. Thönges-Stringaris, "Das griechische Totenmahl," *Mitteilungen des Deutschen Archäologischen Instituts, Athenische Abteilung* 80 (1965): 1–91, esp. 65–68; Boardman and Kuntz (as cited in the introduction to this fragment) 40, 66, 75–76, 214–215, and Garland (as there cited), general index *s.v.* "feeding the dead"; J.-M. Dentzer, *Le motif du banquet couché dans le proche-orient et le monde grec du VIIc au IVc siècle avant J.-C.* (Rome 1982) 529–556, esp. 534–536. Most recently, E. P. Baughan, *Couched in Death: Klinai and Identity in Anatolia and Beyond* (Madison 2013) 182–192, with bibliography 392n48.

    3. ποτήρια: the word does not occur in Homer, but is early, being attested on the famous "Nestor's cup" (750–700 BC: cf. Meiggs-Lewis, *Selection of Greek Historical Inscriptions*, p. 1). The use to which the object is here put is even less Homeric. "The dead are always thirsty" (Boardman and Kurtz, 209; cf. W. K. C. Guthrie, *Orpheus and Greek Religion* [London 1935] 192n14; G. Zuntz, *Persephone* [Oxford 1971] 373–374). See further Garland, general index *s.v.* "drink offerings"; and Meuli, Thönges-Stringaris, and Dentzer as cited above on lines 2–3. **στεφάνους τ' ἐπὶ κρασὶν ἔθηκεν**: again, the picture is doubly un-Homeric: Homer does not mention the use of garlands by the living (see Severyns and Schmidt as cited in n6; G. Murray, *Rise of the Greek Epic*[4] [Oxford 1934] 122; M. Blech, *Studien zum Kranz bei den Griechen* [Berlin 1982] 390–391). Besides, in funeral ceremonies "the head of the dead person was generally decked with garlands and fillets, in a manner unknown to the Homeric age, as a sign, it appears, of respect for the higher sanctity of the departed" (Rohde 1.220 = Engl. trans. 164). In view of our discussion above, we may doubt whether Homer's silence was due to ignorance, but it certainly exists and contrasts with the present explicitness. For ancient evidence as to the crowning of the dead with garlands see Köchling, as cited, in 1n, 48–52; Rohde 1.220n2 = Engl. trans. 189n40; M. Blech 81–108. For a survey of the archeological data see Boardman and Kurtz; *Index s.v.* "Wreaths"; and Blech as cited.

F3 *(see page 146 for text)*

On the constitution of the *Etymologicum Gudianum*, our source for this fragment, see F. Schironi, *I frammenti di Aristarco di Samotracia negli etimologici bizantini* (*Hypomnemata* 152 [2004]) 22–24. The views of Aristarchus on Homer are sometimes reported in this lexicon (see Schironi's index p. 604), and since the present fragment is, like the two preceding, very un-Homeric, one might speculate that it was originally quoted by Aristarchus to contrast Homer's practice with that of οἱ νεώτεροι (see Schironi's index p. 608). A. Henrichs, "Philodems *De pietate* als mythographische Quelle," *Cronache Ercolanesi* 5 (1975): 36–38 discusses this and other lexicographical references to Zagreus' role in Greek poetry and derives them from Apollodorus' περὶ θεῶν. On the identity of the Seleucus mentioned in the present context see Henrichs 37n172.

As said, another very un-Homeric fragment.[7] Homer does not personify or have his characters apostrophize Γῆ or Γαῖα (with the exception of *Iliad* III 278 = XIX 259, on which see Dodds, *The Greeks and the Irrational* 158n10, stressing the archaic nature of these oath-formulae). On Homer's aversion to chthonic deities in general see Rohde 220 = Engl. trans. 161 (cf. Griffin, *Homer on Life and Death* 186–187). On his conception of Ge in particular see L. R. Farnell, *Cults of the Greek States* (Oxford 1937) 3.4–6 (esp. 5: he does not "anywhere expressly ascribe to Gaea any kind of personal activity").

Zagreus is even more conspicuously absent from Homer. For a brief survey of references to this deity in Greek literature and of ancient etymologies of his name see Nilsson, *GGR* 1³.686n1; West, *The Orphic Poems,* 152–154. On the connection with Ge see Rohde 1.209 = Engl. trans. 160. On his identification with Zeus (which explains why his name is here linked "with a phrase specially appropriate" to that deity) see Cook, *Zeus* (Cambridge 1925) 1.644–651, esp. 647.[8]

πότνια Γῆ: cf. [Homer] *Epigram* 7.1. Homer never uses the epithet of this divinity. Indeed the nearest parallel in early Greek literature is *Homeric Hymn to Demeter* 54 | πότνια Δημήτηρ. Compare in later writers ὦ πότνια χθών (Aeschylus *Libation Bearers* 722; Euripides *Hecuba* 70; cf. Sophocles *Philoctetes* 395 [addressed to the earth] μᾶτερ πότνι'). θεῶν πανυπέρτατε πάντων: add this occurrence of the adj. to LSJ *s.v.* 2 ("supreme"), in front of the reference to Callimachus *Hymn* 1.91. For the construction compare Sophocles *Antigone* 338 θεῶν ... τὰν ὑπερτάταν, Γᾶν, Aristophanes *Birds* 1765 δαιμόνων ὑπέρτατε (with Dunbar *ad loc.*), Plato *Timaeus* 40ᶜ γῆν ... πρώτην καὶ πρεσβυτάτην θεῶν. Compare too ὕψιστος as used of Zeus (cf. LSJ *s.v.* 2):[9] see Wackernagel 1916:213–214 ("sind ὕπατος ὑπέρτατος *summus* die normalen Ausdrücke für das, was ὕψιστος ausdrücken soll"). According to Guthrie, *Orpheus and Greek Religion*, 146n36, "the whole jingle with which the line ends does not otherwise occur in extant epic." Perhaps it is hymnic in origin: compare the *figura sermonis* at Aeschylus *Agamemnon* 1485–1486. Διὸς παναιτίου πανεργέτα; *Eumenides* 200 εἶς τὸ πᾶν ἔπραξας ὧν παναίτιος; and cf. Norden, *Agnostos Theos* (Leipzig 1913) index (p. 410) *s.v.* "πᾶν, πάντα u.ä. in Prädikationen Gottes"; D. Fehling, *Die Wiederholungsfiguren und ihr Gebrauch bei den Griechen vor Gorgias* (Berlin 1969) 201–202.

For a bibliography of speculations as to the original context of the fragment, see G. Arrigoni, "La maschera e lo specchio: Il caso di Perseo e Dioniso a Delfi e l'enigma dei Satiri," *Quaderni Urbinati di Cultura Classica* 73 (2003): 38n91.

---

7   W. K. C. Guthrie, *Orpheus and Greek Religion* (Princeton 1935) 146n36 states that its source (the *Etymologicum Gudianum*) was not put together before the twelfth century and adds "the experiment of reading the line aloud has made me at least hope that it was not composed until after the classical age." But see Henrichs as cited.

8   Against Jane Harrison's treatment of our passage in *Prolegomena to the Study of Greek Religion*² (Cambridge 1908) 480–481 see Zuntz, *Persephone* (Oxford 1971) 81n5.

9   For studies of the adjective's application to Zeus see Cook, *Zeus* (Cambridge 1925) 2.876–890; Nock, "The Gild of Zeus Hypsistos," *Harvard Theological Review* 29 (1936): 56–87 = *Essays on Religion and the Ancient World* 1.416–442.

F4 (*see page 147 for text*)

"The accounts differ as to whom Tydeus killed, but they agree that he fled from Calydon to Adrastus at Argos, and that Adrastus purified him from the murder ... and gave him his daughter to wife": Frazer, Loeb Apollodorus 1.72n1. For lists of these variant accounts see Frazer; Erbse on Σ T *Iliad* XIV 114 (3.584); Pfeiffer on Callimachus fr. 680; J. Fontenrose, "Daulis at Delphi," *California Studies in Classical Antiquity* 2 (1969): 123n39. Cf. Fowler 2013:413. Note especially Hesiod fr. 14 MW ("Tydeus fratres patris insidiantes interfecit et ad Adrastum fugit," as Merkelbach and West *ad loc.* summarize its contents). For an interesting study of the different versions see Fontenrose 118–124. Immediately after citing the *Alcmaeonis* and Pherecydes, Apollodorus' narrative (I 8.5–6) proceeds to describe how Tydeus was arraigned by Agrius for his murderous act, and how he fled into exile, joined the expedition against Thebes, and met his death there. We are next told how the sons of Agrius (including Thersites and Onchestus) deposed and imprisoned Oeneus and gave the kingship to their father. Diomedes then returns secretly from Argos with Alcmaeon, puts to death most of the sons of Agrius, and (in view of Oeneus' extreme old age) sets Oeneus' son-in-law Andraemon in charge of the kingdom. However, Thersites and Onchestus have escaped to the Peloponnese, and there they ambush and kill Oeneus. Diomedes conveys his corpse to Argos, buries it there, and then proceeds to Troy.

Because of its position, and its unexpected mention of Alcmaeon, several scholars have derived this account too from the *Alcmaeonis*. They are then obliged to explain its relationship to the state of affairs implied by two passages in the *Iliad* where Thoas son of Andraemon is represented (II 638–639) as leader of the Aetolians (οὐ γὰρ ἔτ' Οἰνῆος μεγαλήτορος υἰέες ἦσαν, | οὐδ' ἄρ' ἔτ' αὐτὸς ἔην, θάνε δὲ ξανθὸς Μελέαγρος) and Tydeus' exile is mentioned (XIV 115–132) but not its cause, even though Agrius, Melas, and Oeneus are specifically named.

Homer's avoidance of tales of internecine strife, and his employment of Tydeus as a paradigm for his son Diomedes (see page 37 above), will amply explain the lack of detail in the latter passage. The relationship between the two epics remains problematic. Are the two brief and elliptical Iliadic references dependent upon the fuller account of the *Alcmaeonis*, as W. Kullmann, *Die Quellen der Ilias* (*Hermes* Einzelschriften 14 [1960]) 144–148 assumes? Or did the *Alcmaeonis* expand and elaborate the passing and riddling allusions contained within the *Iliad*? The whole question received an appropriately cautious and circumspect treatment from Ø. Andersen ("Thersites und Thoas vor Troia," *Symbolae Osloenses* 57 [1982]: 7–34), who tends (rightly, I think) towards the latter hypothesis. He observes (among other things) that the three different versions of the identity of Tydeus' victim which we find in Apollodorus I 8.5 look like different attempts to clarify the vague words of Homer at *Iliad* XIV 115–125.

F5 *(see page 147 for text)*

On Atreus' golden lamb see in general Cook, *Zeus* 1.405–409; Burkert, *Homo Necans* 122 = Engl. trans. 106; Davies, "'Sins of the Fathers': Omitted Sacrifices and Offended Deities in Greek Literature and the Folk-Tale," *Eikasmos* 21 (2010): 338–339. We cannot hope to know how the *Alcmaeonis* came to mention the story of the golden lamb.[10] Bethe (1891:134–135) links it with the tradition of Agamemnon's role in Diomedes' Aetolian expedition, which numerous scholars have attributed to our epic: see Appendix 1 below.

We do at least know enough to say that this fragment too is highly un-Homeric, since the description of the descent of Agamemnon's scepter from generation to generation of the Pelopid family in *Iliad* II 100–108 sedulously avoids the least suggestion of internecine strife.

F6 *(see page 148 for text)*

The mention of Leucadius here is generally regarded as a precious indication that our epic must postdate the Corinthian founding of Leucas during the reign of Cypselus: cf. Prinz 1979:39n13. Kullmann (as cited on page 121 above) 380–381 protests[11] that "der Name ... schon vor der Korinthischen Gründung an der Gegend (wenigstens dem Felsen) oder der Insel gehaftet haben kann," but his citation of the suspect (and undatable) *Odyssey* xxiv 11 and 377–378 hardly proves (see, e.g., Heubeck *ad loc.*) that "die *Odyssee* scheint Leukas noch als Halbinsel zu kennen ... vor dem Korinthischen Durchstoss."

F7 *(see page 148 for text)*

On the papyri that are our source for Philodemus' *On Piety*, see D. Obbink's edition, vol. 1 (Oxford 1996) 24–80; on the work itself, 81–99.

---

[10] Most scholars (e.g. Burkert, *Homo Necans* [Berlin 1972] 122 = Engl. trans. 104) assume it pre-supposes the cannibalistic feast of Thyestes; and J. G. Howie ("The Revision of Myth in Pindar *Olympian* 1," *Papers of the Liverpool Latin Seminar* 4 [1983]: 279 = *Exemplum and Myth: Criticism and Creation* [Leeds 2012] 164) thinks it entails Pelops' murder of Myrtilus.

[11] The dating of the *Alcmaeonis* assumes great importance for Kullmann, since he supposes that it will supply a *terminus ad quem* for the *Iliad*: against this notion that the *Iliad* presupposes the existence of the *Alcmaeonis* see page 121 above.

Appendix 1
Eriphyle in the Theban Epics

I T SEEMED BEST TO SEGREGATE THIS DIFFICULT PROBLEM and treat it here. Consideration of the question will also give us an insight into the ways in which past scholars resurrected the plots of lost epics. Bethe's method was to isolate patterns and tendencies among the forms of the myth preserved by late sources such as the mythographers, and to identify these *mutually incompatible* patterns and tendencies with the different versions employed by different epics. In addition, Friedländer picked out symmetrically *parallel* traditions, which could be assigned to the *Thebais* and its matching sequel, the *Epigoni*.

Bethe was tireless in his search for examples of "Doppelüberlieferung," but the energy he put into it was often totally wasted: consider, for instance, his intuition (1891:169) that because Sicyon loomed large in one early epic's presentation of the Oedipus story (the Ἀμφιάρεω Ἐξελασία), Oedipus' clash with his father must have taken place between Thebes and Sicyon; whereas because Delphi was significant in the *Thebais*, he reasoned, the clash took place at the Phocian pass, before Delphi (cf. page 9 above). With Robert's demolition of the existence of any independent poem called the Ἀμφιάρεω Ἐξελασία (see pages 99–103 above) this distinction can be seen to have been built on sand, and Bethe's further portentous deductions (1891:169–171) as to why the *Thebais* eliminated Sicyon in favor of Delphi are so much wasted paper. It is, of course, crucial to this type of approach (cf. Bethe 1891:116) that two different traditions be interpreted as summarizing and representing two different (and specific) sources, rather than being two chance strands that happen to have survived out of any number of variants that have since vanished. The basic implausibility of this presupposition should be instantly obvious, and the need to identify the two alleged sources with two *epics* totally baffling, even to those who do not bear in mind Stesichorus' *Eriphyle*. It further overlooks the possibility that mythographers themselves might be capable of reshaping myths.[1]

We begin with an unusually favorable instance, involving the death of Tydeus. From his study of this (1891:76–77), Bethe soon broadened the issue to a discussion of the contents of the *Thebais* as a whole, and of Eriphyle's role in the lost Theban epics. According to one version of Tydeus' death, Amphiaraus killed Melanippus and, on Tydeus' request, gave him Melanippus' severed head to gnaw on (regarding our sources for this, see page 82 above). The other version had Amphiaraus himself suggest the disgusting act to Tydeus because Amphiaraus was Tydeus' enemy and wished by this ruse to discredit him in Athena's eyes (Apollodorus III 6.8: see page 82 above). Bethe thinks this second form of the story more sophisticated and therefore more recent. He then proceeds to build upon this fairly innocuous platform some far weightier and wide-reaching hypotheses involving the contexts of the two strands. The first version (which Bethe attributed to the Ἀμφιάρεω Ἐξελασία) had as its background a stress upon Eriphyle's right, as sister of Adrastus and wife of Amphiaraus, to decide the original quarrel between those two worthies. In this account, Amphiaraus was conceived of as a free ruler, though one obliged by the terms of his oath to her to accept Eriphyle's advice thenceforth.

The second version (which Bethe [1891:78], largely followed by Robert [1915:1.211–212], attributed to the *Thebais*) stressed Amphiaraus' hatred of Tydeus (cf. Aeschylus *Seven Against Thebes* 377–383, 571–575; see page 82 above). To explain this hatred, Bethe argued that (a) it was Tydeus who had persuaded the Argive nobility to take part in the war against Thebes (cf. Statius *Thebais* III 345–365) and (b) Amphiaraus was consequently no free ruler or agent but was somehow forced against his will to fight. How forced? Bethe (1891:79) here brought in the tradition found in Hyginus *Fabulae* 73 and Statius *Thebaid* III 572,[2] and ultimately reflecting Amphiaraus' original status as an "Unterweltgott" (see page 90 above), whereby Amphiaraus concealed his whereabouts with Eriphyle's connivance, but was betrayed by his wife, who thus earned his enmity. In this version (cf. Bethe 1891:78 and 82), Eriphyle's intervention in an original quarrel will not have been relevant, nor would her status as Adrastus' sister; she will not, then, have been his sister and Talaus' daughter, but rather the daughter of Iphis, as Σ *Odyssey* xi 326 records her[3] and, as such, will have functioned merely

---

1 A point stressed in his critique of Bethe's treatment by Prinz (1979:166–168); cf. Ø. Andersen, "Thersites und Troas vor Troia," *Symbolae Osloenses* 57 (1982): 15–19.

2 Cf. Servius on Vergil *Aeneid* VI 445; Vatican Mythographer, ed. G. H. Bode (Cellis 1834) I.15.11; Σ *Odyssey* xi 326.

3 Apollodorus III 6.2 (Πολυνείκης δ' ἀφικόμενος πρὸς Ἴφιν τὸν Ἀλέκτορος ἠξίου μαθεῖν, πῶς ἂν Ἀμφιάραος ἀναγκασθείη στρατεύεσθαι. ὁ δ' εἶπεν· εἰ λάβοι τὸν ὅρμον Ἐριφύλη) was also taken to

as Amphiaraus' wife, with none of the important "Entscheidungsrecht" that belongs to her in the first version. But she will still have merited the ultimate punishment from Alcmaeon for revealing his father's hiding place.

This version's attribution to the *Thebais* is perhaps the most plausible of Bethe's reconstructions, as witnessed by the uncharacteristic way in which it elicited Robert's support (1915:1.211: "von nun an freue ich mich Bethe eine ganze Strecke weit folgen zu können"). Not so the obverse side of the coin, for we have already seen how valueless was Bethe's laborious reconstruction of a whole epic tradition allegedly deriving from a large-scale poem called the Ἀμφιάρεω Ἐξελασία (see pages 99–103 above). This in itself is a heavy blow for believers in epic "Doppelüberlieferung." But worse will come.

Scholars have seen further scope for the detection of mutually incompatible epic traditions in the case of the bribing of Eriphyle. This is almost invariably undertaken by Polyneices (see page 48 above), and scholars have generally assumed that he occupied this role in the *Thebais*. *Odyssey* xi 326 and Hyginus *Fabulae* 73, however, represent Adrastus as the briber of his own sister. This would seem to belong to a tradition whereby Adrastus is the bitter enemy of Amphiaraus, and finally assuages his hatred by having his foe dispatched to the war, from which he will never return. Such a scheme is apparently inconsistent with the *Thebais*'s treatment of the story, for there Adrastus eulogized Amphiaraus after his death (F7: see commentary *ad loc.*). It may be consistent, however, with the tradition passingly presupposed by Pindar *Nemean* IX 11–27, and reproduced in detail by Σ *ad loc.* (3.152–153 Dr.) and Menaechmus of Sicyon (*FGrHist* 131 F10), where we have a long and complex account of the origins and prehistory of Adrastus' grudge against Amphiaraus: the former was expelled from Argos by the latter and perforce took refuge for a time in Sicyon, where he married Polybus' daughter and succeeded that worthy in the kingship.

Friedländer (1914:331 = 1969:44–45) supposed the ultimate source of all this to be the *Alcmaeonis*. Its very complexity was taken by him (334 = 47) as a guarantee of its relatively later origin, which fitted his view of this epic. The tradition's explanation of Adrastus' temporary links with Sicyon led him further to the extremely weighty conclusion (334 = 47) that one of the *Alcmaeonis*'s aims was to reconcile the two ancient traditions of Adrastus as king of Argos and recipient of cults in Sicyon (cf. Herodotus V 67). He therefore presumed the epic to have originated in the northeastern Peloponnese.

---

reflect this variant by Bethe (1891:50); *contra* Robert 1915:1.210: "Iphis im Kreis der argivischen Fürsten der älteste war, der Vertreter einer längst im Grabe ruhenden Generation, wie Nestor in der *Ilias*."

This final stage of the argument certainly needs to be treated with extreme caution. For objections of principle to its approach to the origins of myths see page 124 above.

Σ Pindar *Nemean* IX 30 (3.15.3 Dr.) contrasts with the version of Menaechmus of Sicyon (*FGrHist* 131 F10: see above) the account given by οἱ δέ. According to this latter account, the Proetids (Capaneus and Sthenelus) rather than the Anaxagorids helped Amphiaraus in his expulsion of the Talaids from Argos. Amphiaraus killed Talaus, and Adrastus fled into exile. The issues were finally resolved when Eriphyle was betrothed to Amphiaraus. She was to act as arbitrator εἴ τι μέγ ἔρισμα μετ' ἀμφοτέροισι (to wit Adrastus and Amphiaraus) γένηται. The dactylic rhythm of these words and their close resemblance to *Iliad* IV 38 (σοὶ καὶ ἐμοὶ μ.ε.μ.α. γένηται) long ago convinced scholars that they derive from some lost epic, which will be the source also of the preceding narrative attributed to οἱ δέ. What is the identity of this epic?

Welcker (1865:2.345n49) thought it the *Thebais*, and Bethe (1891:46–47) the Ἀμφιάρεω Ἐξελασία. Robert (1915:1.222) irrefutably pointed to the unlikeliness of the very existence of the latter poem (see pages 99–103 above). The former, he thought, could similarly be excluded from consideration. The narrative of the *Thebais* is nowhere explicitly said to have made Eriphyle the sister of Adrastus. But her status as just that is surely implied by her role as arbitrator between Adrastus and her husband. And yet Robert supposed Bethe to have established that the *Thebais* did not portray Eriphyle as sister of Adrastus (see page 124 above).

Robert stressed the multiplicity of possible sources, mentioning in particular (1915:1.222–223) Hesiodic catalogue poetry and, more specifically, the *Melampodia*.[4] Whatever our views as to those specific candidates, we must surely applaud this open-mindedness. With our improved and augmented state of knowledge, we may even observe that the dactylic rhythm and epic structure noted above need not be absolutely inconsistent with derivation from Stesichorus' *Eriphyle*.

Bethe (1891:128–135), followed with some modifications by Friedländer (1914:330–332 = 1969:43–44), detected another fine example of "Doppelüberlieferung" in the next major stage of Eriphyle's story, Alcmaeon's act of matricide. One version locates it before the expedition of the Epigoni against Thebes. This is preserved in Apollodorus III 6.2 and Σ *Odyssey* xi 326:[5] Amphiaraus, setting out against the enemy, orders Alcmaeon not to join any further assault upon

---

[4] Cf. I. Loffler, *Die Melampodie: Versuch einer Rekonstruktion des Inhalts* (Beiträge zur klassischen Philologie 7 [Meisenheim 1963]) 41–43 and 53–55.

[5] Asclepiades of Tragilus (*FGrHist* 12 F29) is also credited with a dating of the matricide before the expedition by Bethe (1891:120) and Robert (*Heldensage* 2.956–957). *Contra* Jacoby *ad loc.* ([1^.489] followed by Prinz [1979:178]), observing (rightly) that Asclepiades offers *no* dating.

the city until he has punished Eriphyle. It is also implied, according to Bethe and Friedländer, by Ephorus (*FGrHist* 70 F123a–b), whose account of a wholly successful campaign by the Epigoni leaves no room for Eriphyle's vengeful Erinyes (her murder is not so much as mentioned) and thus supposedly entails the prior purification of Alcmaeon. Bethe (and Friedländer) derives this version from the *Alcmaeonis*.[6]

The other version (which is found in Apollodorus III 7.2–3 and 7.5, and Diodorus IV 66.3) presents Thersander as the second briber of Eriphyle (Polyneices being the first) and locates her murder after the expedition. This Bethe would attribute to the *Thebais*. Friedländer similarly interprets the second employment of the bribery motif as a deliberately symmetrical counterpart to the first: Polyneices and Thersander, father and son, are neatly paired in an original and sequel identifiable as *Thebais* and *Epigoni*. The alternative and incompatible tradition (on which see page 125 above) whereby Adrastus is the original briber of Eriphyle is assigned by Friedländer to the *Alcmaeonis*.

Prinz objects on general grounds (1979:184–186) to the improbability of an epic (or, indeed, any) version wherein the matricidal act predates the expedition of the Epigoni: such a crime entails madness (or at least a hounding by the Erinyes), and this must be incompatible with Alcmaeon's leadership of, or even participation in, the campaign. The epic version, he argues, placed the murder of Eriphyle after the expedition. Ephorus' narrative certainly seems to have no place for Alcmaeon's madness, but this is explained by Prinz (185) as the fruit of Ephorus' own invention, intended to solve (among other problems; on these see page 130 below) the riddle of Alcmaeon's absence from the Trojan War: by reversing the usual sequence (employed by the epic tradition) in which Eriphyle's death postdates the expedition of the Epigoni, he could represent Alcmaeon as occupied in Aetolia and unable to join the Greeks against Troy.

Thersander's bribe may well have been a constant feature of epic tradition (cf. Prinz 1979:175–176) as Hellanicus (*FGrHist* 4 F98) implies. Likewise the πέπλος of Harmonía may imply a second stage to the bribing of Eriphyle (cf. Prinz 1979:176n27), though this should be distinguished from the question[7] of the relatively late origin of the whole story of the Epigoni.

Yet another opportunity for the detection of significantly variant traditions was exploited by Bethe (1891:110–112) in connection with the Epigoni: their leadership, their identity, the locale, and the outcome of their battle against

---

[6] A derivation that has won the acceptance of many scholars: see the bibliography in Prinz 1979: 183n44.

[7] As Wilamowitz observed (1891:239–240 = 1971:74), the ultimate root of the problem lies in the difficulty of connecting the originally independent story of Alcmaeon's matricide with the relatively late tradition (see page 103 above) of the *Epigoni*.

the Thebans were differently treated in different epics, he insists (116–117); the contents of the two epic traditions as thus reassembled are usefully summarized by Prinz (1979:172).

According to Bethe, one strand makes Alcmaeon leader by the command of Apollo's oracle (Apollodorus III 7.2, Diodorus IV 66 = no. 203 Parke-Wormell [2.85], L 38 Fontenrose [*Delphic Oracle*, p. 370]; cf. Pindar *Pythian* VIII 39–58),[8] and this derives from the *Alcmaeonis*. The other (represented by Euripides *Suppliant Women* 1214–1221; cf. Σ *Iliad* IV 404 [1.517 Erbse]) bestows this place of honor upon Adrastus' son Aegialeus. Here we have, according to Bethe, the version of the *Epigoni*.[9]

Prinz (1979:180) surmises the second version to be explicable in terms of the date of Euripides' play and interprets it as equivalent to a friendly gesture by an Athenian towards Argos, his city's ally. Since we know relatively little about the date of the *Suppliant Women* (see Collard's edition 1.8–14, which concludes that 428–422 is the likeliest range), it may be safer to prefer the explanation given by Collard *ad loc.* (2.419), that we have to do with an autoschediasm devised by Euripides himself "for congruence with the role" of Aegialeus' father Adrastus in the play. Either explanation neatly dispenses with the notion of two equally long-standing and popular versions, each equally epic in origin. Besides, as Prinz (1979:173) further observes, the differences between what are allegedly two separate epic traditions are suspiciously small: Alcmaeon is important to both accounts, for instance.

As for the lists of the Epigoni offered by various ancient sources, it is particularly perverse of Bethe (1891:110–111) to try to establish two separate traditions here (Pausanias X 10.4 and Apollodorus III 7.2 reflecting the *Alcmaeonis*; Σ T *Iliad* IV. 406 [1.517 Erbse] the *Epigoni*) since, as Prinz rightly stresses (1979:169, with a useful tabular presentation of the five different lists presented by various late authors), there is, on the contrary, a bewilderingly wide range of differing and incompatible versions (perhaps indicative of ignorance of any authoritative epic source) with Aegialeus, Thersander, and Alcmaeon (not surprisingly) the only common elements in all five. Bethe's selection of two of these lists as reflecting two epics, and his indifference to the other three, is precisely as arbitrary as Prinz (173) finds it.

Aegialeus' death at the hands of Laodamas, king of the Thebans, is a fixed feature of tradition (a symmetrical reversal of the fate that befell the Seven,

---

[8]   The epic language of this portion of the poem is observed by B. Forssman (*Untersuchungen zur Sprache Pindars* [Wiesbaden 1966] 109–110), who considers the *Epigoni* a possible source. The same conclusion is reached by Stoneman (1981:54–55), on independent grounds.

[9]   So too, for instance, W. Kullmann, *Die Quellen der Ilias* (*Hermes* Einzelschriften 14 [1960]) 148–149n2.

where only the leader, Adrastus, survived). No double tradition can even begin to be alleged here, then. Laodamas is either killed at some unspecified locale (Apollodorus III 7.3) or survives after defeat in a battle at Glisas (Pausanias IX 8.3, 9.2; 1.44.4; Hellanicus *FGrHist* 4 F100; cf. Fowler 2013:414). Bethe (1891:113) attributes the first of these accounts to the *Epigoni* and the second to the *Alcmaeonis*. But since Glisas stands some distance from Thebes, and Apollodorus (III 7.3), Diodorus (IV 66), and Pindar (*Pythian* VIII 47) (not to mention common sense and the usual presuppositions of epic battles) seem to envisage the clash as taking place directly before Thebes itself, there may be something in Prinz's suggestion (1979:182) that the idea of an "Entscheidungsschlacht" was the actual invention of Hellanicus (perhaps by analogy with the famous field battle at Plataea, and appropriately located by him in the vicinity of the recent clashes at Tanagra and Oenophyta [457/6 BC]).

Even without that solution, the idea of two differing epic treatments of the battle with quite incompatible details is very difficult to justify. Laodamas' death (*pace* Bethe 1891:113n8) seems as essential as that of Aegialeus, not least because it so economically explains the Theban defeat and retreat.

What of the movements of the worsted Theban forces after the battle? According to Apollodorus (III 7.3–4) and Diodorus (IV 67.1), they move, on Teiresias' advice, to Tilphusa, and from there to Thessaly (Hestiaeotis, more specifically Homole), whence they later returned, on the Delphic oracle's bidding (Pausanias IX 8.6; Herodotus I 56 and IV 147), to live under Thersander's governance at Thebes. Bethe takes the *Epigoni* to be responsible for this particular set of details. According to Pausanias (IX 5.13), however, they go (under the leadership of Laodamas) to Illyria, and this would seem to correspond to the version presupposed by the Delphic oracle's advice in Herodotus V 61, which connects them with the Ἐγχελεῖς, a mythical race located in Illyria. The *Alcmaeonis* utilized this second version, if Bethe is to be believed.

Here too, however, it is not difficult to conceive an alternative explanation of the variants. Prinz (1979:183) supposes the tradition of the flight to Illyria to be another relatively late invention reflecting historical events, in this case the bad reputation of Thebes after the Battle of Plataea (cf. Herodotus IX 86–87): "dass sie aber die Dorier, die Helden der Perserkriege, aus der Landschaft Hestiaiotis vertrieben haben sollten, war schlechterdings absurd. Deshalb liess man nun ihren König Laodamas überleben und feige mit den Thebanern zu den mythischen Encheleern bzw. Illyriern fliehen."

Prinz (1979:177–178) rightly stresses the likelihood that tragedy (especially Euripides' *Alcmaeon in Psophis,* on which cf. Kannicht, *TrGF* 5.1.206–210; H. D. Jocelyn, *The Tragedies of Ennius* [London 1967] 188–189) has greatly influenced the accounts of Alcmaeon's final fate we encounter in the mythographers and other late writers. This standpoint is inevitably at odds with Bethe's notion (1891:135) that Apollodorus III 7.5 and Pausanias VIII 24 can once more be used as a quarry for ancient epic tradition, this time to reconstruct the *Epigoni*'s version.

Prinz strengthens his position by citing (179) Thucydides II 102.5–6, with its picture of an Alcmaeon finally and peacefully setting in the territory of the Achelous. As a far earlier author than Apollodorus or Pausanias, the historian might be thought likelier to reflect epic, and he certainly omits just those elements found in late writers—Psophis as a first, abortive, place of refuge; Callirhoe's greed as the cause of Alcmaeon's death—which one would independently attribute to Attic tragedy and a later impulse to complicate and elaborate an initially simple and straightforward story. If one believes that the consultation of the Delphic oracle in Apollodorus III 7.5 and Diodorus IV 66.3 (= 204 Parke-Wormell; L 39 Fontenrose)—with its order that Alcmaeon be appointed leader of the Epigoni and afterwards punish his mother—derives from epic, then the epic sequel, as Prinz (178) observes, should be fairly predictable.

Ephorus (*FGrHist* 70 F123^A–B) describes how Alcmaeon accompanied Diomedes to Aetolia and assisted him in punishing the enemies of Oeneus (similarly Apollodorus I 8.6: see the commentary on F4 of the *Alcmaeonis*). Diomedes then returned home, but Alcmaeon stayed behind and proceeded to subdue Acarnania and found Amphilochean Argos. Ephorus dates these events to a period after the Epigoni's assault on Thebes, in which both Alcmaeon and Diomedes participated. The tradition is thus consistent with a placing of Eriphyle's death before rather than after the defeat of Thebes, and those scholars who attribute that state of affairs to the *Alcmaeonis* naturally associate the Aetolian expedition with that epic too (see Bethe 1891:130–135; Friedländer 1914: 330–331 = 1969:43–44 etc.).

Now the founding of Amphilochean Argos by Alcmaeon should give us pause (as it does Prinz [1979:185]), since, even without the explicit testimony of Thucydides (II 68.3), we should have guessed that Amphilochean Argos was originally conceived of as founded by Alcmaeon's brother Amphilochus (cf. Gomme and Hornblower *ad loc.* etc.). Furthermore, according to Euripides' *Oeneus* (cf. Kannicht, *TrGF* 5.2.584–585), it was, as their close friendship in the *Iliad* might lead us to expect, Sthenelus who accompanied Diomedes in the expedition against Aetolia. Prinz (1979:184) would derive this Euripidean account from the *Alcmaeonis*, whose titular hero, he thinks, cannot have participated in the Aetolian expedition because of his mother's vengeful Erinyes (page 127 above). He would attribute Ephorus' incompatible version not to any alternative epic tradition, but rather to the fertile invention of Ephorus himself (185), as part of a complex and elaborate λύσις ("ein rechtes Kunststück antiker Homerphilologie") designed to solve three related problems: Why did the Acarnanians take no part in the Trojan War? Why did Alcmaeon (in strong contrast to his fellow epigone Diomedes) likewise fail to participate? Why does the *Iliad* represent Diomedes as ruling over all Argos and Agamemnon merely king of Mycenae?[10] Answer: because Agamemnon establishes his rule in Argos while Diomedes is absent in Aetolia; he then relinquishes power to him upon his return, but obliges him to participate in the war against Troy. Alcmaeon, however, angrily stays behind (ἀγανακτοῦντα).[11]

On the other hand (to stress once more and finally the difficulties inherent in this kind of enquiry), Andersen (16) is right to observe that Alcmaeon and Diomedes constitute an obvious partnership because of the Theban exploits of their fathers, Amphiaraus and Tydeus (an antithetical pair of heroes: see page 82 above); this could conceivably justify the hypothesis that a tradition of an expedition against Aetolia led by Alcmaeon and Diomedes existed before Ephorus. Whether such a tradition was (a) available to the composer of the *Iliad*; and (b) incorporated in the *Alcmaeonis* must remain unanswerable questions, as we have already seen in connection with F5 of the latter.

---

[10] The problem of the Iliadic picture of who rules Argos has always been difficult to resolve: see Page, *History and the Homeric Iliad* (Berkeley 1959) 127–132, Andersen 30n14. Andersen further claims that Prinz does not explain how and why an Aetolian expedition featured in the *Alcmaeonis*, when the titular hero of that epic did not participate in that expedition. But since Prinz believes the *Alcmaeonis* and the *Epigoni* to be one and the same poem (see page 115 above), this objection is not very damaging: an epic largely devoted to the doings of the sons of the Seven might well treat of Diomedes' Aetolian exploits. Prinz's theory is thus at least self-consistent. One might alternatively hold (as I do) that the *Alcmaeonis* and the *Epigoni* were two separate epics, and that the source of Euripides' version (Diomedes and Sthenelus in Aetolia) was the *Epigoni*.

[11] Cf. Andersen, "Thersites und Thoas vor Troia," *Symbolae Osloenses* 57 (1982): 13–14.

Appendix 2

Source Texts and Translations

Oedipodeia

T *Tabula Borgiana*

Nap. Mus. Naz. Inv. 2408 = *IG* XIV 1292 ii 11 (p. 341 Kaibel) = Jahn-Michaelis K =10
K. Sadurska, *Les Tables Iliaques* (Warsaw 1964), p. 60, L 3 (plate XI); Squire p. 400.

> τ]ὴν Οἰδιπόδειαν τὴν ὑπὸ Κιναίθωνος τοῦ
>]τες ἐπῶν οὖσαν ϝχ´

> > καὶ τ]ὴν Οἰδιπόδειαν τὴν ὑπὸ Κιναίθωνος τοῦ][Λακεδαιμονίου λεγομένην
> > πεποιῆσθαι παραλιπόν]τες ἐπῶν οὖσαν ϝχ´ suppl. Wilamowitz exempli
> > gratia;][Λακεδαιμονίου πεποιημένην προαναγόν]τοϲ suppl. West

the *Oedipodeia*, composed by Cinaetho, consisting of 6,600 epic verses

F1 Scholion on Euripides *Phoenician Women* 1760

Cod. Monac. 560 (1.414–415 Schwartz) = arg. min. in *Phoen.* 11.27 (p. 11 Mastronarde).

> οἱ τὴν Οἰδιποδίαν γράφοντες †οὐδεὶς οὕτω φησὶ περὶ τῆς Σφιγγός†.
> > ἀλλ᾽ ἔτι κάλλιστόν τε καὶ ἱμεροέστατον ἄλλων
> > παῖδα φίλον Κρείοντος ἀμύμονος Αἵμονα δῖον...
> καὶ φασιν ὅτι οὐκ ἦν θηρίον ὡς οἱ πολλοὶ νομίζουσιν ἀλλὰ χρησμολόγος
> δύσγνωτα τοῖς Θηβαίοις λέγοντα καὶ πολλοὺς αὐτῶν ἀπώλλυεν
> ἐναντίως τοῖς χρησμοῖς χρωμένους.

> > οὐδεὶς – Σφιγγός del. Schwartz post Valckenaer, alii alia coniecerunt [ex. gr.
> > ἄλλος δ᾽ post γράφοντες add. Allen, οἱ τὴν Οἰδ. γράφοντες, οἵτινές εἰσιν, οὕτω
> > φασὶ tempt. Vian]; recte iudicavit Marckscheffel: "ex hoc loco misere corrupto
> > nihil licet colligere. ne id quidem constat, utrum versus ex Oedipodia sumpti

sint, an, quod mihi quidem minus uerisimile videtur, alius carminis nomen exciderit." **1-2 ἔπι, ἤμερ-, ἀμύμονα** codd. : corr. Valckenaer

The author of the *Oedipodeia* (<no one else says this about the Sphinx>):
But by far the fairest and most desirable of all,
the dear son of blameless Creon, noble Haemon, <the Sphinx destroyed>.

And they say that it was not a beast, as the majority suppose, but a deliverer of impenetrable oracles to the Thebans, and destroyed many of them when they gave an answer contrary to the oracles.

F2   Pausanias IX 5.10

(3.10–11 Rocha-Pereira)

ὁ δὲ [*scil.* Οἰδίπους] καὶ τὸν πατέρα ἀποκτενεῖν ἔμελλεν, ὡς ηὐξήθη, καὶ τὴν μητέρα ἔγημε, παῖδας δὲ ἐξ αὐτῆς οὐ δοκῶ οἱ γενέσθαι, μάρτυρι Ὁμήρωι χρώμενος, ὃς ἐποίησεν ἐν Ὀδυσσείαι [11.271–274]·

μητέρα τ' Οἰδιπόδαο ἴδον, καλὴν Ἐπικάστην,
ἣ μέγα ἔργον ἔρεξεν ἀϊδρείηισι νόοιο
γημαμένη ὧι υἱεῖ· ὁ δ' ὃν πατέρ' ἐξεναρίξας
γῆμεν· ἄφαρ δ' ἀνάπυστα θεοὶ θέσαν ἀνθρώποισιν.

πῶς οὖν ἐποίησαν ἀνάπυστα ἄφαρ, εἰ δὴ τέσσαρες ἐκ τῆς Ἐπικάστης ἐγένοντο παῖδες τῶι Οἰδίποδι; ἐξ Εὐρυγανείας <δὲ> τῆς Ὑπέρφαντος ἐγεγόνεσαν. δηλοῖ δὲ καὶ ὁ τὰ ἔπη ποιήσας ἃ Οἰδιπόδια ὀνομάζουσι· καὶ Ὀνασίας Πλαταιᾶσιν ἔγραψε κατηφῆ τὴν Εὐρυγάνειαν ἐπὶ τῆι μάχηι τῶν παίδων.

Οἰδιπόδειαν Porson, Οἰδιποδίαν Marckscheffel.

Oedipus was fated to kill his father when he grew up and marry his mother. But I do not believe he had any children, in view of the testimony of Homer. His account in the *Odyssey* [11.271–274] runs: "I saw the mother of Oedipus, fair Epicaste, who did a monstrous deed by marrying her own son. And he married her after killing his own father. But the gods at once revealed these things to mankind." How then could the gods have at once revealed things, if four children were born to Oedipus by Epicaste? No, they were born to him instead by Teuthras' daughter Euryganeia. The author of the epic which is called the *Oedipodeia* makes this clear, and Onesias has painted a picture at Plataea showing Euryganeia in grief over the combat of her sons.

Thebais

Herodotus V 67

Κλεισθένης ... ῥαψῳδοὺς ἔπαυσε ἐν Σικυῶνι ἀγωνίζεσθαι τῶν Ὁμηρείων ἐπέων εἵνεκα, ὅτι Ἀργεῖοί τε καὶ Ἄργος τὰ πολλὰ πάντα ὑμνέαται.

> Haec ad Thebaida pertinere coniecerunt Wilamowitz, alii, haud scio an
> recte.

Cleisthenes stopped the rhapsodes' poetic contests at Sicyon involving
the epics by Homer, because the Argives and their city are frequently
mentioned in those poems.

T1   Pausanias IX 9.1 and 5

(3.17–18 Rocha-Pereira)

τὸν δὲ πόλεμον τοῦτον, ὃν ἐπολέμησαν Ἀργεῖοι, νομίζω πάντων,
ὅσοι πρὸς Ἕλληνας ἐπὶ τῶν καλουμένων ἡρώων ἐπολεμήθησαν ὑπὸ
Ἑλλήνων, γενέσθαι λόγου μάλιστα ἄξιον. [*sequuntur septem contra
Thebas, epigoni*] ... τῶν δὲ Θηβαίων οἱ μὲν αὐτίκα ὡς ἡττήθησαν ὁμοῦ
Λαοδάμαντι ἐκδιδράσκουσιν, οἱ δὲ ὑπολειφθέντες πολιορκίαι παρέστη-
σαν. ἐποιήθη δὲ ἐς τὸν πόλεμον τοῦτον καὶ ἔπη Θηβαΐς [Hemsterhuis:
Θηβαίοις codd.]· τὰ δὲ ἔπη ταῦτα Καλλῖνος [Sylburg: Καλαῖνος codd.]
ἀφικόμενος αὐτῶν ἐς μνήμην ἔφησεν Ὅμηρον τὸν ποιήσαντα εἶναι [fr.
6 W], Καλλίνωι [Sylburg: Καλαίνωι codd.] δὲ πολλοί τε καὶ ἄξιοι λόγου
κατὰ ταὐτὰ ἔγνωσαν· ἐγὼ δὲ τὴν ποίησιν ταύτην μετά γε Ἰλιάδα καὶ τὰ
ἔπη τὰ ἐς Ὀδυσσέα ἐπαινῶ μάλιστα.

This war [against Thebes] waged by the Argives was, I think, the most
noteworthy of all the wars of Greeks against Greeks in the so-called
heroic age.... [*there follow the contents of the story of the war*]. As for the
Thebans, some, as soon as they were defeated, at once fled, together
with their leader Laodamas, while the remainder endured a siege of
their city. On the subject of this war the epic called the *Thebais* was
composed. This epic happens to be mentioned by Callinus, who says
that Homer was the author. Many notable writers are of the same opinion as Callinus, and I myself rank the poem third only to the *Iliad* and
the *Odyssey*.

T2 The *Contest of Homer and Hesiod* 15

(265–267 Allen = 15.42–43 Wilamowitz = p. 344 West)

ὁ δὲ Ὅμηρος ἀποτυχὼν τῆς νίκης περιερχόμενος ἔλεγε τὰ ποιήματα, πρῶτον μὲν τὴν Θηβαΐδα, ἔπη ͵ζ, ἧς ἡ ἀρχή [F1 infra] … εἶτα Ἐπιγόνους ἔπη ͵ζ [*Epig.* T2] ὧν ἡ ἀρχή [*Epig.* F1] … φᾶσι γάρ τινες καὶ ταῦτα Ὁμήρου εἶναι.

Homer, having failed to win the contest, continued a peripatetic existence, reciting first of all the *Thebais* … for some say these poems too are Homer's.

T3 *Tabula Borgiana*

Nap. Mus. Naz. Inv. 2408 = *IG* XIV 1292 ii 12 (p. 341 Kaibel) = Jahn-Michaelis K = 10 K Sadurska, *Les Tables Iliaques* (p. 60) L 4 sq. (plate XI), Squire p. 400.

ὑποθήσομεν Θηβαΐδα
]ν τὸν Μιλήσιον λέγουσιν ἐπῶν ὄντα ͵θφ´

͵θφ´ suppl. Wilamowitz ex. gratia

the *Thebais*, said to have been composed by a Milesian and consisting of 7,000 epic verses.

T4 Tzetzes *Life of Hesiod*

(p. 49. 27–28 Wilamowitz = Hesiod T 80 Jacoby [p. 113])

τὸν παλαιὸν δ' Ὅμηρον Διονύσιος ὁ κυκλογράφος [*FGrHist* 15 F8] φησὶν ἐπ' ἀμφοτέρων ὑπάρχειν τῶν Θηβαικῶν στρατειῶν καὶ τῆς Ἰλίου ἁλώσεως.

Dionysius says that Homer composed on both the Theban campaign and the sack of Troy.

F1 The *Contest of Homer and Hesiod* 15 (= T2 above)

τὴν Θηβαΐδα, … ἧς ἡ ἀρχή ·
Ἄργος ἄειδε θεὰ πολυδίψιον ἔνθεν ἄνακτες …

The *Thebais*, of which the first verse is:
Of Argos sing, goddess, the thirsty city from which the lords <of the expedition against Thebes set forth…>

F2   Athenaeus *Sophists at the Feast* 14.465b

(3.14 Kaibel)

ὁ δὲ Οἰδίπους δι' ἐκπώματα τοῖς υἱοῖς κατηράσατο, ὡς ὁ τὴν κυκλικὴν
Θηβαΐδα πεποιηκώς φησιν, ὅτι αὐτῶι παρέθηκαν ἔκπωμα ὃ ἀπηγορεύκει,
λέγων οὕτως

> αὐτὰρ ὁ διογενὴς ἥρως ξανθὸς Πολυνείκης
> πρῶτα μὲν Οἰδιπόδηι καλὴν παρέθηκε τράπεζαν
> ἀργυρέην Κάδμοιο θεόφρονος· αὐτὰρ ἔπειτα
> χρύσεον ἔμπλησεν καλὸν δέπας ἡδέος οἴνου.
> αὐτὰρ ὅ γ' ὡς φράσθη παρακείμενα πατρὸς ἑοῖο   5
> τιμήεντα γέρα, μέγα οἱ κακὸν ἔμπεσε θυμῶι,
> αἶψα δὲ παισὶν ἑοῖσι μεταμφοτέροισιν
> ἐπαρὰς ἀργαλέας ἠρᾶτο (θεῶν δ' οὐ λάνθαν' ἐρινύν)
> ὡς οὔ οἱ †πατρωίαν εἴη φιλότητι†
> δάσσοντ', ἀμφοτέροισι δ' ἀεὶ πόλεμοί τε μάχαι τε ...   10

hinc pendet Eustathius *Odyssey* 1796.3:

> ὧν [scil. αἱ τοῦ πατρὸς ἀραί] αἴτιον κατά τινας ὅτι παρέθεντο ἐκεῖνοι
> τῶι πατρὶ ἐκπώματα ἅπερ ἐκεῖνος ἀπηγορεύκει. ἦσαν δὲ ἐκεῖνα κατὰ
> τὸν πεποιηκότα τὴν κυκλικὴν Θηβαΐδα πατρὸς ἑοῖο τιμήεντα γέρα,
> τουτέστι τοῦ Λαίου. ἐλύπησε γὰρ ὡς ἔοικε τὸν γέροντα οὐ μόνον ἡ
> τῶν τέκνων παρακοὴ ἀλλὰ καὶ ἡ ἀνάμνησις τοῦ πατρικοῦ φόνου.

δι' ἐκπώματα del. Kaibel, def. Robert   **7 μεταμφοτέροισιν** Meineke:
μετ' ἀμφοτέροισιν complures   **8 θεῶν** Meineke: **θεόν**   **9** locus vexatus:
fortasse **πατρῶϊ' ἐνηέι [ἐν] φιλότητι** (W. Ribbeck: **πατρῶϊ' ἐνηείηι
φιλότητος** iam Hermann) legendum   **10 δάσσοντ'** Wackernagel (**δάσ-
σαιντ'** iam Hermann): **δάσαντο**

Oedipus cursed his sons because of the cups, as the author of the cyclic
Thebais relates, because they had set before him the cup which he had
forbidden. The poet tells the story thus:

> But the godly hero, yellow-haired Polyneices, first of all set before
> Oedipus the fair table made out of silver, which had belonged to Cad-
> mus. But next he filled the golden fair goblet full of sweet wine. But
> Oedipus when he perceived that there had been set before him his
> own father <Laius'> honored possessions, a great evil fell upon his
> heart and straightaway he invoked baleful curses upon his two sons,
> both of them (and the curses did not go unnoticed by the Erinys of
> the gods), to the effect that they would not divide their patrimony

on friendly terms, but rather would ever have wars and battles
between them both ...

The above is the source of Eustathius' summary [commentary on the
Odyssey 1796.3]:

The reason for these curses, according to some, is that the sons of
Oedipus had set before him cups which he had forbidden. These cups
were, according to the author of the cyclic *Thebais*, the esteemed possessions of his father, that is, Laius. It would seem that the old hero
was vexed not only at his sons' disobedience, but at being reminded
how he had murdered his own father.

F3   Scholion on Sophocles' *Oedipus at Colonus* verse 1375

(pp. 54–55 de Marco; cf. eundem ap. *Reale Accad. Naz. dei Lincei* 6 [p. 111])

τοῦτο ἅπαξ ἅπαντες οἱ πρὸ ἡμῶν παραλελοίπασιν, ἔχει δὲ τὰ ἀπὸ τῆς
ἱστορίας οὕτως· οἱ περὶ Ἐτεοκλέα καὶ Πολυνείκην δι' ἔθους ἔχοντες
τῶι πατρὶ Οἰδίποδι πέμπειν ἐξ ἑκάστου ἱερείου μοῖραν τὸν ὦμον,
ἐκλαθόμενοί ποτε εἴτε κατὰ ῥαιστώνην εἴτε ἐξ ὁτουοῦν ἰσχίον αὐτῶι
ἔπεμψαν· ὁ δὲ μικροψύχως [μὲν add. Nauck] καὶ τελέως ἀγεννῶς ὅμως
δ' οὖν [Nauck: γοῦν] ἀρὰς ἔθετο [L: ἄρα τίθετο M, ἀνατέθετο R] κατ'
αὐτῶν δόξας κατολιγωρεῖσθαι· ταῦτα ὁ τὴν κυκλικὴν Θηβαΐδα ποιήσας
[L: ταῦτα ὁ ποιητὴς RM]ἱστορεῖ οὕτως· [LRM])

ἰσχίον ὡς ἐνόησε χαμαὶ βάλε εἶπέ τε μῦθον·
'ὤμοι ἐγώ, παῖδες μέγ' ὀνείδειον τόδ' ἔπεμψαν.'
εὖκτο δὲ Δὶ βασιλῆι καὶ ἄλλοις ἀθανάτοισι
χερσὶν ὑπ' ἀλλήλων καταβήμεναι Ἄιδος εἴσω.

τὰ δὲ παραπλήσια τῶι ἐποποιῶι καὶ Αἰσχύλος ἐν τοῖς Ἑπτὰ ἐπὶ Θήβας
(785 sqq.). LR

Cf. Zenobius of Athos' *Collection of Proverbs* 2.88 = vulg. 5.43 (1.138 Leutsch-
Schneidewin)

ἱστορεῖται δὲ ὅτι Ἐτεοκλῆς καὶ Πολυνείκης, δι' ἔθους ἔχοντες πέμπειν
τῶι Οἰδίποδι ἑκάστου ἱερείου τὸν ὦμον, ἐπιλαθόμενοι ἰσχίον (-ία
codd.) ἔπεμψαν· ὁ δὲ νομίσας ὑβρίσθαι κατηράσατο αὐτοῖς.

Eustathius *Odyssey* 1684.9

ἄλλοι δέ γε βρωμάτων τινῶν χάριν τὸν Οἰδίπουν καταράσασθαι τοῖς
τέκνοις ἱστόρησαν.

fragmentum valde corruptum alios secutus sanavi 1 ἰσχίου om. R 2
παῖδες μέγ' Schneidewin: παῖδες (παῖδε R) μέν ὀνείδειον τόδ'
Buttmann: ὀνειδείοντες post ἔπεμψαν lacunam posuerunt complures

Hermannium secuti; post hoc verbum 'signum diacriticum (:-) quo scholii finem indicare solet habet R', litteram ζ ÷ (id est ζήτει) 'fortasse ob vocem ὀνειδείοντες' habet L   teste de Marco   **3 εὖκτο δὲ Διì** Buttmann: **εὖκτο δὲ Διì** (ex **Δυì**) R, **εὖκτο Διì** L   **βασιλῆι** Triclinius: – **ιλεῖ** codd.   **4 καταβήμεναι** R (quod coniecerat Lascaris): **καταβῆναι** L

This detail has been omitted by all my predecessors, but the details of the story are as follows: Eteocles and Polyneices were accustomed to send their father Oedipus from each sacrifice a portion of the victim's shoulder. On one occasion they completely forgot, either from indifference or for some other cause, and sent him the haunch. And he, in a petty and quite ignoble manner, invoked curses upon them, supposing he was being slighted. These events the author of the cyclic *Thebais* related as follows:

> When Oedipus noticed the haunch he cast it upon the ground and uttered a speech: "Woe is me! My sons have sent this to me as a great insult." And he prayed to Zeus the king and the other immortals that <the sons> should descend to the house of Hades slain at each others' hands.

Zenobius of Athos' *Collection of Proverbs* 2.88

> The story is told that Eteocles and Polyneices, being accustomed to send Oedipus the shoulder of each sacrificial victim, completely forgot and sent the haunch. And he, supposing himself to have been brutally treated, cursed them.

Eustathius' commentary on the *Odyssey* 1684.9

> Others say that the reason for Oedipus' curse on his sons related to food.

F4   Pausanias IX 18.6

(3.34 Rocha-Pereira)

πρὸς δὲ τῆι πηγῆι τάφος ἐστὶν Ἀσφοδίκου· καὶ ὁ Ἀσφόδικος οὗτος ἀπέκτεινεν ἐν τῆι μάχηι τῆι πρὸς Ἀργείους Παρθενοπαῖον τὸν Ταλαοῦ, καθὰ οἱ Θηβαῖοι λέγουσιν, ἐπεὶ τά γε ἐν Θηβαΐδι ἔπη τὰ ἐς τὴν Παρθενοπαίου τελευτὴν Περικλύμενον τὸν ἀνελόντα φησὶν εἶναι.

By the spring [of Oedipus] is the grave of Asphodicus. And this Asphodicus was the man who killed Parthenopaeus son of Talaus in the battle against the Argives, as the Thebans state. But the verses in the *Thebais* relating to the death of Parthenopaeus state that Periclymenus was the man who killed him.

F5 Scholion on *Iliad* V 126

(2.63 Nicole: cf. 2.22 Erbse)

Τυδεὺς ὁ Οἰνέως ἐν τῶι Θηβαϊκῶι πολέμωι ὑπὸ Μελανίππου τοῦ Ἀστακοῦ ἐτρώθη· Ἀμφιάρεως δὲ κτείνας τὸν Μελάνιππον τὴν κεφαλὴν
ἐκόμισε <Τυδεῖ > καὶ ἀνοίξας αὐτὴν ὁ Τυδεὺς τὸν ἐγκέφαλον ἐρρόφει
ἀπὸ θυμοῦ. Ἀθηνᾶ δὲ κομίζουσα Τυδεῖ ἀθανασίαν ἰδοῦσα τὸ μίασμα
ἀπεστράφη αὐτόν. Τυδεὺς δὲ γνοὺς ἐδεήθη τῆς θεοῦ ἵνα κἂν τῶι παιδὶ
αὐτοῦ παράσχηι τὴν ἀθανασίαν. ἡ ἱστορία παρὰ τοῖς Κυκλικοῖς.

   ad Thebaida referunt complures

Tydeus son of Oeneus was wounded in the war against Thebes by
Melanippus son of Astacus. And Amphiaraus, after killing Melanippus,
brought his head to Tydeus and Tydeus, cutting it open, slurped up
its contents in a frenzy. Athena was bringing immortality for him,
but when she saw the disgusting act she turned away from him. And
Tydeus, realising this, begged the goddess to give the immortality to
his son [Diomedes]. The story is in the Cyclic Poets.

F6a Pausanias VIII 25.7–8

(2.273 Rocha-Pereira)

τὴν δὲ Δήμητρα τεκεῖν φασιν (scil. τινες) ἐκ τοῦ Ποσειδῶνος θυγατέρα
ἧς τὸ ὄνομα ἐς ἀτελέστους λέγειν οὐ νομίζουσι, καὶ ἵππον τὸν Ἀρίονα·
ἐπὶ τούτωι δὲ παρὰ σφισιν Ἀρκάδων πρώτοις Ἵππιον Ποσειδῶνα
ὀνομασθῆναι. ἐπάγονται δὲ ἐξ Ἰλιάδος ἔπη καὶ ἐκ Θηβαΐδος μαρτύριά
σφισιν εἶναι τῶι λόγωι, ἐν μὲν Ἰλιάδι ἐς αὐτὸν Ἀρίονα πεποιῆσθαι [*Iliad*
XXIII 346–347; cf. F6b, F6c] ἐν δὲ τῆι Θηβαΐδι ὡς Ἄδραστος ἔφευγεν ἐκ
Θηβῶν

   εἵματα λυγρὰ φέρων σὺν Ἀρίονι κυανοχαίτηι.

αἰνίσσεσθαι οὖν ἐθέλουσι τὰ ἔπη Ποσειδῶνα Ἀρίονι εἶναι πατέρα.

   φέρων (R¹Pa Vb: **φερίων β**) suspectum: fort. φορῶν scribendum, nisi
   εἵματα lectionem veram celat (σήματα coni. Beck, coll. Aesch. *S.C.T.* 49-51)

Some say that Demeter bore to Poseidon a daughter whose name they
do not see fit to reveal to the uninitiated, together with a horse, Arion.
And therefore the name Poseidon of the Horse was received by them
first among the Arcadians. They quote from the *Iliad* and the *Thebais*
as evidence for this tradition. In the *Iliad* Arion himself is mentioned

[XXIII 346], while in the *Thebais* it is related how Adrastus was able to escape from Thebes,

With begrimed clothes and riding on Arion the dark-maned horse.

They take this reference to mean that Poseidon was father to Arion.

F6b   Scholion on *Iliad* XXIII 347

(5.424–423 Erbse)

(ὃς ἐκ θεόφιν γένος ἦεν ·) Ὅμηρος μὲν ἁπλῶς ὅτι θειοτέρας ἦν φύσεως [scil. Ἀρίων], οἱ δὲ νεώτεροι Ποσειδῶνος καὶ Ἁρπυίας αὐτὸν γενεα-λογοῦσιν, οἱ δὲ ἐν τῶι Κύκλωι Ποσειδῶνος καὶ Ἐρινύος.

[pergit Σ idem] καὶ Ποσειδῶν μὲν αὐτὸν Κοπρεῖ τῶι Ἁλιαρτίωι δίδωσιν. ὁ δὲ Κοπρεὺς Ἡρακλεῖ, <ὃς> καὶ Κύκνον ἀνεῖλεν ἐν Παγασαῖς ἐπ’ αὐτοῦ μαχόμενος. ἔπειτα αὐτὸν δίδωσιν Ἀδράστωι.

Apropos of the phrase "who was of divine race": Homer simply says that Arion was of more divine nature, while the genealogy given in later poets is that he was offspring of Poseidon and a Harpy, and the Cyclic poets say that he was offspring of Poseidon and an Erinys. Poseidon gives him to Copreus, son of Haliartus; and Copreus gave him to Heracles; and he killed Cycnus at Pagasae in combat with him. Then he gave him to Adrastus.

F6c   Scholion on *Iliad* XXIII 346

(cf. 5.424 Erbse, 2.205 Nicole; Janko, *Classical Quarterly* 36 [1986]: 51–52)

Ποσειδῶν ἐρασθεὶς Ἐρινύος, καὶ μεταβαλὼν τὴν αὑτοῦ μορφὴν εἰς ἵππον, ἐμίγη κατὰ Βοιωτίαν παρὰ τῆι Τιλφούσηι κρήνηι. ἡ δὲ ἔγκυος γενομένη ἵππον ἐγέννησεν, ὃς διὰ τὸ κρατιστεύειν Ἀρίων ἐκλήθη. Κοπρεὺς δὲ Ἁλιάρτου βασιλεύων [πόλεως Βοιωτίας] ἔλαβε δῶρον αὐτὸν παρὰ Ποσειδῶνος. οὗτος δὲ αὐτὸν Ἡρακλεῖ ἐχαρίσατο γενομένωι πρὸς αὐτόν. τούτωι δὲ ἀγωνισάμενος Ἡρακλῆς πρὸς Κύκνον Ἄρεως υἱὸν καθ’ ἱπποδρομίαν ἐνίκησεν ἐν τῶι τοῦ Πηγασαίου Ἀπόλλωνος ἱερῶι, [ὅ ἐστι πρὸς Τροιζῆνι]. εἶθ’ ὕστερον αὖθις Ἡρακλῆς Ἀδράστωι τὸν πῶλον παρέσχεν· ὑφ’ οὗ μόνος ὁ Ἄδραστος ἐκ τοῦ Θηβαϊκοῦ πολέμου διεσώθη, τῶν ἄλλων ἀπολομένων. ἡ ἱστορία παρὰ τοῖς Κυκλικοῖς.

πόλεως Βοιωτίας del. Janko p. 52 n. 75   ὅ ... Τροιζῆνι del. van der Valk, prob. Janko ib.: deest ap. ΣB sec. Dindorf (4.317)

Poseidon fell in love with an Erinys, and, changing his shape to a horse, had intercourse with her in Boeotia by the stream of Tilphusa. She became pregnant and gave birth to a horse which was called Arion because he was preeminent [Greek *aristos*]. And Copreus, king of Haliarthus, received him as a gift from Poseidon. Copreus in turn gave him to Heracles in gratitude, when he was staying with him. Heracles used him to compete in a horse race with Cycnus, son of Ares, which he won at the temple of Apollo at Pagasae. Then later, Heracles in turn gave the stallion to Adrastus.

It was thanks to Arion that Adrastus was the only survivor of the war against Thebes, all the other leaders meeting their death. The tale is related by the Cyclic poets.

F7   Scholion on Pindar *Olympian* VI 15–17

ἑπτὰ δ' ἔπειτα πυρᾶν νεκρῶν τελεσθέντων Ταλαϊονίδας | εἶπεν ἐν Θήβαισι τοιοῦτόν τι ἔπος· ποθέω στρατιᾶς ὀφθαλμὸν ἐμᾶς | ἀμφότερον μάντιν τ' ἀγαθὸν καὶ δουρὶ μάρνασθαι.

ad haec ΣΑ (1.160 Dr.)

ποθέω· ὁ Ἀσκληπιάδης [scil. ὁ Μυρλεανός] φησὶ ταῦτα εἰληφέναι ἐκ τῆς κυκλικῆς Θηβαΐδος.

   quid dixerit poeta noster incertum

(lines of Pindar's ode represent Adrastus saying, after the corpses on seven pyres had been cremated, "I long for the 'eye' of my army [Amphiaraus], both a good seer and skilled at fighting with a spear.")

Apropos of the verb "long for": Asclepiades says Pindar took this from the Cyclic epic the *Thebais*.

F8   Apollodorus *Library* I 8.4

(p. 26 Wagner)

Ἀλθαίας δὲ ἀποθανούσης ἔγημεν Οἰνεὺς Περίβοιαν τὴν Ἱππονόου. ταύτην δὲ ὁ μὲν γράψας τὴν Θηβαΐδα πολεμηθείσης Ὠλένου λέγει λαβεῖν Οἰνέα γέρας [sequitur Hesiod fr. 12 MW].

When Althaea died, Oeneus married Periboea, daughter of Hipponous. The author of the *Thebais* says Oeneus received her as war booty after the sack of the city of Olenus.

Etiam inter Thebaidos fragmenta numerandum, ut credunt complures.

Ἀμφιάρεω ἐξελασία

Pseudo-Herodotean *Life of Homer* 9

(p. 197 Allen = pp. 7–8 sqq. Wilamowitz = p. 362 West)

(Ὅμηρος ... ἀπικνέεται ἐς Νέον τεῖχος) κατήμενος δὲ ἐν τῶι σκυτείωι παρεόντων καὶ ἄλλων τήν τε ποίησιν αὐτοῖς ἐπεδείκνυτο, Ἀμφιάρεώ τε τὴν ἐξελασίαν τὴν ἐς Θήβας καὶ τοὺς ὕμνους τοὺς ἐς θεοὺς πεποιημένους αὐτῶι.

When Homer arrived, among the poems displayed was "Amphiaraus' Setting Forth for Thebes."

Suda s.v. Ὅμηρος (3.526 Adler = Homeri T1)

ἀναφέρεται δὲ εἰς αὐτὸν καὶ ἄλλα τινὰ ποιήματα· Ἀμαζονιά ... Ἀμφιαράου Ἐξέλασις.

Among the poems ascribed to Homer was "Amphiaraus' Setting Forth for Thebes."

> **Ἀμφ. Ἐξ.** partem fuisse nostri carminis potius quam carmen diversum intellegunt complures

Epigoni

T1   Herodotus IV 32 (= F2 below)

ἔστι δὲ καὶ Ὁμήρωι ἐν Ἐπιγόνοισι, εἰ δὴ τῶι ἐόντι γε Ὅμηρος ταῦτα τὰ ἔπεα ἐποίησε.

This is in the *Epigoni* of Homer, if this epic really is by Homer.

T2   The *Contest of Homer and Hesiod* 15 (= *Thebais* T2 above)

(265–267 Allen = 15 p. 42 sq. Wilamowitz = p. 344 West)

ὁ δὲ Ὅμηρος ἀποτυχὼν τῆς νίκης περιερχόμενος ἔλεγε τὰ ποιήματα, πρῶτον μὲν τὴν Θηβαΐδα [*Thebais* T2] ... εἶτα Ἐπιγόνους [Barnes: ἐπειγομένου] ἔπη ͵ζ ἧς ἡ ἀρχή (F 1 infra) ... φασὶ γάρ τινες καὶ ταῦτα Ὁμήρου εἶναι.

The *Epigoni* ... for some say these poems are by Homer.

Cf. the *Tabula Borgiana* [= *Thebais* T3]

the *Epigoni*, consisting of 7,000 epic verses.

F1 The *Contest of Homer and Hesiod* (= T2 above)

Ἐπιγόνους ... ἧς ἡ ἀρχή·
νῦν αὖθ' ὁπλοτέρων ἀνδρῶν ἀρχώμεθα Μοῦσαι.

Now again let us begin, Muses, the tale of younger men, < who...>

hunc versum παρωιδεῖ Aristophanes (*Peace* 1270–1271):

(παιδίον ά)· νῦν αὖθ' ὁπλοτέρων ἀνδρῶν ἀρχώμεθα –
(Τρυγαῖος)   παῦσαι
              ὁπλοτέρους ἄιδων.

haec Antimacho Colophonio perperam trib. Σ ad loc. (schol. *Ar.* II.2 p. 178 Holwerda):

ἀρχὴ τῶν Ἐπιγόνων Ἀντιμάχου.

F2 Herodotus IV 32 (= T1 above)

ἀλλ' Ἡσιόδωι μέν ἐστι περὶ Ὑπερβορέων εἰρημένα (fr. 209 Rz.: cf. fr. 150.21 MW),

The Hyperboreans are mentioned... also by Homer in the *Epigoni*.

F3 Scholion on Apollonius of Rhodes' *Argonautica* 1.308

(p. 35 Wendel) = *Delphic Oracle* 20 Parke–Wormell (2.9)

οἱ δὲ τὴν Θηβαΐδα [sic] γεγραφότες φασὶν ὅτι ὑπὸ τῶν Ἐπιγόνων ἀκροθίνιον ἀνετέθη Μαντὼ ἡ Τειρεσίου θυγάτηρ εἰς Δελφοὺς πεμφθεῖσα, καὶ κατὰ χρησμὸν Ἀπόλλωνος ἐξερχομένη περιέπεσε Ῥακίωι τῶι Λέβητος υἱῶι Μυκηναίωι τὸ γένος. καὶ γημαμένη αὐτῶι – τοῦτο γὰρ περιεῖχε τὸ λόγιον, γαμεῖσθαι ὧι ἂν συναντήσηι – ἐλθοῦσα εἰς Κολοφῶνα καὶ ἐκεῖ δυσθυμήσασα ἐδάκρυσε διὰ τὴν τῆς πατρίδος πόρθησιν. διόπερ ὠνομάσθη Κλάρος ἀπὸ τῶν δακρύων.

The author of the *Thebais* says that Manto, the daughter of Tiresias, was dedicated by the Epigoni as spoil of war and sent to Delphi. In accordance with an oracle from Apollo, as she came from his temple, she encountered Rhiacus, son of Lebes, a Mycenean by birth. She married him—for this was the term of the oracle's pronouncement, that she marry whomever she met—and went to Colophon and there, in a fit of sorrow, fell a-weeping for the sack of her native land. For this reason she got called Clarus, because of her tears [Greek *klaio* meaning "I weep"].

Fragmentum spurium

Σ Soph. *O. C.* 378 (p. 25 de Marco) κοῖλον Ἄργος· πολλαχοῦ τὸ Ἄργος κοῖλόν φησι, καθάπερ καὶ ἐν Ἐπιγόνοις (Soph. *TrGF* 4 F 190 Radt)· 'τὸ κοῖλον Ἄργος οὐ κατοικήσαντ' ἔτι' καὶ ἐν Θαμύραι (Soph. *TrGF* 4 F 242 Radt)· 'ἐκ μὲν Ἐριχθονίου ποτιμάστιον ἔσχεθε κοῦρον | Αὐτόλυκον, πολέων κτεάνων σίνιν Ἀργεϊ κοίλωι.' Ὅμηρος· (*Od.* 4.1).

> titulos sic transposuit Kirchhoff: καθάπερ καὶ ἐν Θαμύραι· τὸ κοῖλον κτλ.
> ... καὶ ἐν Ἐπιγόνοις· ἐκ μὲν κτλ. qui duos hexametros ad carmen nostrum
> retulit; vid. contra Radt ad locc. (pp. 186 et 237). duos versus nostro epico
> aliter vindicant Pearson (*Soph. Frag.* 1.182) qui post Θαμύραι verba excidisse
> quae versus Sophocleos continerent coni, et Powell (*Collectanea Alexandrina*
> 247) qui lacunam propositam sic ex. gr. suppl.: (... καὶ ὁ τοὺς Ἐπιγόνους
> ποιήσας)· ἐκ μὲν ἄρα κτλ. sed de hexametri usu apud tragicos vid. Radt supra
> cit. p.237.

(The two hexameters quoted are probably from a lost Sophoclean trag-edy [*Thamyras*] rather than from the cyclic *Epigoni* cited in a supposed lacuna.)

Alcmaeonis

F1   Scholion on Euripides *Andromache* 687

(2.295 Schwartz)

(οὐδ' ἂν σὲ Φῶκον ἤθελον·) ὥσπερ ἐγὼ [scil. Μενέλαος] οὐκ ἐφόνευσα τὴν Ἑλένην, οὕτως οὐδὲ σὺ [scil. Πηλεύς] ὤφελες τὸν Φῶκον ἀνελεῖν, καὶ ὁ τὴν Ἀλκμαιωνίδα πεποιηκὼς φησι περὶ τοῦ Φώκου ·
> ἔνθα μιν ἀντίθεος Τελαμὼν τροχοειδέϊ δίσκωι
> πλῆξε κάρη, Πηλεὺς δὲ θοῶς ἀνὰ χεῖρα τανύσσας
> ἀξίνηι ἐϋχάλκωι ἐπεπλήγει μέσα νῶτα.

> **1 μιν** Schwartz: **κεν** MNO **καὶ** A **ἀντίθεος: αὐτόθεος** A **κύκλω**
> **δίσκω** A **2 πλῆξε: πλῆξαι** M **ἀναχεῖρα τανύσας** MNO **ἀνὰ χεῖρα**
> **πετάσας** A **ἐνὶ χειρὶ τινάξας** coni. Schwartz **3 ἀξίνηι ἐϋχάλκωι**
> Kinkel: **ἀξίνη εὐχάλκω** A **ἀξ ..... κου** M contra detrita **ἀξίνην**
> **εὐχαλκου** NO **μέσα: μέγα** O

A propos of a reference to Peleus' killing of Phocus: the author of the *Alcmaeonis* says of Phocus:

Then did godlike Telamon strike him with a circular discus; and Peleus, swiftly raising up his hands, smote him full on the middle of his back with a bronze axe.

F2   Athenaeus *Sophists at the Feast* 11.460b

(3.2 Kaibel)

ποτήρια δὲ πρῶτον οἶδα ὀνομάσαντα τὸν Ἀμόργιον ποιητὴν Σιμωνίδην ἐν Ἰάμβοις οὕτως [fr. 26 W] ... καὶ ὁ τὴν Ἀλκμαιωνίδα δὲ ποιήσας φησίν·
νέκυς δὲ χαμαιστρώτου ἐπὶ τείνας
εὐρείης στιβάδος παρέθηκ᾽ αὐτοῖσι θάλειαν
δαῖτα ποτήριά τε, στεφάνους δ᾽ ἐπὶ κρασὶν ἔθηκεν.

1 **χαμαιστρώτους ἐπί τινας** A: corr. Welcker   2 **παρέθηκ᾽** Meineke: **προέθηκ᾽** A   3 **δαῖτα** Fiorillo: **δὲ τὰ** A   **δ᾽** Kaibel: τ᾽ A

(The first poets to mention, unlike Homer, drinking cups: Simonides fr. 26 W)... and the author of the *Alcmaeonis* says:
And stretching the corpses on a broad couch spread on the ground, he set before them a rich feast, and cups, and he placed garlands on their heads.

F3   The *Etymologicum Gudianum* s.v. *Zagreus*

(2.578 de Stefani) = Cod. Barocc. 50 ap. Cramer, *Anecd. Oxon.* 2.443

ὁ μεγάλως ἀγρεύων ὡς·
πότνια Γῆ, Ζαγρεῦ τε θεῶν πανυπέρτατε πάντων
ὁ τὴν Ἀλκμαιωνίδα γράψας ἔφη.

Seleuci gloss. 17 sec. Reitzenstein (*Geschichte der gr. Etym.* (Lipsiae 1897) p. 159): vid. contra de Stefani ad loc. ('auctoris nota Σε^λ quam lemmati praefixit Reitz. ... non huc pertinet sed ad gl. Ζεύς') **Ζαγρεῦ: Ζαγρεύς** cod. Barocc. **πάντων – ἔφη** om. cod. Barocc. qui et **ὦ** pro **ὡς** praebet

The name signifies "he who hunts mightily" [Greek *za-* = "very much"] as in
Lady Earth, and Zagreus, all highest of all the gods
as the author of the *Alcmaeonis* said.

F4 Apollodorus *Library* I 8.5

(p. 27 Wagner)

Τυδεὺς δὲ ἀνὴρ γενόμενος γενναῖος ἐφυγαδεύθη κτείνας, ὡς μέν τινες λέγουσιν, ἀδελφὸν Οἰνέως Ἀλκάθοον, ὡς δὲ ὁ τὴν Ἀλκμαιωνίδα γεγραφώς, τοὺς Μέλανος παῖδας ἐπιβουλεύοντας Οἰνεῖ Φηνέα [Φινέα Heyne] Εὐρύαλον Ὑπέρλαον [Περίλαον Heyne] Ἀντίοχον [Faber: -ιόχην] Εὐμήδην Στέρνοπα (Στέροπα Heyne) Ξάνθιππον Σθενέλαον.

Tydeus, growing up to a noble manhood, had to go into exile for having killed, as some relate, Alcathous, brother of Oeneus, but as the author of the *Alcmaeonis* says, the sons of Melas, who were plotting against Oeneus: Pheneus, Euryalus, Hyperlas, Antiochus, Eumades, Sternops, Xanthippus, Sthenelus.

F5 Scholion on Euripides *Orestes* 995

(1.197–198 Schwartz)

ἀκολουθεῖν ἂν δόξειε [scil. Εὐριπίδης] τῶι τὴν Ἀλκμαιωνίδα πεποιη-κότι εἰς τὰ περὶ τὴν ἄρνα, ὡς καὶ Διονύσιος ὁ κυκλογράφος [FGrHist 15 F7] φησί [sequitur Pherecydes FGrHist 3 F133] ... ὁ δὲ τὴν Ἀλκμαιωνίδα γράψας τὸν ποιμένα τὸν προσαγαγόντα τὸ ποίμνιον τῶι Ἀτρεῖ Ἀντίοχον καλεῖ.

Euripides would seem to be following the author of the *Alcmaeonis* regarding details about the sheep, as Dionysus the cyclographer also says ..... the author of the *Alcmaeonis* calls the shepherd who brought the flock to Atreus by the name of Antiochus.

F6 Strabo 10.2.9

452 C (3.180–182 Radt)

ὁ μὲν οὖν Μένανδρος λέγει... [Leucad. fr. 1 KA].. ὁ δὲ τὴν Ἀλκμαιωνίδα [-ονίδα codd. praeter Dac xyq] γράψας Ἰκαρίου τοῦ Πηνελόπης πατρὸς υἱεῖς γενέσθαι δύο, Ἀλυζέα καὶ Λευκάδιον, δυναστεῦσαι δ' ἐν τῆι Ἀκαρνανίαι τούτους μετὰ τοῦ πατρός · τούτων οὖν ἐπωνύμους τὰς πόλεις Ἔφορος [FGrHist 70 F 124] λεγέσθαι δοκεῖ.

λέγει post υἱεῖς suppl. Madvig, φησί post δύο Groskurd, sed cf. F4

(*Following a quotation of the comic poet Menander*) The author of the *Alcmaeonis* says Icarius, father of Penelope, had two sons, Alyzus and Leucadius, and that they reigned in Acarnania, together with their father. Ephorus seems to say that the relevant cities are named after them.

F7   Philodemus' *On Piety*

N 1609 IV 8–13 (B 6798 Obbink)

κα[ὶ τῆς | ἐπ]ὶ Κρόνου ζω[ῆς | εὐ]δαιμονεστά[της | οὔ]ϙης, ὡς ἔγραψ[α|ν Ἡ|σί]οδος [*Op.* 109 sqq.] καὶ ὁ τὴ̣ν̣ [Ἀλ|κμ]εωνίδα ποή[σας| καὶ] Σοφο-κλῆς (*TrGF* 4 F 278 Radt).

> **11 ἔγραψ[αν** suppl. Nauck **-ψ[εν** Gomperz   **12 ὁ τὴν** Nauck: **της**

Life in the time of Cronus was most happy... [*sources cited include* "the author of the *Alcmaeonis*"]

Bibliography of
Most Frequently Cited Works

Andersen, Ø. 1978. *Die Diomedes-Gestalt in der Ilias*. *Symbolae Osloenses* suppl. 25. Oslo.

Bethe, E. 1891. *Thebanische Heldenlieder*. Leipzig.

Burkert, W. 1981. "The Seven Against Thebes: An Oral Tradition between Babylonian Magic and Greek Literature." In *I Poemi epici rapsodici non omerici e la tradizione orale* (ed. C. Brillante, M. Cantilena, and C. O. Pavese) 29–48. Padua. [= *Kleine Schriften* 1 (2001) 150–165. Göttingen.]

Chantraine, *Gramm. hom.* = P. Chantraine, *Grammaire homérique*, 1: *Phonétique et morphologie* (Paris 1942); 2: *Syntaxe* (Paris 1953).

Davies and Finglass = Malcolm Davies and Patrick Finglass, *Stesichorus: The Poems* (Cambridge 2015).

De Kock, E. L. 1961. "The Sophoclean *Oedipus* and Its Antecedents." *Acta Classica* 4:7–28.

———. 1962. "The Peisandros Scholium: Its Sources, Unity, and Relationship to Euripides' *Chrysippus*." *Acta Classica* 5:15–37.

Deubner, L. 1942. "Oedipusprobleme." *Abhandlungen der Preussischen Akademie der Wissenschaften* 4:1–43. [= *Kleine Schriften zur klassischen Altertumskunde: Beiträge zur Klassischen Philologie* 140 (1982): 635–677. Königstein.]

Dirlmeier, F. 1954. Review of J. Reiner, *Zeven tegen Thebe* (Amsterdam 1953). *Gnomon* 26:151–158. [= *Ausgewählte Schriften zu Dichtung und Philosophie* (1970): 48–54. Heidelberg.]

Edmunds, L. 1981a. *The Sphinx in the Oedipus Legend*. Beiträge zur klassischen Philologie 127. Königstein.

———. 1981b. "The Cults and the Legend of Oedipus." *Harvard Studies in Classical Philology* 85:221–238.

Fowler, R. 2013. *Early Greek Mythography*, vol. 2: *Commentary*. Oxford.

Fraenkel, Ed. 1957. "Die Sieben Redepaare im Thebanerdrama des Aeschylus." *Sitzungsberichte der Philosophisch-philologischen und der Historischen Klasse des Königlich Bayerische Akademie der Wissenschaften* 3 = *Kleine Beiträge zur klassischen Philologie* 1 (1964) 273–328. Rome.

Friedländer, P. 1914. "Kritische Untersuchungen zur Geschichte der Heldensage." *Rheinisches Museum* 69:299–341. [= *Studien zur Antiken Literatur und Kunst* (1969) 19–536. Berlin.]

Griffin, J. 1977. "The Epic Cycle and the Uniqueness of Homer." *Journal of Hellenic Studies* 97:34–59. [= *Oxford Readings in Homer's* Iliad (ed. D. L. Cairns) 365–389. Oxford 2000.]

Howald, E. 1939. "Die Sieben gegen Theben." *Rektoratsrede.* Zurich.

Huxley, G. L. 1969. *Early Greek Epic Poetry from Eumelus to Panyassis.* London.

Kühr, A. 2006. *Als Kadmos nach Boiotien kam: Polis und Ethnos im Gründungsmythen.* *Hermes* Einzelschriften 38. Stuttgart.

Lloyd-Jones, H. 2002. "Curses and Divine Anger in Early Epic: The Pisander Scholion." *Classical Quarterly* 52:1–14. [= *Further Academic Papers* (2003) 18–35. Oxford.]

Mastronarde = D. Mastronarde, ed., *Euripides, Phoenician Women.* Cambridge 1994.

Nauck, *Mélanges gréco-romains* = A. Nauck, *Mélanges gréco-romains. Bulletin de l'Académie impériale des sciences de St. Pétersbourg* 4 (1875/80).

Prinz, F. 1979. *Gründungsmythen und Sagenchronologie.* Zetemata 72.

Richardson, N. J., ed. 1974. *The Homeric Hymn to Demeter.* Oxford.

Robert, C. 1915. *Oidipus.* 2 vols. Berlin.

Rzach, A. 1922. "Kyklos." In *RE* 11.2.2347–2435.

Severyns, A. 1928. *Le cycle épique dans l'école d'Aristarque.* Liège.

Simon, E. 1981. *Das Satyrspiel Sphinx des Aischylos. Sitzungsberichte der Heidelberger Akademie der Wissenschaften, Philosophisch-historische Klasse* 5. Heidelberg.

Stephanopoulos, Th. K. 1980. *Umgestaltung des Mythos durch Euripides.* Athens.

Stoneman, R. 1981. "Pindar and the Mythological Tradition." *Philologus*: 44–63.

Vian, F. 1963. *Les origines de Thèbes: Cadmos et les Spartes.* Paris.

Wackernagel, J. 1916. *Sprachliche Untersuchungen zu Homer.* Göttingen.

Watson, L. 1991. *Arae: The Curse Poetry of Antiquity.* Leeds.

Wehrli, F. 1957. "Oedipus." *Museum Helveticum* 14:108–117. [= *Theoria und Humanitas* (1972) 60–71. Zurich.]

Wecklein, N. 1901. "Die kyklische *Thebais,* die *Oedipodee,* die Oedipussage und der *Oedipus* des Euripides." *Sitzungsberichte der Philosophisch-philologischen und der Historischen Classe des Königlich Bayerische Akademie der Wissenschaften* 5 (1901): 670–710.

Welcker, F. G. 1865. *Der epische Cyclus* (1841; 2nd ed. 1865). Bonn.

West, M. L. 2003. *Fragments of Greek Epic* (Loeb text and translation). Cambridge, MA.

———. 2013. *The Epic Cycle.* Oxford.

Wilamowitz, U. 1884. *Homerische Untersuchungen*. Berlin.

———. 1931–1932. *Der Glaube der Hellenen*. Berlin.

———. 1891. "Die Sieben Tore Thebens." *Hermes* 26:191–241. [= *Kleine Schriften* 5.1 (Berlin 1971): 26–76.]

———. 1914. *Aischylos Interpretationen*. Berlin.

Willcock, M. "Mythological Paradeigma in the *Iliad*." *Classical Quarterly* 14 (1964): 141–154. [= *Oxford Readings in Homer's* Iliad (ed. D. L. Cairns) 435–455. Oxford 2000.]

General Index

Index Verborum

Index Locorum Apollodoreorum

CPSIA information can be obtained
at www.ICGtesting.com
Printed in the USA
FSHW010646091119

9 780674 417243